W9-BUO-869

Assessing Affective Characteristics in the Schools

Second Edition

Assessing Affective Characteristics in the Schools

Second Edition

Lorin W. Anderson
University of South Carolina

Sid F. Bourke
University of Newcastle

LEA

LAWRENCE ERLBAUM ASSOCIATES, PUBLISHERS
2000   Mahwah, New Jersey   London

Copyright © 2000 by Lawrence Erlbaum Associates, Inc.
All rights reserved. No part of this book may be reproduced in any form, by photostat, microfilm, retrieval system, or any other means, without prior written permission of the publisher.

Lawrence Erlbaum Associates, Inc., Publishers
10 Industrial Avenue
Mahwah, NJ 07430

Cover design by Kathryn Houghtaling Lacey

Library of Congress Cataloging-in-Publication Data

Anderson, Lorin W.
Assessing affective characteristics in the schools /
Lorin W. Anderson and Sid F. Bourke.—2nd ed.
    p. cm.

Includes bibliographical references and index.
ISBN 0-8058-3197-5 (cloth : alk. paper) —
ISBN 0-8058-3198-3 (pbk. : alk. paper)
1. Educational tests and measurements. 2. Teaching.
I. Bourke, S. F. II. Title.
LB3051.A698   2000   99-054005
371.26—dc21   CIP

Books published by Lawrence Erlbaum Associates are printed on acid-free paper, and their bindings are chosen for strength and durability.

Printed in the United States of America
10   9   8   7   6   5   4   3   2   1

Contents

Preface

One of the reviewers who commented on the first edition of this book said, in essence, "good book, bad timing." The timing was bad because in 1981, at least in the United States, education had entered a renewed basic skills phase. Traditionally, concerns for the affective domain have been lost when attention is focused exclusively on readin', 'ritin,' and 'rithmetic.

We hope this is a "better book" with "better timing." In making this a "better book," we have made substantial changes, while preserving what we believe to be the best of the first edition. The majority of the differences between the two editions can be summarized in a series of first edition–second edition bullets.

- Whereas the first edition focused on selecting appropriate instruments, the second edition has a dual focus on selecting and designing instruments.
- Whereas the first edition discussed a wide range of strategies for designing self-report instruments, the second edition focuses primarily on instruments designed in accordance with the principles of Likert scaling.
- Whereas the first edition focused on instruments containing single affective scales, the second edition recognizes that most current instruments contain multiple affective scales.
- Whereas the first edition assumed, for the sake of simplicity, the data obtained from affective assessment instruments were interval in nature, the second edition acknowledges the ordinal nature of affective data and its consequences for scale development.

- Whereas the first edition focused on the use of instruments to understand individual students, the second edition has a dual focus on individual students and groups.
- Whereas the first edition has a somewhat instrumental focus (i.e., using affective data to maximize student success and retention in education), the second edition takes a somewhat broader view—that in addition to its instrumental utility, affect is valuable in and of itself.

There are two other noteworthy differences that we believe make this a "better book." The first is the use of a single, small data set to illustrate the concepts and principles in chapter 6 ("Treating and Analyzing Affective Data") and chapter 7 ("Interpreting Affective Data"). In addition to facilitating understanding, we believe the use of this data set enables the reader to mimic our efforts in treating, analyzing, and interpreting affective data.

The second difference, which also pertains to these two chapters, is the suggested use of the Statistical Package for the Social Sciences (SPSS) in the treatment, analysis, and interpretation of the data. Our suggested use is not meant as an endorsement of this statistical package. Rather, as we state in chapter 6, we believe that SPSS is "by far the most available statistical software for social science students," "its syntax is more readily understandable than many other statistical packages," and "it is a reasonably powerful and comprehensive package."

Whether our timing is any better is more debatable. In the 20 years since the publication of the first edition, basic skills have given way to accountability. However, we see accountability as more of an opportunity for affective assessment than a prohibition of it. As written in chapter 5:

> We believe that school accountability may in fact be a new, potentially rich area for affective assessment. Accountability legislation has been enacted in many states in the United States; accountability expectations exist in numerous countries throughout the world. In most cases, neither educators nor the public seem to want accountability programs that rely exclusively on standardized academic achievement tests. Good, solid affective assessment instruments have potential to provide data that can be incorporated into more broadly conceptualized school accountability programs. (p. 104)

Over and above accountability issues, what students think about themselves, their peer relationships, their schools, and their integration into the wider society, is increasingly recognized as important for the students' mental health. In light of the rate of social change and consequent change in our schools, these issues are important also for the health of our societies and the schools within them.

ACKNOWLEDGMENTS

We would like to express our appreciation to Lane Akers, our editor at Lawrence Erlbaum Associates, for giving us the opportunity to revise the book. Although we have not yet checked with the Guiness people, we suspect that 19 years may be a record for the longest time span between two editions of the same book. The senior author also thanks Rick Stiggins and Jim Popham for encouraging him over the years to rework and re-issue the book. Finally, we are grateful to Joan Herman for her careful reading and constructive comments of the manuscript. We hope they, and others, find it to be worth the wait.

—*Lorin W. Anderson*
—*Sid F. Bourke*

1

Gathering Information About Students' Affect: Why Bother?

In 1894 Alfred Binet was commissioned by the French Ministry Of Education to devise a testing instrument that could be used to identify those students who could not benefit from the French educational system because of their "subnormal" intelligence. The instrument that he and Theodore Simon designed became the model for future intelligence tests in particular and cognitive tests in general.

Although most people in education realize Binet's impact on the field of intelligence testing, few recall much of his thinking at the time he was devising this instrument. Perhaps some examples of this thinking will help the reader understand why a reference to Binet is used to introduce a book dealing with affective characteristics and affective assessment. The following three excerpts are taken from Binet and Simon's (1916) now classic book, *The Development of Intelligence in Children*:

> Our examination of intelligence cannot take account of all [the] qualities, attention, will, regularity, continuity, docility, and courage which play so important a part in school work, and also in after-life; for *life is not so much a conflict of intelligence as a combat of character.* (p. 256)

> We must expect in fact that the children whom we judge the most intelligent, will not always be those who are the most advanced in their studies. An intelligent pupil may be very lazy. We also notice that the lack of intelligence of

certain subnormal pupils does not account for their retardation. We recall what we saw when we followed the lesson for many hours in a subnormal class. It was surprising to see how restless they were, always ready to change their places, to laugh, to whisper, to pay no attention to the teacher. With such instability, it would require double the intelligence of a normal pupil to profit from their lessons. (p. 256)

And now as a pedagogical conclusion, let us say that what ... [pupils] should learn first is not the subjects ordinarily taught, however important they may be; they should be given lessons of will, of attention, of discipline; ... in a word they must learn how to learn. (p. 257)

These passages reflect some very nonintellectual thoughts for someone who is considered the father of intelligence testing. In these three excerpts, Binet and Simon (1916) clearly stated the predominant role of nonintellectual characteristics in school learning. These characteristics serve two functions. First, they are necessary for successful learning in school. As such, Binet indicated that they should be developed *before* traditional subject matters are taught. Those students who do not possess these nonintellectual characteristics will have difficulty learning the traditional subject matters, because they would need "double the intelligence of a normal pupil" (to do so. Second, these nonintellectual characteristics are important as end products of schooling because "life is not so much a conflict of intelligence as a combat of characters." Thus, according to Binet, children's development of nonintellectual characteristics in the schools is at least as important as the development of intellectual characteristics.

Concerns for noncognitive[1] student characteristics continue today. Interestingly, their importance as both means and ends is still recognized. Popham (1994), for example, suggested that:

the reason educators attend to affective variables is because such variables influence students' future behaviors. Students who have a positive attitude toward learning will be inclined to continue learning after they leave school. Students who have an interest in art will tend to volitionally seek out artistic experiences. Students who value freedom will be more likely to behave in a manner that increases their freedom rather than constrains it. (p. 405)

Similarly, Messick (1979) linked noncognitive characteristics with motivation. "Since a motive is any impulse, emotion, or desire that impels one

---

[1]The core of noncognitive characteristics lies in the beliefs that people hold As we see in chapter 2, beliefs that have emotional components can be classified as affective. In many cases, however, it is difficult to determine the extent of the emotional component of particular beliefs. Nonetheless, they do exist on a continuum related to some target and can be arranged in terms of their direction and intensity. Throughout this book, we error on the side of calling some beliefs affective that others would not label affective. Raven (1992) and Berlack (1992), for example, suggested that what they call conative factors (e.g., will, determination, persistence) are often erroneously subsumed under the affective label.

to action, almost all ... noncognitive variables ... qualify as motivational to some *degree*" (p. 285). Among the affective characteristics empirically connected with motivation are locus of control and interest (Messick, 1979), expectancies for success and the value attached to academic success (Berndt & Miller, 1990), and a sense of school belongingness (Goodenow & Grady, 1993).

With respect to affective outcomes of education, there is strong public support. In the United States, a Gallup poll taken in 1994 asked three questions concerning character education. A majority of those polled favored courses on values and ethical behavior (an increase from 1987, the last year this same poll was taken). In addition, more than 90% of those surveyed favored the teaching of core citizenship values. Finally, two thirds favored nondevotional instruction about world religions (Elam, Rose, & Gallup, 1994).

Consistent with these public perceptions, educators have begun to argue for the importance of character education. Some support the need for specific character education programs (Lickona, 1997; Power & Higgins, 1992; Watson, Battistich, & Solomon, 1998). Others argue that character education is, has been, and should be a part of the overall educational program.

> A fundamental premise of traditional education has been that every teacher is a teacher of morals. This premise can be construed in two ways: first, that every teacher should be a teacher of morals and, second, that every teacher is—willingly or not—a teacher of morals. It seems to me that both construals are correct. Teachers—even when they deny that they do so—transmit something of moral values and, since this transmission is inevitable, they should seek to do a responsible job of it. (Noddings, 1997, p. 1)

The purpose of this book is to present a conceptualization of the domain of affective characteristics and a discussion of how information about affective characteristics can be collected, analyzed, and interpreted. In writing this book, we hope that concern for affective characteristics will become an integral part of schooling in this country and throughout the world. By using the phrase "integral part" we are conveying our hope that concern for the affective domain will supplement rather than replace the current concern for the cognitive domain. This integration of intellectual and emotional is needed if schools are to fulfill their responsibility for providing high-quality education for all students.

DEFINITIONAL CONCERNS

In order to facilitate communication between us and the readers, several terms need to be defined. Three of the most important terms are those in the title of the book: *affective characteristics, assessment,* and *school.*

Affective Characteristics

Humans possess a variety of characteristics, that is, attributes or qualities that represent their typical ways of thinking, acting, and feeling in a wide variety of situations. These characteristics often are classified into three major categories. The first category, *cognitive characteristics,* corresponds with typical ways of thinking. A second category, *psychomotor characteristics,* corresponds with typical ways of acting. A third and final category, *affective characteristics,* corresponds with typical ways of feeling. Thus, within this configuration, affective characteristics can be thought of as the feelings and emotions that are characteristic of people, that is, qualities that represent people's typical ways of feeling or expressing emotion.

Despite this traditional differentiation, it is important to remember that:

> few, if any, human reactions fall completely into one of these categories [cognitive, affective, and psychomotor]. It is important that the affective domain be understood to be a construct, not a real thing, and that labeling of certain reactions as affective ... is to point out aspects of these reactions which have *significant emotional or feeling components.* (Tyler, 1973, p. 1)

Messick (1979) echoed these same sentiments when he wrote:

> it is clear that simple contrasts such as "cognitive" versus "noncognitive" are popularly embraced in spite of the dangers of stereotyping, probably because they highlight major distinctions worth noting. It is in this spirit, then, that some major features of cognitive and noncognitive assessment are addressed-with an insistence that *cognitive* does not imply *only* cognitive and that *noncognitive* does not imply the *absence* of cognition. (p. 282)

The word "typical" is important in the definition of affective characteristics. Humans are not computers; their emotions cannot be programmed to be constant. Rather, the emotional states of humans vary from day to day and from situation to situation. Some days people are up emotionally, other days they are down. Some situations are stressful, others are relaxing. Despite this variability, however, people tend to have typical ways of feeling. Some people generally tend to be up, whereas others tend to be down across a variety of days and situations. In order to understand the affective domain, we must focus on these typical feelings and emotions. Such focus is not intended to downplay the variability of these feelings and emotions. Indeed, this variability must be considered if we are to understand the affective realm. Rather, this focus on typical feelings and emotions is meant to provide an understanding of the general way of feeling so that deviations can be noted and understood as well.[2]

---

[2]Many psychologists make a distinction between affective characteristics (which they refer to as traits) and affective reactions induced by certain situations (which they refer to as states) The Spielberger State-Trait Anxiety Inventory (Spielberger, 1972) is one example.

In summary, then, a specific human characteristic must meet two general criteria to be classified as affective. It must involve the feelings or emotions of the person. In addition, it must be typical of the feelings or emotions of the person. Three more specific criteria must be met by all affective characteristics: intensity, direction, and target.

Intensity refers to the degree or strength of the feelings. Some feelings are stronger than others. "Love," for example tends to be a stronger emotion than "like." Similarly, some people tend to have stronger feelings than other people. Some people, for example, are extremely tense, others are only moderately tense.

Direction is concerned with the positive or negative orientation of feelings. Put simply, direction has to do with whether a feeling is good or bad. Some seem to be innately good or bad: Pain is bad, and pleasure is good. Others are considered good or bad depending on their definitions within particular cultures. In U.S. culture, for example, enjoying school is thought of as a positive feeling, whereas anxiety usually takes on a negative connotation. Most positive feelings have negative counterparts and vice versa. Hating school is the negative counterpart of truly enjoying school. Similarly, being relaxed is the positive counterpart of being tense.

When both intensity and direction of feelings are considered, it becomes apparent that most affective characteristics exist along a continuum. The midpoint of the continuum differentiates the positive from the negative direction, whereas the distance from the midpoint indicates the intensity of the feelings. A graphical representation of a continuum of feelings is displayed in Fig. 1.1.

Five boys' names have been written along the continuum: Phil, Rich, Tom, Art, and Bob. As can be seen, these boys differ from one another in the intensity of their feelings, the direction of their feelings, or both. Phil and Bob have equally intense feelings, but the feelings differ in direction. The same is true of Rich and Art. In contrast, Art's feelings and Bob's feelings lie in the same direction but differ in intensity; so do Phil's feelings and Rich's feelings. Finally, Tom's feelings have neither direction nor intensity. One may say they are neutral.

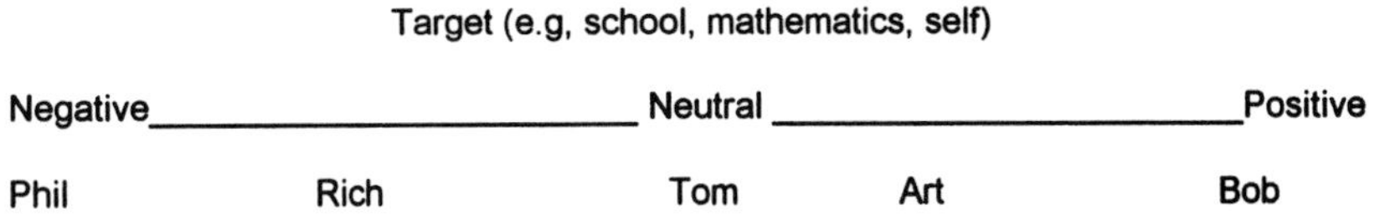

Target (e.g, school, mathematics, self)

Negative_____ Neutral _____Positive

Phil   Rich   Tom   Art   Bob

FIG. 1.1   An illustration of the continuum of feelings.

The third specific critical feature of affective characteristics can be termed the *target*. Target refers to the object, activity, or idea toward which the feeling is directed. If, for example, anxiety is the affective characteristic under consideration, several targets are possible. A person may be reacting to school, mathematics, social situations, or teachers. Each can be a target of the anxiety. Once identified, the name of the target can be placed above the affective characteristic continuum as shown in Fig. 1.1.

Sometimes the target is known by the person, sometimes it is not. That is, a person may begin to feel tense when a test is distributed in class. This person is likely to be aware that the target of the tenseness is the test. Another person, on the other hand, may be sitting in his or her living room and suddenly begin to feel tense. This person might wonder, "Why am I tense?" Perhaps some fleeting thought triggered the tension, a thought that cannot be recalled. In this case the target is not consciously known. This latter type is referred to as *free-floating anxiety*.

Sometimes the target is implicit in the stated affective characteristic. For example, the target of self-esteem is obviously "the self." In other cases, the target is connected to the affective characteristics (e.g., attitude toward mathematics, interest in learning science). In these situations, the affective assessment instruments tap what might be termed *affect-target combinations*. That is, it is not general attitude that is assessed (an affective characteristic); rather, it is attitude toward mathematics (an affect-target combination).

In sum then, affective characteristics possess five defining features. Two are general, and three are specific. First, they are feelings or emotions. This feature differentiates affective from other human characteristics. Second, they are typical ways of feeling. This feature differentiates affective characteristics from affective reactions induced in certain situations. Third, they possess some degree of intensity. Fourth, they imply direction. Fifth, there is some target (either known or unknown, implicit or explicit) toward which the feelings are directed.

Assessment

Let us turn now to a consideration of the term *assessment*. As used in this text, to assess a human characteristic simply means to gather meaningful information about that characteristic. Such information permits one to determine whether a person possesses a particular characteristic or how much of a particular characteristic a person possesses. For example, the information can tell us whether Cathy is anxious about taking tests *(Does Cathy possess test anxiety?)*, or it can tell us how anxious Cathy is about taking tests *(How much* test anxiety does Cathy possess?). In the first instance, the information is seen *as dichotomous* (that is, she does or she doesn't). In the second it is seen as *continuous* (that is, she does to varying degrees). Both types of information are useful in certain situations and for certain purposes.

This last statement leads to an important aspect of educational assessment in general and of affective assessment in particular. Assessments are usually made for some reason. That is, there generally is some purpose for which information is gathered. A teacher, for example, may gather information about his or her students' interests in a particular topic for the purpose of deciding whether or not to include the topic in the curriculum. A principal may be interested in gathering information about a prospective teacher's educational values for the purpose of seeing whether the prospective teacher's values are consistent with those of the present staff, the current philosophy of the school, or both. Whatever the reason for making the assessment, it should be clearly stated before the information is gathered. (More is said about the purposes of affective assessment in chap. 5, this volume.)

We now arrive at an important distinction between assessment and evaluation. As we suggested, assessment refers to the gathering of information about affective characteristics. Evaluation, on the other hand, refers to either a judgment of the worth or value of the characteristics per se or the worth or value of the amount of the characteristic actually possessed by a particular individual. Thus, whereas assessment tells you what affective characteristics a person possesses (e.g., what educational values does this teacher hold?), evaluation considers the worth or value of these characteristics (e.g., does this teacher hold the right values?). Likewise, whereas assessment tells how much of a particular characteristic a person possesses (e.g., how much interest in a particular topic do students have?), evaluation makes a value judgment regarding that amount of that characteristic (e.g., is that sufficient interest to include the topic in the curriculum?).

One final point must be made about the relation of assessment and evaluation. Evaluations, like other educational decisions, should be made on the basis of high-quality information. If they are not, the tendency is to make poor evaluations and decisions, no matter how good the evaluator or decision maker may be. At the same time, however, the possession of high-quality information cannot guarantee that sound evaluations and decisions will be made.

If sound evaluations and decisions are to be made, two conditions must be in place. First, high-quality information must be available. Second, a carefully planned and defensible procedure for using the information to conduct the evaluation or make the decision must be formulated and im-plemented. That is, the steps involved in the evaluation or decision-making process must be carefully thought out and carefully spelled out.

School

The term *school* is included in this section more for the purpose of discus-sion than of definition. The reader undoubtedly knows what a school is. The concept of school is important here because it serves as a context within which to view affective characteristics. Only those affective charac-teristics that are relevant to schools and learning are discussed in this text. Furthermore, although the principles and procedures described and illus-trated here apply to the assessment of affective characteristics of teachers, administrations, parents, and the like, the assessment of students' affective characteristics is the focus of this book.[3]

Affective characteristics can be related to school learning in one of three ways. First, students possess affective characteristics when they arrive at their schools and classrooms. These have been termed "affective entry characteristics" (Bloom, 1976). Second, when in schools and classrooms, affective characteristics form an important part of the lens through which students perceive and react to the events and activities that take place within them. A student who likes a particular teacher, for example, may put a positive spin on a certain behavior (e.g., a comment made by the teacher), whereas a student who dislikes the teacher may put a negative spin on the very same behavior. Third, when they leave their schools and classrooms, students take with them a set of affective characteristics. If these affective characteristics are incorporated into school or classroom goals, they are referred to as *affective outcomes*. If, instead, they are unin-tended results of schooling, they are termed *affective consequences*. A vi-sual summary of these three relationships between affective characteristics and schooling is shown in Fig. 1.2.

AFFECTIVE CHARACTERISTICS AS MEANS TO ENDS

In line with the thinking of Binet and Simon (1916) and Tyler (1973), stu-dents enter school situations with varying degrees of a variety of affective characteristics (e.g., attitudes, interests, values, and self-esteem). These

---

[3]Affective instruments for use with teachers and administrators can be found in a compendium prepared by Paula E Lester and Lloyd K. Bishop. The title is the *Handbook of Tests and Measure-ments in Education and the Social Sciences* and the publisher is Technomic Publishing Co., Inc., 851 New Holland Avenue, Box 3535, Lancaster, PA 17604. It contains instruments that assess af-fective characteristics such as anxiety, job commitment, job satisfaction, morale, motivation, self-esteem, self-efficacy, stress–burnout, and teacher attitudes–beliefs.

FIG. 1.2. Affective characteristics and schooling.

entering characteristics tend to be related to attentiveness and perseverance in class and ultimately to the acquisition of various cognitive, psychomotor, and affective objectives. That is, students possessing more positive affective entry characteristics tend to be more attentive, more persistent, less disruptive, and they tend to achieve more. On the other hand, students possessing more negative affective characteristics tend to be just the opposite—they are less attentive, less persistent, more disruptive, and they tend to achieve less. In the context of this discussion, then, affective characteristics are means to ends. The ends in this case are attentiveness, persistence, lack of disruptiveness, and learning.[4]

Interest as a Means to an End

"Learning is relatively inefficient, if effective at all, when it is stimulated by coercion rather than by the genuine interest of the learners" (Tyler, 1973, p. 2). That is, for students to learn well (effectively) and to learn quickly (efficiently), they must have some interest in learning what they are expected to learn. A noteworthy converse of Tyler's statement is that without interest, some form of coercion is necessary. Perhaps the lack of concern for student affective characteristics, such as interest, has led to the increased use of more coercive programs, such as behavior modification.

    Interest in learning, particularly interest in learning specific subjects, is an important means to valued ends. As Messick (1979) contended: "Since interests serve to sustain self-determined activities not only in the absence

---

[4]In situations in which instructional units or programs are highly sequential (i.e., the outcomes of one unit or program facilitate or inhibit the outcomes of subsequent units or programs), the ends of one unit or program become the means for the other units and programs. In these situations the distinction between means and ends become blurred over time.

of external reinforcement but often in the face of negative reinforcement, they are important examples of intrinsic motives" (p. 285).

Internal Locus of Control as a Means to an End

A widely investigated affective characteristic is *locus of control*, which contrasts individuals who believe they are responsible for their success and failures (*internals*) with individuals who believe the reasons for successes and failures rest with force of circumstances, powerful others, or luck (*externals*). Within attributional theory (Weiner, 1992), a person with an internal locus of control attributes his or her successes and failures to personal characteristics and qualities (e.g., ability, hard work).

Students who attribute their successes to their abilities and efforts (i.e., internal students) tend to be more self-motivated than their external counterparts. They also tend to work more independently and are able to provide their own reinforcement for their work, rather than seeking reinforcement from external sources (DeCharms, 1976; Fanelli, 1977; Lefcourt. 1976).

Equally if not more importantly, internal students see a connection between their actions and the results of these actions. Thus, for example, they are more likely to believe that their efforts lead to achievement. This effort–achievement connection is an important component of most theories of motivation (see chap. 8, this volume, for a more detailed discussion of this point).

Having an internal locus of control is not always good. Attributing failure to low ability (e.g., "I'm not smart enough to learn it") is a powerful motivational inhibitor that "generates low expectations for future success (because ability is perceived as stable) and feelings of shame as well as expressions of pity from others (because it is perceived as uncontrollable)" (Weiner, 1992, p. 861).

Self-Efficacy as a Means to an End

Whereas causal attributions refer to inferences made by students as to why they succeeded or failed in the past, self-efficacy is concerned with students' beliefs about the future. *Self-efficacy* was defined as a "person's belief in his or her capability of performing a behavior required to reach a goal" (Weiner, 1992, p. 861). In the vernacular, self-efficacy is a "can-do" attitude. Self-efficacy influences what students choose to do (i.e., the goals they select), their persistence, and the quality of their performance relative to goal attainment (Smith, 1989). Finally, as seen in chapter 8, this volume, self-efficacy combines with the value students place in learning to form the cornerstones of one of the most widely accepted theories of motivation.

The opposite of a can-do attitude is a can't-do attitude. A can't-do attitude lies at the heart of a concept known as *learned helplessness* (Seligman, 1975). The symptoms of learned helpless include lack of persistence in the face of failure, negative affect, and negative expectations about the future. Consequently, learned helpless has an adverse effect on motivation and, ultimately, learning (Weiner, 1992).

Anxiety as a Means to an End

Unlike interest and internal locus of control for success, which are believed to positively influence motivation and achievement, anxiety (like low-ability ascription for failure and learned helplessness) is seen as a "motivational inhibitor" (Weiner, 1992, p. 863). Although there are many sources or targets of anxiety, test anxiety has consistently been found to be negatively related to academic performance in a variety of settings (Sarason, 1986). The way in which test anxiety operates also has been studied. In general it is believed that test anxiety produces thoughts that are irrelevant to the task at hand. This is a form of mental withdrawal. This mental withdrawal, in turn, is debilitative in terms of academic performance (Schwarzer, 1986). A similar argument can quite likely be made for other types of anxiety: math anxiety, school anxiety, and the like.

These examples of affective entry characteristics are not intended to exhaustive. Rather, they are meant to illustrate ways in which the affective characteristics of students are important means to a variety of important educational ends. In addition, however, several of the affective characteristics mentioned can be considered both means and ends. For example, as Tyler (1973) wrote, "interest in school work not only furnishes positive motivation for school learning, but in addition, most schools *attempt to help children develop interests* [italics added] in many areas of school learning" (p. 2).

AFFECTIVE CHARACTERISTICS AS ENDS

Just as students enter school situations possessing different degrees of various affective characteristics, they leave school situations with different degrees of various affective characteristics. In some cases students may leave with the same levels or same characteristics with which they entered. In other cases students may leave with different levels (greater or lesser) of particular characteristics or with different characteristics altogether. If these "leaving characteristics" are intended (in the sense they are stated as goals with efforts made to attain them) the are termed affective outcomes. One planned affective outcome suggested by Tyler (1973), for example, is the development of an objective attitude—that is, an increased openness to new ideas, activities, standards, and goals. If, on the other hand, the leaving characteristics are unintended, we call them *affective consequences*. The discussion in this section focuses on affective outcomes. Affective consequences are discussed in chapter 8.

The discussion begins with a question. Just how important are affective outcomes of the schooling process? Perhaps three quotations will help to answer this question. Hesburgh (1979) stated his belief in the importance of affective outcomes quite clearly:

> I realize full well that education is essentially a work of the intellect, the formation of intelligence, the unending search for knowledge. Why then be concerned with values? Because wisdom is more than knowledge, man is more than his mind, and without values, man may be intelligent but less than fully human. (p. xi)

Klausmeier and Goodwin (1971) echoed this belief: "Attitudes and values are among the most vital outcomes learned in schools, for they are important in determining how individuals react to situations, and also what they seek in life" (p. 382).

Finally, Messick (1979) stated this point slightly differently emphasizing the role of the schools in the development of affective outcomes:

> Since human beings learn to value certain objects, activities, and ideas so that these become important directors of their interests, attitudes, and satisfactions, the school should help the student discover and reinforce values that might be meaningful and significant to him in obtaining personal happiness and making contributions to society. (p. 6)

At this point the reader may ask a related question: If affective outcomes are so important, why have they not become a central part of schooling in many countries? Although this is a difficult question, educators have offered several reasons. Tyler (1973), for example, suggested two possible reasons for the lack of emphasis on affective outcomes:

> In the past, affective learning in the schools was not systematically planned or even considered. To a large extent, two prevalent beliefs operated to inhibit analyses of the learning of affective behavior. One was the view that the development of appropriate feelings was the task of home and church, not the school. The other was the belief that appropriate feelings developed automatically from knowledge and experience with content and did not require any special pedagogical attention. Today educators recognize that although the home and other nonschool institutions still have important

roles to play in affective learning, there are objectives in the affective domain that are appropriate to the educational functions of the school and college. They also recognize that these objectives are not automatically attained when students develop relevant knowledge and have experiences with phenomena and their derivative content. (p. 2)

A third reason for the avoidance of affective outcomes in schooling was proposed by Bloom, Hastings, and Madaus (1971). This reason falls under the heading "fear of indoctrination," or, as Bloom, Hastings, and Madaus wrote:

One of the reasons for the failure to give instructional emphasis to affective outcomes is related to the Orwellian overtones which attitudinal and value-oriented instruction often conjures up in the minds of teachers and the public. Can we teach values without engaging in indoctrination and brainwashing techniques so foreign to our concepts of education? (p. 226)

More recently, Popham (1994) offered a fourth reason, one that updates and expands on Tyler's (1973) first reason.

Folks who formally oppose the schools' involvement in affective education tend to recognize [that] *affect influences future behavior.* The stronger the affect, the stronger its impact on one's future actions. If Christian parents truly believe that a child's future behaviors will determine the child's entry into heaven, then it is all too clear why quite many members of the new religious right would rather have values fostered in the home than the classroom. (p. 406)

To overcome this problem, Popham (1994) suggested educators pursue what he terms "noncontroversial affective outcomes." He then provided three examples:

A *noncontroversial attitude to be sought*: Students will regard opposing views circumspectly, that is, will consider the potential merits of intellectual positions that are in opposition to their own.

A *noncontroversial interest to be fostered*: Students will become sufficiently interested in the content they study so that, after formal schooling has ceased, they will still wish to learn more about such content.

A *noncontroversial value to be promoted*: Students will subscribe to the inherent importance of an individual's or a society's property rights so that malicious defacement of public property or theft of another person's goods will be regarded as unacceptable.(p. 407)

In sum, then, educators seem to agree that affective outcomes of schooling are critical. Attitudes, interests, and values are frequently suggested as the most important affective goals. Despite this perceived importance, however, an emphasis on affective outcomes has been avoided by schools in the past. As seen previously, several reasons for this avoidance can be offered. Given both the importance of affective outcomes and educators' reluctance to pursue them, let us conclude this section with one final question. What role should schools play in the learning or acquisition of affective outcomes?

Many people believe that schools should play no part in the development of affective characteristics; rather, they would have schools be value free. Unfortunately for these people, this is an impossible dream. They are forgetting the accidental or incidental development of affective characteristics mentioned earlier and discussed in greater detail in chapter 8. In schools today, affective characteristics such as values are being learned and are being taught. Thus, whether they should or should not be taught is moot. Students learn teachers' values by observing their behaviors. What rules do teachers reinforce? What rules do they not reinforce? How do they react to different types of questions posed by their students? How do teachers react to different types of students—for example, fast versus slow learners and members of different ethnic groups? How enthusiastic are teachers about teaching? About teaching a particular topic? Through answers to these questions students infer the values, attitudes, and interests of their teachers. In a similar manner, they infer the values and attitudes of various administrators. And from out-of-class discussions with peers, they hear encounter a wide variety of attitudes, interests, and values.

Numerous affective characteristics are being formed or changed by a variety of people in the school setting. To the extent that it is desirable for affective characteristics to be formed or changed in such an unplanned, haphazard manner, little needs to be done about schools' working toward the development of affective characteristics. On the other hand, if various affective characteristics are as important as previously indicated, can we afford to leave the development of these characteristics to chance? We think not. Because affective characteristics are being affected by the schooling process, the least we can do is ensure that critical affective characteristics are developed as effectively as possible. Davis (1981) made this point very clearly:

> Most of us are willing to take the position that many old-fashioned values and virtues are good for every individual and for society. Further, the values are worth cultivating in fertile young minds. The alternative is to hang up your hoe and watch the values grow—along with plenty of weeds—as chance side effects of, for example, lessons in history, English, or social studies. Depending upon the particular community, students have many opportunities to acquire maladaptive or even self-destructive values, for example, appreciation for successful lying, cheating, stealing, sitting on the curb drink-

ing wine, using heroine or other hard drugs. Surveys among slum young-sters have shown that many of them admire, respect, and hope to emulate the pimps, prostitutes, and drug dealers whose fine clothes and air-conditioned Cadillacs are obvious testimony to their "success" in Ameri-can society. More productive values deserve equal time. (p. 273)

AFFECTIVE CHARACTERISTICS IN SCHOOLS AND CLASSROOMS

Affective entry characteristics are brought to schools and classrooms by students. Affective outcomes and consequences are taken from schools and classroom by students. What about affective characteristics of students while they are in specific schools and particular classrooms? What beliefs do students have about the schools they attend? What attitudes do they have about specific aspects of their classrooms and their teachers?

Answers to questions such as these require fairly specific targets. There is a substantial difference between attitudes toward school in general and their general satisfaction with the particular school they are currently at-tending. Similarly, there is a large difference between attitudes toward sci-ence and attitude toward the way in which science is taught in this particular classroom. Since the publication of the original edition of this book, there has been an explosion of research related to what may be termed "in-flight" affective characteristics.

Classroom environment instruments originated in the late 1960s as part of the evaluation of Harvard Project Physics (Walberg & Anderson, 1968). These instruments make use of students' perceptions to assess key dimen-sions of specific classrooms, generally as the students believe them to be (the "actual" environment) and as they would prefer them to be (the "ideal" environment). Since their inception, classroom environment in-struments have been used for a multitude of purposes. Examples include comparing students' and teachers' perceptions of actual and preferred classroom environments, examining whether students have greater achievement in their preferred classroom environments, evaluating teach-ers' attempts to improve classroom environments, and investigating cross-national differences in classroom environments (Fraser, 1998).

Quality of school life or school environment instruments are a some-what more recent phenomenon (Ainley & Bourke, 1992; Halderson, Kelley, Keefe, & Berge, 1989). In principle, they are quite similar to the classroom environment instruments in terms of the constructs they include. Teacher support (classroom environment) becomes teacher–student rela-tionships (school environment). Task orientation (classroom environment) becomes student academic orientation (school environment). Cohesive-ness (classroom environment) becomes student–peer relationships (school environment). The primary difference is the target: classroom versus school. The shift from classroom to school is consistent with the belief among some educators that the school is the smallest meaningful unit of educational improvement (Pellicer & Anderson, 1994) and the call from legislators and the public for school accountability (Macpherson, 1995; Maxwell, 1996; Public Agenda Foundation, 1996; Townsend, 1996).

Finally, a sense of school belonging (also known as school membership) is the most recent of the in-flight entries. Operating from the belief that "academic motivation is not a purely individual, intrapsychic state [but also] grows out of a complex web of social and personal relationships," Goodenow and Grady (1994) argued that the "extent to which [students] feel personally accepted, respected, included, and supported by others" (pp. 60–61) determines not only their participation in school but, conversely, their disengagement from school that ultimately leads to leaving school. Their research suggests that the degree of school belongingness, as expressed by students, predicts their general school motivation, expectancy for academic success, and the value students attributed to their school work.

Since the publication of the first edition of this book, then, affective assessment has expanded from an exclusive focus on "before and after" to a concern for "during," and from the use of fairly global targets to more specific ones. Students' beliefs about and attitudes toward their specific schools and classrooms provide a useful source of information that can be used for a variety of purposes.

THE IMPORTANCE OF AFFECTIVE ASSESSMENT

Suppose by reading this far you have become convinced that affective characteristics are important as means of education, as ends of education, and as barometers of education-in-process. If this is true, the importance of assessing these characteristics should be obvious. In simplest terms, we need to know (a) what affective characteristics students possess when they enter schools and classrooms, (b) how students' perceive their schools and classrooms, and (c) the extent to which they are achieving important affective goals. On a group basis, this information should enable the design of more effective school and classroom environments. On an individual basis, it should allow for the identification of those students who do not possess or have not developed desirable or useful affective characteristics or, perhaps more importantly, those whose affective characteristics inhibit them from succeeding in their classes or participating fully in their schools. Early identification of these students may enable us to provide the type of assistance they need to increase their likelihood of academic success and decrease the likelihood they will drop out of school.

This seems so straightforward and reasonable that the reader may ask, once again, why affective assessment is not a regular and ongoing part of our assessment process. Again, there are no easy answers. Bloom, Hastings, and Madaus (1971) offered one possible answer. They suggested that many people believe either that affective outcomes are nebulous or that they cannot be attained in the typical periods of instruction offered in schools today:

> This belief is implied in the statements of teachers who claim their goals are intangible or so long range that the attitudes, values, interests, and apprecia- tions they have tried to develop in their students may not reveal themselves until much later in lifelong after formal education has been completed. (p. 227)

A second answer to the question is that affective characteristics are considered to be private rather than public matters (Bloom et al. 1971). Unlike cognitive achievement, about which the public has a right to know for purposes of credentialing and certification, the public does not have the right to know about ones attitudes, interests, values, and the like. These are private concerns.

There is a third answer to the question, one we attempt to address directly in this book. Many people believe that it is virtually impossible to gather valid and reliable information about affective characteristics. This belief is predicated on the related belief that there simply are no sound methods for gathering such information. Each of these possible answers are briefly addressed.

Affective Goals are Intangible or Long Term

This belief actually consists of two separate but related beliefs. The first is that affective goals are intangible; the second is that affective goals take a long time to accomplish. Let us consider each of these.

Are affective goals intangible? Yes, to the same extent that cognitive goals are intangible. Consider the following cognitive goal: The learner is to understand the factors that contributed to the outbreak of World War II. This is an abstract goal. What is meant by "understand"? Precisely when was the "outbreak" of the Second World War? When has a factor contributed to the outbreak of a war? Educators have long recognized the abstractness of cognitive goals. In response to this abstractness, many have supported what has been called the *behavioral objective movement*. This movement was an attempt to make such abstract goals concrete. An advocate of behavioral objectives might have stated the goal in the previous example as follows: "The learner is to write in his or her own words three events that led to the involvement of the United States in World War II." In this and similar ways, attempts are made to make the intangible tangible.

Goals by their very nature are abstract and intangible. In order to assess them we must work toward making the goal statements more concrete. In fact, in order to facilitate the teaching and learning of goals, goal statements must be much more concrete than they typically are. We use the term *conceptual definition* to describe a definition of an affective characteristic with respect to its abstract meaning. In contrast, we use the term *operational definition* to describe an affective characteristic in more concrete terms. Thus, although it is true that affective goals are intangible, it also is true that these goals must be made more concrete if they are to be useful, either from an instructional or an assessment perspective, in educational settings. Because this is a critical issue, a more detailed discussion of conceptual and operational definitions is presented in chapter 2 of this volume.

One final point should be made concerning the belief in the intangibility of affective goals. Many educators use this belief to avoid facing the recent trend toward accountability in education. That is to say, they exchange cognitive for affective goals and then argue that their instructional programs cannot be evaluated because affective goals are too intangible to be assessed. Hopefully, this book will contribute to the removal of this belief by demonstrating that affective goals can be made tangible and consequently can be assessed. For whatever the goals of an instructional program may be, it is important to gather information concerning the effectiveness of the program with respect to those goals. And if the goals are truly important, it is necessary to know which students have and have not attained those goals.

Are affective goals long-term goals? Certain affective goals do require a long time to accomplish. Similarly, however, there are many cognitive goals that take a long time to develop (e.g., that the learner be able to critically evaluate an essay). Those affective goals that do take a long time to develop can still be periodically assessed to chart their development. In this situation the purpose of assessment is to see if the development is taking place as expected. By monitoring the development of long-term affective goals, modifications in instructional programs can be made as needed to increase the program's effectiveness with respect to those goals. Naturally, it is important to keep in mind that these interim assessments are only progress checks and that the final assessment of the affective goal will be made only after the necessary amount of time has elapsed.

It is important to note, however, that many affective goals are not long-term goals, just as many cognitive goals are not long term. Affective goals can be short term in nature. For example, an affective goal may be that students become interested in learning more about matrix algebra after a 2-week introductory unit on the topic.

Let us summarize at this point. Affective goals can differ in two respects: (1) the degree of abstractness (or intangibility) and (2) the time needed for their attainment. Abstract goals must be made concrete if they are to be taught and assessed. When properly selected or designed, affective assessment instruments are concrete representations of abstract goals. The time that is needed for students to attain these goals must be taken into consideration if the results of affective assessments are to be interpreted properly. Assessment made before their time are best considered progress reports.

Affective Characteristics are Private Rather Than Public Matters

The right of privacy is an important value underlying the American way of life. Thus, the issue of privacy with respect to assessment of affective characteristics is important. Traditionally, it has arisen because of the potential uses of the information gathered through the assessment process. Unfortunately, a variety of uses can be made of any information; some are good, some are not so good. For example, we may use information about a student's intelligence to label the student "terminally stupid." On the other hand, we may use information about a student's intelligence to better understand the student's present level of functioning. Given this understanding, it may be possible to design a more effective instructional program for the student. These two uses differ greatly in the effect on the student. Too often we seem more willing to label students than to actually help them, hence the concern for privacy. No one likes to be labeled.

Similarly, in the affective domain, the gathering of the information can lead to both good and poor uses of information. A teacher, for example, can use the information that a student has a negative attitude toward his or her course to berate the student in front of others. Or a teacher can use this information to work toward development of a more positive attitude on the part of the student. Because uses of affective information can vary widely, concerns for privacy are justified once again. If, however, information was routinely used for positive ends, such concern would be less important. Unfortunately, those of us in the fields of assessment and measurement cannot guarantee that information will be used wisely or by "wise" people.

The other side of the privacy issue, however, is the public's need to know certain things about individuals. Participation in society carries with it certain responsibilities and obligations. For example, our society does not question whether a state government has the right to determine whether an individual can pass a driving test before being issued a driver's license. Like state government officials, school personnel need to know certain things about students and other school personnel. For example, information about the cognitive, affective, and psychomotor characteristics students possess when entering a course or program is important if appropriate instructional conditions are to be provided for the students.

Thus, the issue of affective characteristics as a private rather than a public matter is complicated by two opposing concerns: the individual's right to privacy and the public's right to information. How can this difficult issue be resolved? The answer lies in the concept of relevancy. If information is needed before a decision can be made and if the information is relevant to the decision to be made, then the gathering of such information is *not* an invasion of privacy. On the other hand, if the information is not being gathered for any particular purpose or if the information is not relevant to the stated purpose, then the gathering of such information is likely to be an invasion of privacy.

In sum then, the belief that affective characteristics are private rather than public matters is partly true and partly false. To the extent that information is needed to make a sound decision—a decision that an institution has a right to make—and to the extent that such information is relevant for the making of the decision, the gathering of such information is a public matter. Even in this case, however, we must respect the individual's right to privacy. Any gathering of information is a potential invasion of privacy because the information can be used in a variety of ways. Hopefully, we will learn to use information for the betterment rather than to the detriment of individuals and institutions. To the extent that this hope is realized, the assessment of affective characteristics is both a private and a public matter.

The Impossibility of Gathering Affective Information

This belief is standard among educators who are generally opposed to testing, measurement, and assessment. Because the belief is derived from a basic philosophy asserting in part that testing destroys the very thing it is trying to measure, it is difficult to deal rationally with this issue. Suffice it to say that one of our purposes is to convince the reader that it is *both important and possible* to gather affective information. As a consequence the authors are willing to let the reader decide for himself or herself whether we have succeeded. (Hopefully, the reader will make this decision after reading the entire book.)

OVERVIEW OF THE REMAINING CHAPTERS

This book is organized around a highly sequential approach to affective assessment. We began with a discussion of the importance of affective characteristics in education and the concomitant importance of affective assessment. In chapter 2 we explore in greater detail definitional considerations by highlighting two types of definitions: *conceptual definitions,* which focus on the meaning of affective characteristics, and *operational definitions,* which focus on more concrete representations of affective characteristics (i.e., affective assessment instruments).

In chapter 3 we describe and contrast two general methods of gathering information about affective characteristics: observational and self-report. In chapter 4 we discuss qualities of sound and defensible affective instruments, with an emphasis on those developed in accordance with the principles of Likert scales. In chapter 5 we present a step-by-step procedure for selecting and for designing affective instruments. We also discuss how to decide whether to select or design an instrument and, if a decision is made to select an instrument, where likely candidates for selection can be found.

In chapter 6, we walk the reader through the data entry, editing, and analysis process. We use an existing data set to illustrate the major concepts and their application. In chapter 7, our attention turns to interpretation of the data obtained from the administration of affective instruments. Finally, in chapter 8, we describe four primary uses of affective assessment data in the context of educational and school improvement. To the extent that we have succeeded in writing an understandable and useful book, the reader should, after finishing it, have achieved the following objectives.

1. Understand the importance of affective characteristics and affective assessment in the context of schools.
2. Know the qualities of sound, defensible, and useful affective assessment instruments.
3. Be able to select an appropriate affective instrument and justify the selection, or design a sound, defensible affective assessment instrument.
4. Be able to enter, edit, and analyze data obtained from the administration of an affective instrument and use the data to examine the technical quality of the instrument, making improvements in the instrument as needed.
5. Be able to interpret the results of the administration of affective instruments and use the results for a variety of educationally-relevant purposes.

SUMMARY OF MAJOR POINTS

1. Affective characteristics are qualities of a person that represent his or her typical ways of feeling or emoting.
2. Affective characteristics possess five defining features, two general (a & b) and three specific (c, d, & e).
   a. They are feeling
   b. They are typical ways of feelings
   c. They have some degree of intensity
   d. They have direction
   e. They are directed toward some target (e.g., idea, activity, or object).
3. It is difficult to completely differentiate affective characteristics from other human characteristics (e.g., cognitive, psychomotor, conative).
4. Assessment refers to the gathering of information about a human characteristic for some stated purpose. Assessment is distinct from evaluation, which refers to the judgment of worth or value of the characteristic (or some amount of the characteristic).
5. For sound evaluations to be made, two conditions are necessary:
   a. High-quality information must be available.
   b. A reasonable procedure for making the judgment must be formulated implemented.
6. School, used in this volume, describes the context within which to view affective characteristics. That is to say, only those affective characteristics that are relevant to schools and learning will be discussed here. Furthermore, students (rather than teachers, administrators, and parents) are the focal point.
7. Affective characteristics are important as means to ends (i.e., they facilitate some desired goal of the schooling process), as ends in themselves (i.e., they *are desired goals* of the schooling process), and as "filters" of the process itself (i.e., the influence the way in which students' perceive and make sense of their schools and classrooms).
8. Several reasons can be given to explain why affective goals have not been actively pursued in schools. Among them are:
   a. A belief that the development of affective characteristics is the task of the home and church,
   b. A belief that affective characteristics develop somewhat "automatically,"
   c. A fear that schools will indoctrinate students or transmit values antithetical to those held by parents and guardians.
9. Schools do have a role to play in the development of affective characteristics. If schools do not assume that role, numerous undesirable people are more than willing to assume it.

10. Affective assessment is important because it provides the information we need to understand students and to improve the quality of education we provide them. In the case of affective goals, affective assessment provides a means of evaluating goal attainment.
11. Despite its importance, there are several reasons why affective assessment is not a regular part of the assessment program in place in schools. Among them are the following:
   a. The belief that affective goals are intangible.
   b. The belief that affective goals take a long time to develop.
   c. The belief that affective characteristics are private, not public, matters.
   d. The belief that assessing affective characteristics is virtually impossible.

Each of these beliefs is partially true and partially false, with the exception of the last one, which is totally false.

2
Affective Characteristics: What Are They?

Most educators agree that well thought out and clearly communicated definitions are the keys to understanding. In few areas of education does this principle seem to hold as well as in the areas of affective characteristics and affective assessment. Good definitions are needed in order to (a) select or design an appropriate assessment instrument, (b) examine the technical quality of the instrument, and (c) interpret (i.e., make sense of) the results. Consequently, this chapter is in many respects the keystone chapter of the entire volume. Without an understanding of what is being assessed, assessment is trivial at best.

The chapter begins with a brief section on the importance of well thought out and clearly communicated definitions. Next, the focus is on the importance of defining both the specific affective characteristics and the target toward which the affective characteristic is directed. The third section describes two types of definitions that are useful in assessment: conceptual and operational. The fourth section is concerned specifically with conceptual definitions of selected affective characteristics, and the fifth and sixth sections discuss two methods of arriving at sound operational definitions for these characteristics. The seventh and final section contains a restatement of the role of definitions in affective assessment.

THE IMPORTANCE OF DEFINITIONS IN AFFECTIVE ASSESSMENT

As mentioned earlier, a sound definition of the affective characteristic under consideration provides a basis for the selection or design of an assessment instrument as well as proper interpretation of the results. This basis is provided for in several ways. First, a clear definition helps to decide on the type of instrument that is needed. Should you use a self-report or an observational instrument? If a self-report is chosen, should you use a Likert scale or some other scaling technique? If a Likert scale is chosen, what format should you use for the response options (e.g., strongly agree to strongly disagree, almost always to never)?

Once the type of instrument decided is on, a clear definition also helps to decide on the specific instrument (from the general type of instrument) that is appropriate for use. Suppose, for example, you determine that an attitude is to be assessed. An instrument you locate is designed to assess values. There is a discrepancy between the specific affective characteristic that you intend to assess and the affective characteristic that is actually assessed by the instrument. This discrepancy suggests a problem with the validity of the instrument and, consequently, will likely lead to other problems.

In addition to aiding in the selection of an appropriate instrument, a sound definition also provides a basis for communication among educators and between educators and noneducators. Such communication is necessary if affective assessment instruments are to be used properly and if the results of the assessment are to be meaningful and useful.

Unfortunately, in the field of education, several definitions often exist for the same word. A term such as *intelligence,* for example, possesses several definitions. The presence of a variety of definitions has contributed to much of the misunderstanding surrounding the concept of intelligence. In order to minimize this misunderstanding, it is necessary to explicitly state the definition of intelligence being used so that everyone will understand it. It is not important that a "right" definition exists. The search for right definitions tends to be long, tedious, frustrating, and futile. What is important is that a definition be accepted at that moment in time so that communication can be enhanced rather than retarded.

In sum, then, the definition of specific affective characteristics should be stated in a clear, concise manner. By stating the definition, confusion can be reduced and communication improved. And, although people may disagree with the definition, they nonetheless have a common understanding of the meaning of the characteristic as used in that particular context.

As indicated in chapter 1, affective characteristics are directed toward some target or targets. Most frequently these targets are objects, activities, or ideas. Thus, for example, one may have a strong negative attitude toward nineteenth-century English literature. One also may be mildly interested in learning a second language. Or one may value democracy greatly. In these three examples, nineteenth-century English literature, learning a second language, and democracy are the object, activity, and idea, respectively, toward which the affective characteristic (attitude, interest, and value) is directed.[1]

The point here is that definitions are needed for both the specific affective characteristics and for the targets toward which the affective characteristics are directed. Because the focus of the remainder of the chapter is on definitions of specific affective characteristics, the focus in the rest of this particular section is on the definition of the targets toward which the affective characteristics are directed.

Suppose you wish to assess students' attitudes toward school. The affective characteristic is attitude, and the target is school. School can be defined or described in many ways. School can refer to the building itself. Because this is not likely to be the referent when assessing a person's attitude toward school, several other possibilities exist. School can refer to the various school personnel (e.g., teachers, counselors, and administrators). School can refer to various subjects taught in scool or the way in which these subjects are taught. Finally, school can refer to what has been referred to by various authors as the milieu, climate, or culture of the school. Whatever meaning the term *school* is to have with respect to the affective characteristic, attitude, should be spelled out in some detail.

One way of delineating the target toward which the affective characteristic is directed is to define it in terms of its important aspects or critical features. School, for example, can be used to refer to the building per se, the people who work in the building, the subjects taught in the building, the norms and expectations for those who inhabit the building, or the social interactions that take place in the building. Each of these can be thought of as an important aspect or critical feature of the concept *school*. Thus, any one or any combination of these critical features can be used to properly define school. Virtually any target (e.g., nineteenth-century English literature or democracy) can be defined in terms of its important aspects or critical features.

The importance of defining the target should be clear from the previous example. If the target is not clearly defined, individuals may react to different aspects or features of the target. When thinking of school Felicia might be reacting to the subjects taught in school, Joan may be reacting to the school personnel, Bill may be reacting to the social interactions in school,

---

[1]The reader should note that two other defining features of affective characteristics are present in these descriptions: intensity (strong, mildly, and greatly) and direction (positive, and negative).

and Manny many be reacting to the norms and expectations. These differences in targets, then, may lead to different responses which, in turn, may lead to very different interpretations of these students' attitudes toward school. Furthermore, comparisons between or among these students will be difficult if not impossible, because they are reacting to different aspects or features of the target.

One final comment is necessary. To alleviate the problems described here, the definition of the target should be communicated to the students who will be responding to the instrument. One way to do this is to include the definition as a part of the instructions given to the students before they respond to the instrument.

CONCEPTUAL AND OPERATIONAL DEFINITIONS

Two types of definitions are important in the context of assessment: conceptual definitions and operational definitions. As mentioned in chapter 1, conceptual definitions are those concerned with the abstract meaning of a characteristic. Operational definitions, on the other hand, refer to a set of behaviors (e.g., spoken words, actions) that, when exhibited, can be used to make inferences about the characteristic. It helps us to make the distinction between conceptual and operational definitions clear if we move outside the affective realm briefly, to consider definitions of intelligence.

Intelligence may be defined conceptually as the ability to discover relationships among objects, activities, or ideas. Alternatively, intelligence may be defined as the ability of a person to adapt effectively to his or her environment. These definitions give meaning to the term intelligence. That is, intelligence is the ability to discover relationships, or intelligence is the ability to adapt effectively to ones environment.

Turning to operational definitions, most human characteristics, especially affective ones, must be inferred from some kind of behavior (e.g., writing, speaking, acting) because they are not directly observable. To continue with the intelligence example, the behaviors most frequently used to make inferences about a person's intelligence are his or her written responses to a number of questions or tasks.

One operational definition of intelligence, for example, consists of a person's responses to the items on the Stanford-Binet Intelligence Test. A second operational definition of intelligence consists of a person's responses to the items on the Raven's Progressive Matrices Test. Because different questions or tasks are included on the two tests and hence different responses are called for, these are two different operational definitions of intelligence.

In order for assessment to provide valid and useful information about a particular characteristic, a close relation must exist between the conceptual definition of the characteristic and its operational definition.[2] Stated simply, there must be a close correspondence between the behaviors required of the person being assessed and the conceptual definition of the human characteristic being assessed. This is perhaps the basic principle of assessment.

Let us return for a moment to the intelligence example in order to see how this principle applies. In the discussion thus far, two conceptual definitions of intelligence have been put forward and two intelligence tests have been mentioned. The first definition (definition A) was concerned with a person's ability to see relations among objects, activities, and ideas. The second definition (definition B) was concerned with a person's ability to adapt effectively to his or her environment. The two intelligence tests were the Stanford-Binet and Raven's.

If a sample of items is examined from the Stanford-Binet Intelligence Test (see Fig. 2.1), you see that the behaviors required by the items are those that enable a student to adapt effectively to an environment, more specifically, a typical school environment. The vocabulary and questions are similar to those that students encounter in classroom situations. If, on the other hand, you examine a task from the Raven's Progressive Matrices Test (see Fig. 2.2), you see that this task requires a student to see relations among objects. A student would rarely encounter such a task in a typical classroom environment. Thus, the Stanford-Binet Intelligence Test seems to be more closely aligned with definition B, whereas the Raven's Progressive Matrices Test seems to be more aligned with definition A. To use the Stanford-Binet for the purpose of assessing conceptual definition A or to use Raven's for the purpose of assessing conceptual definition B would be inappropriate. This inappropriateness stems from the lack of correspondence between the conceptual and operational definitions.

Although this example comes from the cognitive domain, a close relation between conceptual and operational definitions is also critical in the affective realm. As has been mentioned previously, the extent to which this relation exists is typically referred to as the validity of the assessment instrument. Although more is said about the validity issue in later chapters, one point is worth noting at this time. It concerns an important difference between cognitive and affective assessment, a difference that highlights a critical feature of affective assessment.

---

[2]The concept of operational definitions has led cynics to suggest that intelligence is whatever an intelligence test measures. These individuals have missed completely the need for both conceptual and operational definitions and a close relationship between the two.

12-Year Level

1. Vocabulary (same as 6-year level). Fifteen words correct for credit at this level. Words like juggler and brunette.

2. Verbal Absurdities (five statements). "Bill Jones's feet are so big that he has to pull his trousers on over his head. What is foolish about that?" Four out of five right for credit at this level.

3. Picture Absurdities. Picture showing person's shadow going wrong way. "What is foolish about that picture?"

4. Repeating Five Digits Reversed. "I am going to say some numbers, and I want you to say them backwards." One out of three correct for credit.

5. Abstract Words. "What do we mean by pity?" Three out of four for credit at this level.

6. Sentence Completion (four sentences with missing words). "Write the missing word in each blank. Put just one word in each." Three out of four required for credit at this level.

FIG. 2.1. Sample items from the Stanford-Binet Intelligence Test (Thorndike & Hagen, 1977). Copyright © 1960 by Houghton Mifflin Company. Reprinted by permission of Houghton Mifflin Co. All rights reserved.

Cognitive assessment attempts to provide information about various cognitive characteristics by eliciting behaviors that can be classified somehow as correct or incorrect or, increasingly, along a continuum of correctness or quality of performance. Cronbach (1970) used the term *maximal performance* to refer to cognitive tests because students are expected to get the maximum number of items correct that they can. Affective assessment, on the other hand, attempts to provide information about various affective characteristics by eliciting behaviors that are typical of the behaviors exhibited by the person, that is, behaviors that are usually exhibited. As a consequence, Cronbach (1970) used the term *typical performance* to refer to affective instruments.

Messick (1979) addressed directly this distinction between maximal and typical performance instruments. He wrote, "The absence of right-answer keys forces (affective) assessment to draw inferences from *consistency* [italics added] in response rather than *correctness* [italics added] of response" (p. 283). If consistency is a critical feature of affective assessment, then it is impossible to infer an affective characteristic from a single response or reaction. Rather, it is necessary to have a person respond to several statements or questions that are similar in some way or to react in a variety of similar situations if one is to make proper inferences about the affective characteristic under consideration. More is said about this issue (called the reliability issue) in later chapters.

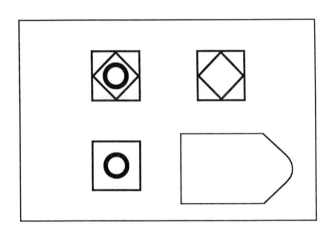

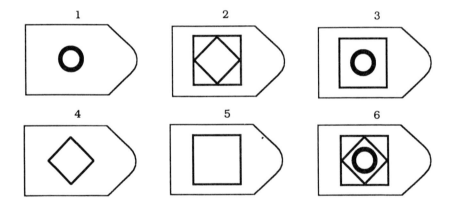

Note. A two-dimensional arrangement of four cells is presented with one cell (in this illustration, the lower right-hand cell) blank. The examinee must select, from the six options given, the one that fits the empty set and completes the arrangement.

FIG 2.2. Sample item from Raven's Progressive Matrices Test (reprinted with permission of John Wiley & Sons, and J. C. Raven Limited).

Both conceptual and operational definitions of selected affective characteristics are presented in this chapter. Following the logic of the previous discussion, conceptual definitions are presented first, followed by a discussion of operational definitions. Two methods for deriving operational definitions are presented. Although these methods are slightly different, both attempt to yield operational definitions that are closely related to the conceptual definitions.

CONCEPTUAL DEFINITIONS OF SELECTED AFFECTIVE CHARACTERISTICS

In chapter 1 we offered a definition of affective characteristics. The definition is, in fact, a conceptual definition of the general category of affective characteristics. Briefly, for a human characteristic to be classified as an affective characteristic, it must possess five critical features: (1) feelings, (2) typical feelings, (3) intensity of feelings, (4) direction of feelings, and (5) target of feelings. Although some educators talk about affective characteristics in general terms (e.g., Huebner & Dew, 1987), most talk about specific affective characteristics such as attitudes, values, and anxiety. Because these specific characteristics are in fact affective, they all must contain feelings. However, because they are distinct affective characteristics, they must differ from each other in some way. Most typically, these differences lie in the intensity of the feelings, in the direction of the feelings, in the target of the feelings, or in some combination of the three.

The purpose of this section is to present conceptual definitions for eight specific affective characteristics that appear to be related to schooling and school learning. These eight characteristics are attitude, value, self-esteem, locus of control, self-efficacy, interest, aspirations, and anxiety. Each of the following subsections discusses one of these characteristics. In each section the characteristic is defined in terms of its critical features (i.e., intensity, direction, and target). After all eight categories have been discussed, a summary table is displayed, and the eight characteristics are contrasted.

Attitudes

Attitude refers to "a learned predisposition to respond in a consistently favorable or unfavorable manner with respect to a given object" (Fishbein & Ajzen, 1975, p.6). As can be seen in this definition, the target of an attitude is usually an object. With respect to direction, an attitude can be either favorable or unfavorable. Furthermore, degrees of favorableness would indicate the intensity of an attitude.

Despite the fact that a range of intensity is possible, attitudes in general can be considered affective characteristics of moderate intensity because the person is responding or reacting to an object already given. Affective characteristics with higher intensity tend to impel a person to seek out things (see *Interests*) or to influence a person to behave in a certain way (see *Values*). Although the intensity of any affective characteristic can and does vary somewhat, the intensities of different affective characteristics do differ on the average. More is said about this point later.

Finally, and quite important from an educational perspective, attitudes are learned. That is, people learn to attach these feelings to particular targets. Note that the feelings themselves may or may not be learned. What is learned, however, is the attachment of the feelings to the particular targets. For example, favorableness may or may not be a learned feeling. However, individuals learn to attach the feeling of favorableness (or its opposite, unfavorableness) to a wide variety of targets (e.g., automobiles, churches, teaching as a profession).

Values

Several definitions of *values* are available. Getzels (1966), for example, defined a value as a "conception of the *desirable*—that is, of what ought to be desired, not what is actually desired—which influences the selection of behavior" (p. 98). Thus, according to Getzels, values can be differentiated from interests, which, as we see later, are clearly related to what is desired. Tyler (1973), on the other hand, defined a value as "an object, activity, or idea that is cherished by an individual which derives its educational significance from its role in directing his interests, attitudes, and satisfactions" (p. 7). Thus, attitudes and interests must differ from values because they are influenced by the values a person holds. Finally, Rokeach (1973) described a value as:

> an enduring belief that a specific mode of conduct or end-state of existence is personally or socially preferable to an opposite or converse mode of conduct or end-state of existence.... It is a *standard* [italics added] that guides and determines action, attitudes toward objects and situations, ideology, presentations of self to others, evaluations, judgments, justifications, comparisons of self with others, and attempts to influence others. (pp. 5, 25)

What can be said about values in light of these three definitions? First, values are beliefs about what should be desired (Getzels, 1966), what is important or cherished (Tyler, 1973), and what standards of conduct or existence are personally or socially acceptable (Rokeach, 1973). Second, values influence or guide behavior (Getzels, 1966); interests, attitudes, and satisfactions (Tyler, 1973); and a whole host of items, including behavior, interests, attitudes, and satisfactions (Rokeach, 1973). Third, values are enduring (Rokeach, 1973). That is, values tend to remain stable over fairly long periods of time. As such they are likely to be more difficult to alter or change than many other affective characteristics.

How are values related to the critical features shared by all affective characteristics? First, based on this combined definition, values tend to be high-intensity feelings. Words and phrases such as *cherished* and *guides* and *determines action* indicate this level of intensity. Second, the possible directions of value would be *wrong or right* (Getzels, 1966), *unimportant or important* (Tyler, 1973), or *unacceptable or acceptable* (Rokeach, 1973). Third, the targets of values are many and varied (e.g., behaviors or activities, attitudes, and endstates of existence). In general, however, the targets of values tend to be ideas (e.g., endstates of existence) more frequently than to be objects or activities. Fourth, values are, in fact, human characteristics because they have an enduring quality. And, finally, it is apparent that values, like attitudes, are learned.

Self-Esteem

Some readers may be surprised at the use of the term *self-esteem* rather than the more popular term *self-concept*. The use is intentional because an important distinction exists between the two terms. Put simply, self-esteem is the affective component of self-concept. Let us explore this distinction in greater detail.

Shavelson, Hubner, and Stanton (1976) defined self-concept simply as "a person's perception of himself" (p. 411). These perceptions that people have of themselves can be classified either as evaluative, more subjective perceptions (e.g., I am a good reader) or nonevaluative, more factual perceptions (e.g., I can read all of the words on this page). Although self-concept is, in fact, the sum total of all of these perceptions, self-esteem would consist of the sum total of only the evaluative perceptions. Eventually, over the period of several years, this sum total will likely impact the feeling of self-worth of the individual (e.g., I am a worthwhile human being vs. I am a worthless human being).[3]

Of the many varieties of self-concept and self-esteem, the one most relevant for educators is academic self-concept and academic self-esteem. Following from Shavelson, Hubner, and Stanton (1976), academic self-concept can be defined as a person's perception of himself or herself as a student in an academic setting (e.g., a school). Academic self-esteem, then, would be the evaluative portion of academic self-concept.

What are the critical feature of academic self-esteem? The target of academic self-esteem is the person himself or herself. However, this target ex-

---

[3]It is likely this cumulative self-perception that educators are referring to when they express their concern about students' self concepts. No one wants schools to contribute to students' beliefs that they are worthless individuals.

ists in a particular setting—namely, an academic one. The direction of academic self-esteem can either be negative or positive. Thus, educators talk of a student with positive self-esteem or negative self-esteem. The intensity of academic self-esteem is an interesting topic. At first blush, the intensity would seem to be high because the target of the feelings is the self. If, however, one remembers that the target exists in an academic setting, it is possible to conceive of academic self-esteem as having low intensity.

Consider a student who has negative academic self-evaluations (e.g., lousy, dumb, and slow) but who believes that school and success in school are unimportant (i.e., is of low value). This student may express himself or herself in the following way: "I get lousy grades in school but I don't care." In this instance the intensity of academic self-esteem might be low. Thus, it seems best to conceive of academic self-esteem as being a moderately high-intensity affective characteristic that can range in intensity from low to high depending on other beliefs and perceptions of the individual.

Locus of Control

According to Messick (1979), *locus of control* is the extent to which individuals tend to accept responsibility for their own behavior, the results of their behavior, or both. In Messick's words, locus of control contrasts "individuals who think of themselves as responsible for their own behavior (internals) against individuals who attribute responsibility to the force of circumstances or powerful others or luck (externals)" (p. 285). Locus of control, then, requires either accepting or denying responsibility for a person's actions or their consequences. When results or consequences are considered, locus of control refers to the attributions individuals make about those results or consequences. Were they the result of what I did or did they result from factors beyond my control?

The target of locus of control, then, is the behavior of people and, generally, the results or consequences of the behavior. The direction would be external (i.e., believing others are responsible) or internal (i.e., believing that you are responsible). The intensity of locus of control is difficult to estimate. Because the target is the person's behavior and the consequence or result of that behavior, the intensity is likely to be moderately high, particularly for individuals with an internal locus of control. For those with an external locus of control, the intensity may be somewhat lower.

Self-Efficacy

Self-efficacy can been defined as a "person's belief in his or her capability of performing a behavior required to reach a goal" (Weiner, 1992, p. 861).

In school, students tend to invest considerable time and effort in those things they believe they are capable of learning. When a task is too difficult, students may not expect to be successful. A typical response in this situation is "I can't learn that." Unfortunately, making the task too easy is not the solution. In this case, success on the task is more likely to be attributed to the low degree of difficulty than to the student's own competence or ability. The response becomes, "Anyone can do those exercises; I still can't learn mathematics."

The target of self-efficacy is a task, a subject, an instructional objective, and the like. The direction is best captured by *I can* versus *I can't*. The intensity of self-efficacy is much like that of self-esteem. In general, it probably is best considered as "moderately high intensity" with a range influenced by a variety of other factors (including other affective characteristics). Finally, like the majority of other affective characteristics, self-efficacy is learned. The learning takes place over time as the student experiences a series of successes and failures. A predominance of successes likely leads to self-efficacy, whereas a predominance of failures likely leads to its negative counterpart, learned helpless (see chap. 1, this volume).

Interests

According to Getzels (1966), an interest is a "disposition organized through experience which impels an individual to seek out particular objects, activities, understandings, skills, or goals for attention or acquisition" (p. 98). Thus the most obvious feature of an interest is its intensity. In general, interests are high-intensity affective characteristics. They impel people to seek out things. The things sought after are the targets of the interests. Because interests tend to be action-oriented, these targets tend to be activities and skills more frequently than they tend to be objects or understandings. Even when the target seems to be an object, it really is an activity because interests impel one to secure the object. Interests tend to be present or absent. Thus the range of interests can perhaps best be expressed by the word-pair "interested–disinterested." In between this pair of words, however, are degrees of intensity. Thus, like attitudes, interests can differ somewhat in their intensity. Interests on the average are higher intensity feelings than attitudes. Finally, interests are learned because, as Getzels indicated, they are organized through experience.

Aspirations (Educational)

Aspirations can be defined as a student's intent to pursue additional education after the age of compulsory school attendance has been reached. The results of several international studies suggest that aspirations are related to student achievement as well as attitudes (Anderson, Ryan, & Shapiro, 1989). The strength of this relationship is particularly impressive in light of the fact that aspirations were assessed using a two-item scale. The first asked students whether they intended to complete high school, the second, whether they intended to pursue higher education.

The key word in understanding aspirations is "intention." Fishbein and Ajzen (1975) argued that intention is a far better predictor of actual behavior than is attitude. Thus, we suggest that aspirations are a moderately high-intensity affective characteristic, the target of which is education, and the direction being either "no more" or "more."

Anxiety

Hall and Lindzey (1970) defined *anxiety* as "the experience of tension that results from real or imaginary threats to one's security" (p. 145). The definition clearly specifies the target of the feeling, namely, real or imaginary threats to one's security. Within the school context, mathematics and tests are considered major targets of anxiety. That is, students perceive tests and mathematics as threats to their security. The use of the term *tension* in the definition suggests that anxiety generally is a high-intensity affective characteristic. Furthermore, the direction of anxiety can be either relaxed or tense.

One point about anxiety is worth noting. Anxiety is an interesting affective characteristic in that people can have too much or too little anxiety. Being overly relaxed during a test, for example, may be just as problematic as being overly stressed. Although difficult to achieve, just the right amount of anxiety seems necessary for a student to function optimally in a testing situation.

A Comparison of Specific Affective Characteristics

The eight affective characteristics can be differentiated in terms of three critical features: direction, target, and, to a somewhat lesser extent, intensity. With respect to intensity, two points can be made. The first is that different affective characteristics possess different degrees of intensity. That is, on average, certain affective characteristics are more intense feelings than others. Anxiety, values, and interests tend to be high-intensity affective characteristics. Academic self-esteem, self-efficacy, and aspirations tend to be moderately high-intensity affective characteristics. Locus of control and attitudes tend to be moderate-intensity affective characteristics.

Differences in the intensity of affective characteristics may cause conflicts in students. As mentioned in the previous paragraph, interests, values, and anxiety are all high intensity emotions. Students may be interested in something that they consider to be of no redeeming social value (e.g., reading pornographic literature). In light of this conflict, these students may follow their interests or values. If they follow the interests, anxiety may result. And, if they follow the values, frustration may follow.

Consider a second example. Suppose a student is interested in learning some new material but he or she finds it very difficult to learn . Suppose this person values doing well in school (i.e., getting good grades). If he or she pursues his or her interests, the result may be poor grades. Initially, this may be anxiety producing; ultimately, it may lead to low self-efficacy. If, on the other hand, the student behaves in accordance with his or her values and chooses not to explore material of interest, frustration may result as a result of missed opportunities.

A second point is that each affective characteristic varies in intensity. Under certain conditions and with certain students, attitudes, for example, may be higher or lower in their intensity. This variation is quite likely attributable to two sources: the target of the affective characteristic and the other affective characteristics that come into play. Attitudes toward school friends may be more intense than attitudes toward the school principal. The difference in intensity here comes from the difference in intensity associated with the two targets: friends versus the principal. Similarly, the attitude toward school held by high school students doing well in school (i.e., having positive academic self-esteem) may be less intense than those doing poorly in school (i.e., having negative academic self-esteem). In this case, the intensity of the attitude is likely influenced by the intensity of the negative academic self-esteem. It is this variation in intensity within each affective characteristics that is the most important in affective assessment.

By combining intensity with direction, it is possible to conceptualize each affective characteristic as existing along a continuum. A continuum for each of the eight affective characteristics is displayed in Fig. 2.3. On each continuum the neutral point or midpoint is indicated by a short vertical line. Direction is designated by whether a person falls to the to the *right* (positive) or *left* (negative) of the neutral point. Intensity is indicated by the distance the person is away from the midpoint. Simply stated, the greater the distance, the greater the intensity. Finally, the targets of the various affective characteristics can be indicated by placing a label representing each target directly over the neutral point on the continuum. This also has been done in Fig. 2.3.

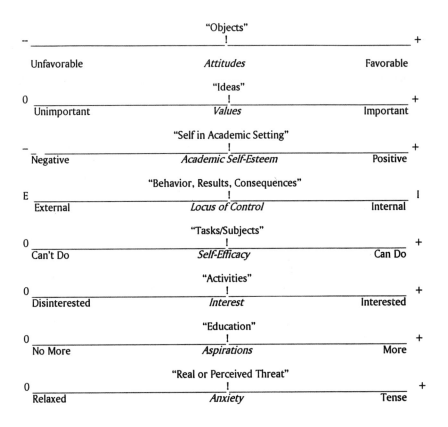

FIG. 2.3. Specific affective characteristics ordered along a continuum of direction and intensity with common targets identified.

Five of the affective characteristics (interest, value, self-efficacy, aspirations, and anxiety) range from neutral to positive as indicted by the "zero" and "plus" signs at the ends' of the continuum. They differ in the label applied to the positive pole (interested, important, can do, more, and tense, respectively). Two of the affective characteristics (attitude and academic self-esteem) range from negative to positive. They too differ in the label applied to the positive pole of the continuum (favorable and positive, respectively. The remaining characteristic, locus of control, is more relativistic in nature. The continuum ranges from denying responsibility (i.e., external) to accepting responsibility (i.e., internal).

Turning to an examination of the targets of the affective characteristics, differences can once again be seen. Attitudes, interests, and values can be differentiated by their most frequent targets: objects, activities, and ideas, respectively. The five remaining characteristics have quite specific targets. Academic self-esteem has the self in an academic setting as its target. For locus of control, the target is a behavior of the person or some result or consequence of that behavior. The target of self-efficacy is a task, subject, instructional objective—something learned or performed. For aspirations, the target is education. Finally, the target of anxiety is some object, activity, or idea that is seen as a threat (real or imagined) by the person.

TWO QUESTIONS ABOUT SPECIFIC AFFECTIVE CHARACTERISTICS

The discussion in the previous section may leave the reader with two questions. First, why was motivation not included in the set of specific affective characteristics? Second, are all of these distinctions among specific affective characteristics really necessary?

Motivation was excluded from the list of relevant affective characteristics because it is believed to be somewhat redundant. Messicks (1979) suggested that "a *motive* is any impulse, emotion, or desire that impels one to action, … [consequently] all the [affective characteristics] under discussion qualify as motivational to some degree" (p. 285). In fact, motivation likely results from the interplay of several affective characteristics (with value and self-efficacy chief among them). The description of the relation between affective characteristics and motivation, in some detail, can be found in chapter 8.

Are all these distinctions really necessary? We think so. Consider the following example. Malik believes mathematics to be dull, boring, worthless, a waste of time, horrendous, frightening, and difficult to learn. It is likely that Malik has a negative attitude toward mathematics (dull, boring), does not value mathematics (worthless), has no interest in learning mathematics (a waste of time), has high levels of math anxiety (horrendous, frightening), and has somewhat negative academic self-esteem with regard to mathematics (difficult to learn). In this instance, because all of the specific affective characteristics are negative, it makes sense to speak of the individual as having negative affect toward mathematics.

Now consider a second student, Crystal. Suppose she also feels that mathematics is dull and boring, but that it is important. Furthermore, for her, mathematics is easy to learn. However, she does not intend to enroll in any more mathematics courses beyond the one in which she currently is enrolled. Crystal has a negative attitude toward mathematics (dull, boring) and little, if any, interest in learning it (she does not intend to enroll in additional mathematics courses). On the other hand, she sees mathematics as having value (important). With respect to mathematics, she also has positive academic self-esteem and self-efficacy (easy to learn).

With respect to Malik, it is not necessary to differentiate among the various types of affective characteristics he possesses. It is possible to generalize about his affect from any one of the specific affective characteristics mentioned. With respect to Crystal, on the other hand, such a differentiation is essential if we are to understand her affect with respect to mathematics. To generalize about her affect from any one of the characteristics is unwarranted and would likely lead to misunderstanding. In some instances and with some individuals or groups, the distinctions made here are probably unimportant. In other instances and with other individuals and groups, however, these distinctions promote a greater degree of understanding than is possible using the generic term, *affect*.

OPERATIONAL DEFINITIONS OF AFFECTIVE CHARACTERISTICS

As indicated earlier in this chapter, the purpose of operationally defining an affective characteristic is to describe in some detail those behaviors that can be used to make inferences about the presence of the affective characteristic in students. Such inferences can be made on the basis of an individual's speech, written responses, or overt actions.

In this section two approaches are presented that can be used to operationally define affective characteristics. The first approach is concerned with specifying what are called *mapping sentences* (e.g., Fiske, 1971). The second approach is similar to that used in constructing domain-referenced achievement tests (e.g., Hively, 1974).

The Mapping-Sentence Approach

Fiske (1971) proposed an approach to operationalizing affective characteristics that is based on answers to a number of important questions. Why should a particular characteristic be assessed? What type of characteristic is it? What is the core of the characteristic? How is it different from similar characteristics? What is represented by the low end of the scale of the characteristics? What mode of assessment is to be used? What are the facets and elements of the characteristic?

Many of these questions have been addressed earlier. Two of them, however, are the keys to the issue of operationally defining affective characteristics: (a) What is the core of the characteristic? (b) What are its facets and elements? Let us consider each of these in some detail.

Kifer (1977) suggested defining the core of the characteristic by thinking about the kinds of beliefs or actions that would be held or exhibited by a person who possesses the characteristic. That is, what would a person possessing this characteristic believe or do? Kifer then presented a useful illustration of this approach. He began with a characteristic that he called "perceptions of adequacy of one's self and abilities as a student" (p. 208). He defined this characteristic as the "extent to which students feel confident about themselves as learners" (p. 207).

With this definition in mind, Kifer (1977) asked, "What kinds of things would be done by a person who possesses 'confidence' in his or her abilities?" (p. 207). He proceeded to answer this question in an interesting and informative manner. A confident student would:

> (1) feel free to state his opinion in a class; (2) deal competently with constructive criticism; (3) ask questions when he or she was confused in class; (4) make decisive academic decisions; (5) enjoy expressing personal opinions; (6) believe that he or she could deal easily with new material; (7) deal effectively with group pressure; and so on. (In this regard, I remember a most creative response to what a confident student might do: the student would fill in the *New York Times* crossword puzzle with an ink pen!). (pp. 207–208)

Once the core of the characteristic has been described, the focus turns to a delineation of the facets and elements of the characteristic. Facets can be thought of as categories, whereas elements are examples of the categories. Kifer (1977) suggested two facets: the behavior to be exhibited by the student if an inference is to be made that some degree of the affective characteristic is present and the situation in which the behavior is likely to be exhibited. For each of these two facets, examples (i.e., elements) can be generated. Once generated, the facets and elements are placed in what is called a mapping sentence (see Fig. 2.4). The mapping sentence is a graphic representation of both facets and their associated elements.

Specific statements are generated by selecting one element from the situation facet and one element from the behavior facet.

> We may wish to write an item which asks the student to respond to a question about expressing unpopular opinions in front of the group (Situation e, Behavior 4). The item could be, "Even if everyone in my class disagrees with me, I will present my opinions for discussion." For elements (Situation a, Behavior 1) during lecture or discussion and answering questions, the item could be, "I want to be called on in class." For elements (Situation e, Behavior 1) an item could be, "I enjoy presenting my interests to my classmates." (Kifer, 1977, p. 210)

In summary, the mapping sentence approach begins by listing the kinds of beliefs or actions that would be held or exhibited by someone who possesses the affective characteristic being assessed. Based on this listing, two

The response of a student (x) to a statement about personal perceptions:

Situation
| a. during lecture or discussion
| b. in small group.
| c. from peer to peer
| d. with teacher
| e. from peer to group

indicates that he or she feels adequate when:

Behavior
| 1. answering questions
| 2. asking questions
| 3. expressing opinions
| 4. expressing unpopular opinions
| 5. involving himself/herself

which indicates a belief in ones self and abilities as a student.

FIG. 2.4. An illustration of a mapping sentence (Kifer, 1977; reprinted with permission of Plenum Publishing Corporation and Edward Kifer).

facets are identified: behaviors and situations. Once identified, the behavior and situational facets (and their associated elements) are represented visually in a mapping sentence. Finally, statements are generated by sampling one element from the behavioral domain and one from the situational domain and writing a sentence that includes both. Kifer (1977) summarized the effectiveness of this approach quite succinctly:

> If the core is well defined, the facets and elements well constructed, and the items consistent with the definition, then one has performed a major step in constructing a measure which could produce consistent results. How good the measure is, though related to how well one has approached the task of specifying the variable, must finally be decided by tryouts of the instrument and thorough scrutiny of the empirical properties of test results. (pp. 210–211)

The Domain-Referenced Approach

The domain-referenced approach begins with an examination of the critical features of the affective characteristics (Hively, 1974). Consideration is first given to the target and direction of the affective characteristics. Subsequently, the intensity of the affective characteristics is considered. Each of these is a domain.

Table 2.1 displays how attitude toward mathematics can be operationalized within this context. The first column outlines a procedure for operationalizing the affective characteristic. The second column indicates the target and the fourth column lists the adjectives that would be appropriate for describing the direction. The third column indicates the links between the targets and the direction. Because these links tend to be verbs, the word "verb" is used to head up the column.

The domain-referenced approach can best be understood by moving down the rows of the table. In row one, we begin with the general affective characteristic, in this case, attitude. Under each column we specify the domain of targets, verbs, and directional adjectives that would be appropriate for assessing attitude toward mathematics. Because in this example the affective characteristic is attitude, the target is mostly likely an object. Thus, any object related to mathematics (see the Target column) defines the domain. In the Verb column, the domain is "any form of the verb 'to be' or any verb denoting favorableness." These verb forms provide an acceptable link between the target and the directional adjectives. Finally, the Adjectives column the domain includes any adjective having a similar meaning to favorable or unfavorable.

In the second row of Table 2.1 examples are listed of each domain. "Mathematics," "numbers," "arithmetic," "algebra," "numerical operations," and "equations" are examples of objects related to mathematics. "Is," "are," and "am" are present tense forms of the verb "to be," "like," and "enjoy" are verbs associated with favorableness.[4] Similarly, "satisfying," "enjoyable," "pleasant," and "nice" (as well as their negative counterparts) are adjectives that are similar in meaning to the adjective pair "favorable–unfavorable."

Once these specific elements or examples are listed, sentences can be formed by sampling randomly from each of the three domain. Row 3 illustrates one such sampling. "Mathematics" is sampled from the target domain. "Is" is sampled from the verbs domain, and "enjoyable" is sampled from the directional adjectives domain. Thus one possible sentence is simply, "Mathematics is enjoyable." A student who would agree that mathematics is enjoyable or would somehow demonstrate that he or she finds it to be enjoyable would be said to have a positive attitude toward mathematics. On the other hand, a student who verbally indicates that mathematics is not enjoyable or demonstrates that he or she does not find

---

[4]Since attitudes tend to be present oriented, present tenses of verbs are the most appropriate.

TABLE 2.1

An Example of Operationalizing "Attitude Toward Mathematics"

Row	Action	Target Domain	Verb Domain	Adjective Domain
1.	Indicate domains for attitude toward mathematics.	Any object related to mathematics	Any form of "to be;" Verbs denoting favorableness	Any adjective having a meaning similar to favorable or unfavorable.
2.	List examples of each domain.	Mathematics, algebra, arithmetic, numbers, operations, equations	Is, are, am, like, enjoy	Satisfying/unsatisfying enjoyable/not enjoyable pleasant/unpleasant nice/awful good/bad positive/negative
3.	Select one example from each domain.	Mathematics	Is	Enjoyable
4.	Generate statement: "Mathematics is enjoyable."			
5.	Transform statement: "I really enjoy mathematics." "Most of the time I find mathematics enjoyable."			
6.	Select another example from each domain.			
7.	Generate statement: "Numbers like positive."			
8.	Transform statement: "I have an positive reaction to numbers;"; "I like working with numbers."			

mathematics to be enjoyable would be said to have a negative attitude toward mathematics.

The original statement can be transformed or reworded as needed. There are three possible reasons for transforming or rewording the original statement. First, transforming or rewording may be necessary in order to make the statement grammatically correct. Second, transforming the statement can change it into a question. Such a transformation may be desirable if affective characteristics of younger pupils are to be assessed. Third, transforming or rewording allows the intensity of the feeling expressed in the statement to be altered. The statement, "I really enjoy mathematics" (Row 5 of Table 2.1), is of higher intensity than the originally generated statement. On the other hand, the statement, "Most of the time I find mathematics enjoyable," is of lesser intensity than the original statement.

Row 6 of Table 2.1 presents a second sampling from each of the three sets. "Numbers" is the target, "like" is the verb, and "positive" is the adjective. The resulting statement is "Numbers like positive" (Row 7). Because this statement is neither meaningful nor grammatically correct, some type of transformation is necessary. Two possible transformations are presented in Row 8: "I have an positive reaction to numbers" (substituting "have" for the selected verb "like"), and "I like working with numbers" (omitting the adjective). In both of these transformations, the active voice is used.

One of the major aspects of the domain-referenced approach is the movement from the specification of the domain to the particular examples within each domain. (Note the consistency with the mapping-sentence approach described earlier.) This movement can be accomplished in at least two ways. First, interviews can be held with students who are similar to those for whom the assessment instrument is being designed. The interviewer should make careful notes of the adjectives, verbs, and target synonyms that are used to describe one's feelings about the target. These adjectives, verbs, and target synonyms become the examples of each of the three domains. Morrison, Gardner, Reilly, & McNally (1993) used a modification of this suggestion. They selected statements taken from a careful reading of the diaries that students kept during a project involving the impact of portable computers on attitudes toward studying.

Second, the adjectives, and possibly the verbs, can be taken from adjective lists. Allport and Odbert (1936) compiled a listing of 17,953 adjectives that has been found useful in designing affective assessment instruments. Although a bit dated, a careful perusal of this list can produce elements that can be included in the various domains. With not much effort, many of these adjectives can be transformed into appropriate verbs.

Tables such as Table 2.1 can be generated for each of the affective characteristics discussed earlier in this chapter. Developing such tables is an important step in moving from conceptual to operational definitions of affective characteristics. The use of these tables, once developed, should enable a close relation between the conceptual and operational definitions to be maintained.

In summary, the domain-referenced approach to developing sound operational definitions begins by identifying appropriate targets (Domain 1) and directional adjectives (Domain 3) for the specific affective characteristic. Next, appropriate verbs (Domain 2) that can link the target and the adjectives are listed. Appropriate examples of each domain are then written down. These specific examples can come from interviews with members of the group for whom the instrument is intended or from an available list of adjectives. Appropriate operational definitions are then formed by sampling the elements within each of the three domains and arranging the elements into an appropriate sentence format. Intensity can be increased or decreased by appropriately modifying the generated sentences.

A COMMENT ON EDITING ITEMS

Self-report measures require, at a minimum, that those responding should find the items meaningful. Consequently, some type of editing is likely to be needed regardless of the approach used to generate or write items. In this regard, Edwards (1957), Thorndike (1982), and Oppenheim (1992) provided excellent guidelines that can be used to edit the initial drafts of the items. The following list was compiled from these three sets of guidelines:

- Write statements that cover the entire range of the affective characteristic (plus its target).
- Ensure that each item involves feeling and affect and is not a statement of fact (or a statement that can be interpreted as factual).
- Keep the language of the statements simple, clear, and direct.
- Write statements in present tense.
- Each statement should contain only one complete thought.
- Avoid statements likely to be endorsed by everyone or almost no one.
- Avoid words that are vague modifiers or words that may not be understood by those who are asked to respond to the scale.
- Avoid statements that involve double negatives.

We would expand slightly on the last bullet. A double negative can also result when a negative in the statement is coupled with a negative in the response options. Suppose, for example, the statement reads: I do not enjoy reading for pleasure. Further suppose the response options are in the standard Likert form: strongly agree, agree, undecided or not sure, disagree, and strongly disagree (see Appendix A). Now consider a person who circles (or otherwise indicates) strongly disagree. The person strongly disagrees that he or she does not enjoy reading for pleasure. What does this mean? So we would suggest the last bullet be rewritten: Avoid the use of items that involve double negatives.

DEFINITIONS REVISITED:
SELECTING AFFECTIVE ASSESSMENT INSTRUMENTS

In the previous section we have focused on designing affective instruments. However, there are numerous situations in which educators will be more likely to select available instruments than to design their own (see chap. 5). What role does well thought out and clearly communicated definitions of affective characteristics play in selecting appropriate affective instruments?

Anyone searching for an appropriate affective instrument should have a clear definition in mind before beginning the search. This definition should be as precise as possible, specify the defining features of the characteristic. When a prospective instrument has been located, the definition suggested by the author or authors of the instrument should be compared with this definition. If the definitions are quite similar, the instrument should be set aside for further examination. If, on the other hand, the definitions are substantially different, two decisions can be made. First, the instrument can discarded. Second, the definition underlying the located instrument can be accepted. If this new definition is accepted, the instrument should once again be set aside for further consideration.

Clear, precise definitions are critically important because they give meaning to words, terms, and ideas. Unless definitions are stated and instruments are derived logically from the definitions, the assessment of affective characteristics will be confusing at best and useless at worst.

SUMMARY OF MAJOR POINTS

1. Clear, precise definitions of affective characteristics are needed in order to: select or design an appropriate instrument, examine the technical quality of an affective instrument, and interpret (i.e., understand) the results obtained from administering the instrument.
2. Clear, precise, and agreed-on definitions enhance communication among educators and between educators and noneducators.

3. Definitions are needed both for the specific affective characteristic (e.g., attitude) and the target toward which the affective characteristic is directed (e.g., homework).

4. Perhaps the best way of defining an affective characteristic and its target is to indicate their important aspects or *defining features.* In simplest terms, the defining features can be identified by asking the questions, "What makes this, this?" "What makes attitude, attitude?" "What makes homework, homework?"

5. Two types of definitions are important in the context of assessment: conceptual definitions and operational definitions.

6. *Conceptual definitions* are concerned with the abstract meaning of the affective characteristics.

7. *Operational definitions,* on the other hand, refer to the set of behaviors (e.g., statements, actions) that when heard, read. or observed can be used to make inferences about affective characteristics.

8. In order for assessment to provide meaningful and useful information about a particular characteristic, a close relation must exist between conceptual and operational definitions.

9. For a human characteristic to be classified as an affective characteristic, it must possess five defining features: (a) feeling, (b) consistency of feeling over some period of time, (c) intensity of the feeling, (d) direction of the feeling, and (e) target of the feeling.

- In light of these defining features, it is not surprising that there are many different affective characteristics. They differ in their intensity, direction, and target. However, in some instances and with some individuals or groups, it is not necessary to maintain distinctions among various affective characteristics. In other instances, however, these distinctions become crucial.

- Two approaches for operationally defining affective characteristics are the mapping sentence approach and the domain-referenced approach. Each is described in some detail in this chapter.

- People searching for an affective instrument (rather than designing one) should have a clear, precise definition of the affective characteristic in mind before beginning the search. Whether a particular instrument is selected should depend in part on the match between the definition used by person searching and the definition used by the instrument designer. If possible, the procedure used by the instrument designer in preparing the statements should be examined by the prospective user.

3

Issues in Affective Assessment: How Can Information Be Gathered?

Chapter 1 presents a rationale for the importance of affective characteristics in the context of schools and schooling. Chapter 2 discusses is conceptual and operational definitions of a variety of affective characteristics. The purpose of this chapter is to examine general approaches to assessing affective characteristics.

We begin by describing two different approaches to gathering information about human characteristics. Next, we discuss problems inherent in each of these approaches. Following this discussion, examined is the appropriateness of the two approaches for gathering affective information; each approach's strengths and weaknesses are described, leading to the identification of our preferred method for assessing affective characteristics.

GATHERING INFORMATION ABOUT HUMAN CHARACTERISTICS

In a very general sense there are only two ways in which we gather information about human characteristics: We look, and we listen. Consider a physician whom you consult for a physical examination. He or she looks in your ears, in your throat, at the pointer measuring your height, at the balances measuring your weight, at the needle on the sphygmomanometer measuring your blood pressure, at the computer printout describing your blood work, and at the x-rays. And he *listens* to your heart and pulse, to your cough, and to you ("where does it hurt?").[1] When a physician looks, two sources of information are available—the person (e.g. ears and throat) and readings from some instrument (e.g. pointers, needles, and printout). When a physician asks and listens, the only source of information is the person himself or herself.

What threats to obtaining good information are inherent in these ways of gathering information? First, the physician may not see something that should be seen. For example, the physician looks at the X-ray and fails to notice the spot on your lung. Second, the instruments used to produce the readings may be faulty. For example, a spring on the weighing scale may be loose or missing. Third, the physician may obtain the wrong information for one of two reasons. The physician may be purposefully misinformed by you because you are afraid of the consequences of telling the truth. For example, the doctor asks you if you have been following your diet, and you answer that you have (when you have not). You are afraid to tell the doctor that you have not because you want to avoid another verbal reprimand. Alternatively, the physician may ask the wrong question. Continuing with the diet example, the doctor may ask whether you understand the importance of the diet he recommended for you. You can honestly answer yes to this question regardless of whether you have been following the diet. Your honest response can be misleading to the doctor who may assume (incorrectly) that if you really understood the importance of the diet, you definitely would be following it.

In sum, then, physicians tend to rely on two primary methods of gathering information: looking and listening. When physicians attempt to gather information by looking, they may get misinformation if they fail to notice something, or if the readings they are looking at come from faulty instruments. When physicians attempt to gather information by listening, they may get misinformation if the person being listened to chooses to provide incorrect or misleading information, or if they ask the wrong question.

The previous example pertains to gathering information about physical characteristics. Can the same reasoning be applied to gathering information about psychological characteristics that are more likely to be related to schools and school learning? Although the latter is likely to be more complex than the former, let us see.

---

[1]The astute reader will note that a physician also touches, feels, and probes in order to gather information. Because an analogy between a physician and an affective assessment specialist is forthcoming and because the affective assessment specialists will not likely touch, feel, or probe, discussion of this tactile approach to gathering information ends with this footnote.

Suppose we are interested in gathering information about a student's learning of physics, specifically aerodynamics. We may ask a few questions such as, "What are the major principles of aerodynamics?" And we may *listen* to his or her answers. We may *look* at drawings of a novel model airplane that the student produced and *listen* to the student's explanation of it. Alternatively, we may *look* at the initial flight of the model airplane, focusing on the results.

Obviously, knowing what we are looking or listening for is crucial. In the example of the physical examination, the things being looked and listened for had been determined on the basis of years of cumulative experience. In the example of learning physics, the items being looked and listened for should correspond with the instructional objectives of the unit, course, or program. That is to say, one of the objectives should state that the student be able to recognize the major principles of aerodynamics. Another objective should state that the student be able to design a novel model airplane based on sound principles of aerodynamics. Yet another objective should state that the student be able to design a model airplane that could fly for a minimum of 2 minutes. As can be seen, then, instructional objectives focus the looking and listening toward certain things and away from other things. The more carefully defined the objectives are, the more focussed the looking and listening can become.

The threats to good information in the learning physics example are similar to those in the physician example. In looking, the person making the assessment may not see something he or she should. The likelihood of this happening is increased if the objectives are not clearly specified. For example, the person might focus on the flight pattern or speed of the plane rather than on the duration of the flight. Alternatively, the person making the assessment may misinterpret what he or she sees. For example, on looking at the sketch of the plane, the person making the assessment may believe that the dotted lines indicate wires connecting the wings of the plane to the body. He or she then decides that the position of the wires would violate basic principles of aerodynamics. This would be an incorrect interpretation if the dotted lines actually represented reinforcing rods built into the wings and body of the plane. (Note that this misinterpretation is comparable to the misinterpretation resulting from faulty instruments in the physician example.)

In listening, the person making the assessment may also gather incorrect information. A student may correctly guess the major principles of aerodynamics (when given a multiple-choice test) without really knowing them. Conversely, although truly knowing the major principles, the student may momentarily forget them (perhaps a result of test anxiety). In either case, the person assessing is listening to what amounts to misinformation.

Hopefully, the previous two examples serve to convince the reader that information about human characteristics (at least physical and cognitive characteristics) tends to be gathered using two methods. Furthermore, each method can be hampered by difficulties that affect the quality of the information gathered. These points can be summarized using somewhat more technical terms. This summary aids in making the transition to the next section, in which the application of these ideas to affective assessment is examined.

There are two global methods of gathering information about the vast majority of human characteristics, especially those relevant within the context of schools and schooling. The first method can be termed the *observational method*. The observational method refers to gathering information by looking at the person being assessed. The second method can be termed the *self-report method*. The self-report method refers to gathering the information by asking questions of the person and listening to the responses provided.

The observational method can yield bad information if the person gathering the information fails to *observe* the relevant characteristics or relevant indicators[2] of that characteristic or misinterprets what he or she observes. The self-report method can yield bad information if the person gathering the information asks a poor question that has the wrong focus (or asks a good question poorly) or if the person providing the information intentionally or accidentally misinforms the person gathering the information. Table 3.1 summarizes this discussion and includes examples of each method of gathering information.

As the reader can surely guess, observational methods and self-report methods can be used to gather information about affective characteristics. The problems inherent in each method (described previously) are also present in the affective realm. In the following two sections, observational and self-report methods are described as they apply to affective assessment. We highlight the problems inherent in both methods and suggest possible solution strategies for the identified problems.

OBSERVATIONAL METHODS AND AFFECTIVE ASSESSMENT

In the affective realm the use of observational methods is based on the assumption that it is possible to infer affective characteristics from overt be-

---

[2]A physician could, for example, use a sphygmomanometer to estimate a patient's respiratory rate. In this example, a respiratory rate may be the relevant characteristic, but an sphygmomanometer does not provide a relevant indicator of it.

TABLE 3.1

**The Relation Between Methods of Gathering Information and
Possible Problems in Using the Methods to Gather Information**

Methods of Gathering Information	Possible Problems in Using the Methods to Gather information
Observational Methods (e.g., systematic behavioral observation, applied performance testing)	Failure to observe relevant characteristics or relevant indicators of those characteristics Misinterpretation of what is observed
Self-Report Methods (e.g., paper-and-pencil achievement tests, questionnaires, interviews)	Inaccurate or incorrect information because the wrong question was asked Misinformation provided by respondent, either intentionally or accidentally

havior, physiological reactions, or both.[3] This is a crucial assumption, one that should be considered carefully.

Making Inferences From Overt Behavior

Arguably, the best known conceptualization of the relation between human characteristics and human behavior is that of Kurt Lewin (1935). Lewin hypothesized that a person's behavior is some function of the person's characteristics (cognitive, affective, and psychomotor) and of the characteristics of the environment in which the person finds himself or herself. Consider, for example, a person who has a negative attitude toward Chinese food.[4] Suppose that person is with a person he or she knows very

---

[3]Many physiological responses have been examined in a search for a good, nonverbal indicator of affective characteristics. Three notable examples are electrical skin conductance (often called the Galvanic skin response or GSR), heart rate, and pupillary dilation. Fishbein and Ajzen (1975) stated the major problem of such responses when they wrote that "one problem is that most physiological measures appear to assess *general arousal* and therefore cannot be used to distinguish between positive and negative affective states" (p. 94). They then concluded that "it would definitely be desirable to have a nonverbal measure of [affect] not under the subject's control, but it appears unlikely that any known physiological reaction will serve this purpose" (p. 94). Using the terminology of chapter 2, these measures can provide information about the intensity of an affective characteristic but not about the direction or the target. This negative evaluation of physiological response measures, in addition to their practical limitations, leads the authors to relegate the discussion of such measures to this endnote.

[4]Jo Anne Anderson provided this example when Lorin was preparing the first edition as a reminder to him to listen to her when it comes to her food preferences (Anderson, 1981). As an indicator of the power of emotion, suffice it to say that she still remembers it to this day.

well. This person suggests they go to a Chinese restaurant. In this situation the person with the negative attitude toward Chinese food might well say, "I don't really like Chinese food. I would rather go to some other type of restaurant."

Now suppose the same person is with a person he or she does not know very well. The person suggests Chinese food. Not feeling comfortable enough with this person to make his or her true feelings known, the person goes along to the Chinese restaurant. Once there, he or she orders and eats Chinese food (because it is the only thing on the menu). Notice that the same attitude leads to completely different behavior in the two situations. The social environment was different in each situation and had a greater effect on the person's behavior than did the person's attitude.

One of the primary questions concerning the use of observational methods to assess affective characteristics is illustrated in this example. Because behavior often tends to be a function of both the human characteristic and environmental demands or expectations, is it possible to infer an affective characteristic from the person's behavior? The best answer to this question is, "Yes, under certain conditions."

What are these conditions? The conditions can best be explained by restating a proposition stated in chapter 2. Affective characteristics can be inferred from overt behaviors to the extent that the overt behaviors are sufficiently consistent across a variety of situations. Because in the previous example the behaviors were drastically inconsistent in the two situations, no inference about the relevant affective characteristic—attitude toward Chinese food—is possible. To the extent that a person's behavior is consistent across a variety of settings, it is possible to make inferences about related affective characteristics.

The importance of consistency of overt behaviors cannot be overestimated. As a consequence, one of the major difficulties in using overt behaviors to assess affective characteristics is the amount of time and effort involved in observing behavior. To decrease the amount of time and effort required, some educators have attempted to create a typical setting or environment in which it is likely that a typical behavior will be exhibited. From this single observation or from some series of observations in this setting, they have attempted to assess affective characteristics of persons placed in the setting. The use of a single observation in a single setting tends not to allow inferences to be made about affective characteristics. Although the use of a series of observations in this setting is potentially useful in this regard, the amount of time and effort is once again increased.

Another attempt to create a typical situation or environment stems from the use of *unobtrusive measures*. Put simply, unobtrusive measures are measures that can be used without people knowing that information is being gathered about them. The underlying assumption of these measures is that people will behave in a more typical manner if they do not know that they are being observed.

Two examples of unobtrusive measures should serve to illustrate more specifically what they are. In one study, an investigator attempted to assess public interest in the various exhibits in the Museum of Science and Industry in Chicago. He went to the custodial staff and asked them how often they had to replace the floor tiles near certain exhibits. The frequency of replacement of floor tiles was taken as an indicator of the public's interest in the various exhibits. The more frequent the replacement, the higher the interest.

In a second study, an investigator attempted to assess the popularity of various radio stations in a particular locale. Posing as a gas station attendant, he examined the radio dial as he worked on the car, pumping gas and cleaning windows. (We understand this would be a difficult study to conduct today in the age of pump-your-own gas.) The number of radio dials turned to a particular radio frequency was taken to be indicator of listeners' preferences for the radio station broadcasting at that frequency.

Note that both of these measures are clearly unobtrusive. In neither instance did the persons on whom the information was being gathered know he or she was being observed by the experimenter–observer. They may have been aware, however, that other individuals in the social setting were watching them and altered their behavior accordingly, thus deviating from the behavior that would be consistent with their affect. The environmental demands may still be there whether or not the observation per se is unobtrusive.

There is another potential problem associated with the use of unobtrusive measures, the ethical question of consent. In particular, educational authorities require that *informed consent* of participants in research is obtained. Informed consent means that potential research subjects must be told the nature of the study so they are in a sound position to agree or not agree to take part in it (Australian Association for Research in Education, 1995). In the case in which the subjects of the research are children, those responsible for these children (e.g., parents, teachers) have the right to know the objectives of the research as well as who and what will be observed. Thus, unobtrusive measures not only do not seem to deal with the demands made by the social environment, but they may be problematic from the viewpoint of research ethics.

In summary, then, it is possible to make some inferences about affective characteristics from behavior: if the behavior is observed across a variety of settings or across a fairly extended time period and if the behavior is found to be fairly consistent across the situations or over time. Attempts to infer affective characteristics from a single observation of behavior or from observation of behavior in a single situation have been (and almost certainly will continue to be) futile.

Problems in Inferring Affective Characteristics From Overt Behavior

In addition to the practical limitations imposed by multiple observations of behavior, other problems arise because of the nature of observational methods in general (as noted in Table 3.1). The observer may observe a behavior that is unrelated to the affective characteristic of interest. Consider, for example, an observer who wishes to assess a person's attitude toward science. The observer decides that paying attention in math class would be a good behavioral indicator of attitude toward science and so observes several students in several science classrooms and laboratories, noting their attentiveness. In one laboratory the observer notes that two students working together are highly task oriented. In a classroom the observer sees one student taking copious notes during the teacher's presentation. These three students are said to have the most favorable attitudes toward mathematics. In light of our discussion it may be wise to consider the possible environmental demands that are influencing the behavior (e.g., working to please the teacher, classroom rules and known consequences of violating these rules).

For the purpose of this illustration, however, a different focus is needed; perhaps the students are not paying attention, at least not to the task or material the teacher has in mind. Suppose the two students in the laboratory are playing a game rather than working on their science experiment. Suppose the attentive note-taking student is working on a class report for next period's social studies class rather than taking notes on the science material being presented by the teacher. The behavior being observed in these situations is completely unrelated to the affective characteristic of interest, namely attitude toward science.

Thus, in using behavioral observations to infer affect, two considerations are crucial. Initially, the behaviors that are believed to be related to the affective characteristics must be clearly specified. Hopefully the reader sees this as the problem of operational definitions that are discussed in chapter 2. In addition, however, it is important to observe these behaviors only when they are related to the relevant affective characteristic. As can be seen in the previous example, this is no easy task. Trained observers must be used to conduct these observations. The necessity of trained observers is an additional drawback to the use of observational methods for the assessment of affective characteristics in schools.

A final problem inherent in observational methods is the misinterpretation of what is observed (see Table 3.1). We all know stories of two people who have witnessed an automobile accident and provided the police with two different accounts. Because they observed the same phenomenon, the most likely cause of this discrepancy is the difference in the interpretations made by the two observers. For example, suppose one car turns left in front of a second car coming around a curve. Further, suppose that second car hits the first car broadside. Suppose that the two witnesses are standing relatively close to one another and that their vision of the accident is not impaired. One observer may say that the first car failed to yield the right of way. A second observer, on the other hand, may say that the driver of the second car was driving too fast for given road conditions (i.e., the curve).

Notice that the different interpretations are based on the same observation; both observers saw the first car collide with the second car from a similar position. If different observations had been made (e.g., if the two persons were standing on opposite sides of the street), then the problem may not be one of different interpretations but simply one of different observations perhaps arising from their different physical viewpoints.

Consider an example more closely aligned to affective assessment. Suppose observational methods are used to assess the frustration tolerance of elementary school children. Two observers enter a free-play setting in order to gather the desired information. Now suppose that Jeannie Smith throws a building block in the direction of Sammy Jones. Both observers watch Jeannie throw the block, but the first observer codes it as an example of frustration, whereas the second observer codes it as an example of anger (at Sammy Jones). (A third observer may see the act as an example of affection toward Sammy Jones because elementary students tend to show affection in strange ways, but that is somewhat beside the point.) In any case, the two interpretations differ. We are faced with a dilemma: Which interpretation should we believe? We could bring in a third observer but if the third disagrees with the other two, as in the parenthetical example, little value comes from this third observer. Besides, we could quickly find ourselves having more observers than children if we are not careful.

The use of multiple observers is useful, however, because it permits taking note of differences in interpretation. Once these differences are noted, discussions among the observers may lead to increasingly similar interpretations in the future.

Let us summarize the fate of observational methods for the purpose of affective assessment. Three problems are immediately apparent. First, there is the problem of inferring affective characteristics from overt behavior. Second, there is the problem of observing behaviors relevant to the affective characteristic. Third, there is the problem of misinterpreting the behavior that is seen by the observer.

These problems are not impossible to solve, but the proposed solutions are costly in time and money and are often somewhat impractical in the context of schools. Nonetheless, it may be informative to summarize these potential solutions. First, correct inferences from behavior to affective characteristics are more likely if these inferences are made from multiple observations. The multiple observations may be made of the same behavior in a variety of settings or the same behavior over time in the same setting. To the extent that the behaviors remain fairly consistent over settings or over time, appropriate inferences are more likely possible.

Second, if the behaviors believed to be linked to the affective characteristic are clearly defined and if care is taken to observe only those behaviors in an appropriate context, appropriate inferences from behaviors to affective characteristics are more likely. Of course, these two "ifs" imply careful thought in the initial conceptualization and operationalization of the affective characteristic, and the use of carefully trained observers.

Finally, if the observers are carefully trained and if at least two observers are used to make the observations, then the likelihood of misinterpretation is greatly reduced. The use of at least two observers allows you either to estimate the degree of misinterpretation present or correct future misinterpretation through discussions between or among observers.

The Florida Key: An Example of a Behavioral Affective Measure

Despite these potential difficulties, several educators have attempted to use observational methods to assess affective characteristics. One of the most noteworthy attempts was made by Purkey, Cage, and Craves (1973). Their measure, which seeks to assess learner self-esteem, is called the *Florida Key*. Because the Florida Key is a very good illustration of an observational method for assessing affective characteristics, it is discussed in some detail.

Purkey and his colleagues (1973) surveyed the literature to identify the general classroom behaviors of students who were considered to possess both positive and realistic academic self-esteem. A random sample of elementary teachers was asked to judge the extent to which the behaviors were useful in inferring students' academic self-esteem; 18 classroom behaviors were identified. Other elementary school teachers were then asked to consider each of their students relative to other students his or her age and to indicate the frequency with which each student exhibited each of the 18 behaviors. Four subsets of behaviors were identified, which Purkey and his colleagues labelled relating behaviors, asserting behaviors, investing behaviors, and coping behaviors.

Various technical qualities of the Florida Key were examined. The main finding of interest for the purpose of this discussion was the correlation between the student scores on the Florida Key and the student scores on the school subscale of the *Coopersmith Self-Esteem Inventory* (CSEI). The CSEI is a self-report measure of self-esteem, and the school subtest of the SCEI represents a measure of academic self-esteem. Thus, the correlation between the Florida Key and the CSEI would be an indication of the strength of the relation between an observational method and a self-report method of assessing academic self-esteem.

Purkey and his colleagues (1973) found the correlation between the Florida Key and the CSEI to be 0.33. Given that a correlation coefficient can range from 0 to 1, a correlation of 0.33 is modest and indicates that the variance in common between the two measures is only a little more than 10%. Quite clearly, the Florida Key and the CESI are not assessing the same characteristic. Because, however, the correlation coefficient was statistically significant, there is some relation between the two measures.

Given that the two measures are not assessing the same characteristic, we are left with that ever-present question: Which of the two measures represents a more accurate assessment of academic self-esteem? To address this question the discussion turns to self-report methods for assessing affective characteristics.

SELF REPORT METHODS AND AFFECTIVE ASSESSMENT

Two major types of self-report methods are used in education: questionnaires and interviews. Although they differ in many respects, they share a common format when used as self-reports. Namely, a person is asked to respond to a series of statements or questions, either by marking a box or an oval or writing a short statement (in the case of questionnaires) or by responding orally (in the case of interviews). Both questionnaires and interviews can be more or less structured.

Highly structured instruments are often referred to as closed. They consist of a fixed set of questions or statements in a format dictated by the designer of the instrument. Questionnaires used to assess affective characteristics are normally closed, although they often include a section at the end for any written (unstructured) comments people may wish to make. Less structured instruments are often referred to as open because the questions are open ended, thereby providing opportunities for extended written responses. In general, interviews are more often open, at least to a greater degree than questionnaires. The comparisons made here between questionnaires and interviews adopt this normal practice. In principle, however, there is nothing to prevent a questionnaire from being more open and an interview from being entirely closed. Telephone interviews, for example, are most often closed. Another term may be introduced here; Oppenheim (1992) referred to closed interviews as standardized interviews.

A summary of the advantages and disadvantages of questionnaires and interviews is given in Table 3.2. Questionnaires are more administratively convenient and provide a firmer base for systematic coding of information obtained. Interviews, on the other hand, are more flexible and may provide the opportunity for probing to a depth not possible with most questionnaires. Following the comparison of questionnaires and interviews in Table 3.2, the major focus of the remainder of this chapter and throughout the book is on structured questionnaires. Consequently, from this point on the terms self-report instrument and structured questionnaire are used synonymously.

With structured self-report questionnaires the persons whose affective characteristic is being assessed are given a set of statements or questions. In the directions, they may be asked to indicate the extent to which they agree or disagree with each statement, to indicate the level of importance they attach to a particular object or idea, or the frequency with which they participate in a particular activity. Each response is scored in terms of its

TABLE 3.2

Comparison of Questionnaires and Interviews as Self-Report Measures

Advantage–Disadvantage	Questionnaire	Interview
Standardization	Responses are readily coded in a standardized way.	Responses are more idiosyncratic and thus less amenable to coding.
Administration–Convenience	Can be completed by large groups simultaneously or by mail or e-mail.	One-to-one administration whether in person or by telephone.
Length	Limited by age and interest of respondents—perhaps from 40 to 60 questions at the most.	Limited in the same way—perhaps from 20 minutes to 1 hour.
Depth–Breadth	Mostly limited to structured questions previously developed.	Can move into other areas or for more detail, as appropriate.

positiveness toward the affective target. More often than not, the responses are summed to attain a total score, although this is not mandatory. (In fact, in chap. 6 we consider the problems in summing of responses under different conditions.) As noted in Table 3.1, a major problem with these methods lies in the fact that the persons being assessed may provide incorrect information. That is, they may not respond to each statement or question in a manner that is consistent with their true feelings.

Social Desirability

Why might persons provide misinformation? The most common reasons fall under a general heading called social desirability. What does social desirability mean? Traditionally, social desirability has meant that a person responds to a question or statement in a way that he or she believes to be socially acceptable (or, at least, acceptable to the person administering the self-report measure) rather than in a way consistent with his or her true beliefs and feelings.

Suppose, for example, a student is responding to a series of statements and comes to the following: "Stealing is wrong." The student remembers the time that he or she stole some money off the teacher's desk to buy lunch for a friend who had no money and came from a poor family. "Surely stealing can be right sometimes," the student thinks. Suddenly in the midst of this thought a very powerful recollection enters the student's mind: "Thou shalt not steal." The student immediately marks the Strongly Agree response option. Why? Because it's more socially acceptable. This is an example of social desirability.

Interviews are even more susceptible to the tendency to give social desirable responses than are questionnaires. This is because the intended reader of questionnaire responses is normally at a greater social distance from the respondent than an interviewer. It is much more likely that a respondent would give a socially desirable response to please a person sitting with them, than feel the need to do this for an unknown person, who will be reading the completed questionnaire at some time in the future. The reader would normally not know the respondent personally, even if he or she did have the respondent's name on the questionnaire.

Research conducted since the 1970s has suggested that social desirability is, in fact, composed of two separate components or factors (Robinson, Shaver, & Wrightsman, 1991). The first can be termed *impression management*. This is consistent with the traditional definition of social desirability: that some people are purposefully tailoring their answers to create the most positive social image. The second is *self-deceptive positivity*. In this case, the responses given are not attempts to deceive others; rather, they represent a tendency for some people to always see themselves in the most positive light. These people engage in self-deception. Self-deceptive positivity is important because controlling for it tends to lower the validity of measures where the target either is or involves the self (e.g., self-esteem, locus of control, and self-efficacy). Stated somewhat differently, there is some degree of self-deceptive positivity in most of us which is manifested in our responses to statements pertaining to our self-esteem, locus of control, self-efficacy, and the like.

Social desirability tends to become a greater concern when extremely personal questions are being asked, when the information is being used to make "selection-type" decisions, or when people differ widely in their tendency to respond in a socially desirable manner. Let us briefly examine each of these.

Many personality inventories, such as the Minnesota Multiphasic Personality Inventory, include statements that deal with extremely personal concerns (e.g., "I am a special messenger from God"; "I sometimes feel like killing myself"). In general, the more personal the statements or questions, the greater the tendency to respond in a socially desirable manner. Most affective scales used in an educational setting do not include such personal statements or questions, although they may well include other sensitive questions. Examples of questions that may be considered as sensitive are (a) questions concerning students' attitudes to school, (b) questions concerning their relationships with teachers, and (c) questions concerning their relationships with their peers or classmates. To the extent that self-report instruments do include such statements or questions, the user of the scales should be alert for evidence of socially acceptable responses. In the first example (perhaps using a statement such as "I enjoy school"), peer pressure, especially for boys, may incline some children to disagree (even though they do enjoy school). In the other two examples (student relationships with teachers and peers), fear of retribution may suggest that it would be prudent to respond positively.

Socially desirable responses also increase in situations where *selection-type decisions* are being made. These are situations in which a student is being considered for entry into a special program, entry into college, or an award. In situations like this, social desirability may be a strong factor influencing responses.

Social desirability in this instance is fairly easy to identify because scores influenced greatly by social desirability tend to lack predictive validity (e.g., Cronbach, 1970, pp. 495–497). That is to say, these scores will not accurately predict success in the program or in college, and some degree of predictive validity is needed before any instrument should be used to make selection decisions. Thus, predictive validity is a check on the presence of social desirability in the responses to affective scales.

Finally, social desirability is a major factor if individuals or cultural groups differ widely in their tendency to respond in a socially desirable manner. If, however, social desirability is a response style that virtually all people possess to the same degree, then it will not affect the relative standing of the people in terms of their scores on the affective scale. That is, if social desirability increases everyone's scores on a particular affective scale by five points, then the amount of the affective characteristic possessed by a person relative to the amounts possessed by all other people will not change. For certain types of score interpretation this alleviates the social-desirability issue; for other types of interpretation, however, social desirability is still a problem (see chap. 7, this volume).

What can be done to minimize the influence of social desirability? Five approaches have been proposed for dealing with social desirability: (1) insuring anonymity or confidentiality, (2) using the Randomized Response Method, (3) obtaining an estimate of social desirability, (4) using appropriate administrative conditions, and (5) estimating the empirical validity of the instrument. Three of these are considered at this time. Appropriate administrative conditions are discussed in chapter 5, this volume. Estimating the empirical validity of the instrument is discussed in chapters 4 and 6.

Anonymity and Confidentiality.   Assuring anonymity is one way of dealing with social desirability. As Stanley and Hopkins (1972) suggested, "anonymity is the key to valid ... assessment of feeling in any situation *in which the subject may be rewarded or punished for his response*" (p. 299; italics added). Permitting students to remain anonymous thus tends to minimize the effect of social desirability on their responses. Anonymity is not a preferable strategy for combatting social desirability. Why? Several reasons can be given. First, a tremendous amount of information is lost. With anonymous responses it is difficult to relate the information gathered about the affective characteristic with any other information (e.g., gender, race, ability, or achievement) unless this information is also provided by the students on the same instrument or an attached general-information page. Second, using the information to identify and help individual students is impossible because we do not know which students made which responses. Third and finally, there is little firm evidence that anonymity really alleviates the social-desirability problem, at least with respect to the assessment of affective characteristics appropriate within the context of schools.

Furthermore, our experience is that concerns for privacy have increased in recent years and are unlikely to decrease. The problem is not only one of the truthfulness of responses obtained; students may decline to participate at all when they believe their responses might be seen by others (whether or not anonymity is ensured). An increased rate of refusal to participate raises other problems related to affective assessment, such as the representativeness of the scores that are obtained from those who agree to participate. This matter is taken up in Chapter 6.

The combination of an increased concern for privacy and problems associated with anonymity suggests the possibility of confidentiality of responses. In contrast with anonymity (where no one knows who responded in what way to which items), confidentiality means that someone does know but that "someone" will not tell anyone else.

Confidentiality has two aspects. First, there is the question of who has access to the responses. The normal guarantee that can be given by researchers is that, apart from a small number of persons on the research team, no one else will see the respondent's answers. Second, there is the question of the identification of any individual student or school (or other institution) in any presentation of the information and in any reports to be written. The researcher simply needs to state that no individual or group will be identified or identifiable and to ensure that this "promise" is kept. We have found that students, teachers and other groups accept such assurances of confidentiality from researchers, especially when the researcher is from outside their school system.

Acceptance of an assurance of confidentiality does enable information gathered from a self-report instrument to be linked with other personal information. Either names or identification numbers on these instruments can be used to enable such links to be made. The names or numbers are then removed from files when data matching is complete. The original instruments are destroyed (e.g., shredded) once the information has been extracted, coded, and stored in computer files. Advising students of disposal arrangements that are in place to protect the confidentiality of the information they provide can contribute to positive relationships between students and researchers.

Using the Randomized Response Method.   The Randomized Response Method (RRM) is an attempt to estimate the amount of social desirability in a set of responses and, based on that estimate, eliminate social desirability so that the presence or amount of the affective characteristic can be determined (Greenberg, Abdula, Simmons, & Horvitz, 1969). RRM consists of seven steps (see Table 3.3).

The key to RRM is the pairing of innocuous questions with socially sensitive questions, but the innocuous questions must be of a special type; namely, those for which answers are known. In the example in Table 3.3, we "know" that about one half of the students will have birthdays in one of the six months listed. We use this knowledge coupled with our knowledge of probability (i.e., flipping a coin) to estimate the percent of students responding affirmatively to the socially sensitive question (Popham, 1994).

The RRM can be expanded beyond one pair of questions. If the affective characteristic is attitude toward school vandalism, for example, a series of socially sensitive questions pertaining to this attitude can be written. Each is paired with an innocuous question. Before responding to each pair of questions, students would flip a coin to determine which of the two questions to answer. The percent of students agreeing to each socially sensitive question can be estimated as shown in Table 3.3. The median percent can be used as the summary statistic representing students' attitudes toward

TABLE 3.3

The Randomized Response Method

Step	Activity
1	Select a fairly large sample of students (e.g., 500).
2	Pair an innocuous question with a socially sensitive question. For example, (1a) Were you born in any of the following 6 months: January, March, May, July, September, or October? Is paired with (1b) Do you believe it is fundamentally wrong for teenagers to deface public property by spray painting it? Make sure something is known about the distribution of the content of the innocuous question in the population (see Step 5).
3	Instruct each student to flip a coin and, without telling anyone of the result, answer the first question (1a) if it turned out "heads" and the second question (1b) if it turned out "tails." Their answer to whichever question they answer goes in space 1 on a separate sheet of paper.
4	Make the assumption that 50% of the population (i.e., 250 students) answered question 1a and 50% answered question 1b. This is a reasonable assumption in light of the random nature of the coin toss.
5	Assume that 50% of those responding to question 1a responded "Yes" and 50% responded "No." Again, 50% would be a reasonable estimate for the percent of students with birthdays in 1 of the 6 months. That would mean that 125 said "yes," and 125 said "no."
6	Calculate the total percent of "yes" responses. Suppose it is 60%. Convert this to numbers in the total population of 500. This would mean that 300 said "yes" and 200 said "no."
7	Subtract the number of "yes" responses in step 5 (125) from the number of "yes" responses in step 6 (300). The result would be 175. This means that 175 of the 250 students (70%) of the students who responded to question 1b, agreed that defacing public property by spray painting it is fundamentally wrong.

school vandalism. The variability of percent agreement across all question pairs would provide useful information about the internal consistency of the entire scale.

Estimating Social Desirability. A third strategy for dealing with social desirability is to obtain an estimate of social desirability—either as an estimate of social desirability inherent in the statements or questions, or an estimate of individuals' tendencies toward social desirability. Edwards (1957, 1962) attempted to elicit both types of estimates.

In order to obtain an estimate of the amount of social desirability present in a self-report instrument, Edwards (1962) asked judges to examine the statements in it and to rate each in terms of its inherent social desirability on a scale of 1 to 11. Statements rated low on the continuum were said to have social undesirability, whereas statements rated high on the continuum were said to possess social desirability. Statements near the center of the continuum were said to be neutral and were in fact the most advantageous in terms of assessing the affective characteristic.

In order to obtain an estimate of the amount of social desirability tendency possessed by people, Edwards (1957) devised a social-desirability instrument. His reasoning in developing this instrument was straightforward. If scores on the social-desirability instrument are highly related with the scores on a particular affective instrument, then the validity of the affective instrument is suspect. Subsequent research has suggested that the Edwards' instrument measures self-deceptive positivity, rather than impression management (Robinson et al., 1991; see our earlier discussion of social desirability). In contrast, instruments such as the Marlowe-Crowne Social Desirability Scale (Crowne & Marlowe, 1960) and the Children's Social Desirability Scale (Crandall, Crandall, & Katkovsky, 1965) appear to measure impression management. Finally, there are instruments that provide data on both of these components of social desirability (e.g., Paulhus, 1984, 1988).

Acquiescence

In addition to social desirability, at least one other factor contributes to the respondent providing misinformation. This factor has been termed acquiescence (Cronbach, 1970). Acquiescence refers to the tendency of a person to agree with a statement (or answer *yes* to a question) when he or she is unsure or ambivalent. Once again, it is more likely that a respondent would want to be agreeable to please an interviewer who is present than be concerned about a future reader of their questionnaire answers who is not present.

Like social desirability, acquiescence tends to be a greater problem under certain conditions. Two conditions can be readily identified. First, acquiescence is likely to increase as a factor if the person has no strong feeling about or understanding of the affective target. We are reminded of a colleague who administered an instrument assessing attitudes toward statistics to his introductory educational statistics classes. The instrument was administered at the beginning and at the end of the course. To the chagrin of our colleague, the scores decreased fairly substantially from the first occasion to the second. His interpretation was that the course had a negative influence on students' attitudes toward statistics. An alternative explanation is that the responses on the first occasion were inflated by a tendency toward acquiescence. It is likely that prior to studying statistics, students had little if any understanding of what statistics really are. As a consequence, the students tended to agree somewhat with the vast majority of statements. Later, armed with more information and a greater understanding, this tendency diminished, and their true feelings were recorded.[5]

Second, acquiescence tends to increase as the length of the scale increases. After agreeing with the first 10 statements, for example, a person, perhaps somewhat unconsciously, tends to agree with the next 25 statements.

The problem of acquiescence can be dealt with in at least two ways. Because people who acquiesce tend to agree with statements or respond affirmatively to questions, one useful strategy for dealing with the problem is to include an equal number of positive statements (e.g., I love school) and negative statements (e.g., I detest school) on the instrument. When this is done the acquiescence effect can be estimated by comparing the responses to the positive statements with those to the negative statements. In general, acquiescence will show up in a fairly low-internal consistency reliability for the entire instrument. More is said about reliability in chapter 4, this volume.

Additionally, it is wise to place the items on the self-report instrument in a random fashion. This is particularly important when multiple affective characteristics are being assessed on a single instrument, and the instrument is fairly lengthy. Alternatively, the instrument should assess only one affective characteristic and the instrument should be kept as short as possible. If the instrument is fairly short, the respondent may see no need to develop a response set because the amount of time and effort needed to respond to the items seems reasonable.

Although these approaches to the control of acquiescence are based on sound, logical considerations, it is also wise to examine the actual responses made to the items. Such an examination can focus on the number of original responses that have subsequently been changed and the num-

---

[5]This may be yet another variation on the theme, "Ignorance is bliss."

ber of items left unanswered. A brief look at erasures, cross-outs, and omissions can provide useful information in this regard. They tend to indicate ambivalence on the part of the respondent, and, as mentioned earlier, the tendency to acquiesce is greater when the respondent is ambivalent about a response.

OUR PREFERRED METHOD FOR ASSESSING AFFECTIVE CHARACTERISTICS

Which of the two general approaches to assessing affective characteristics is preferable? To answer this question let us begin with an examination of the differences between them. Table 3.4 summarizes the problems inherent in each method as well as the proposed solution strategies for each problem.

One fact seems clear from an examination of the information presented in Table 3.4. The solution strategies necessary for sound observation methods are much more costly (in terms of time and human resources) than are those necessary for sound self-report methods. Some of the additional costs can be alleviated by an approach like that of Purkey, Cage, and Graves (1973), who, the reader will remember, used the students' teachers as the observers. In this way, multiple observations in at least a small number of different settings were probably considered by the teachers in arriving at their judgments. Purkey and his colleagues also developed clear operational definitions (i.e., behaviors) as the basis for their instrument. However, the training of teachers as observers was not documented.

The question of how perceptive teachers are has still not been answered satisfactorily. When answers have been sought (e.g., Kounin, 1970), the major finding is that teachers differ greatly in their perceptiveness in classrooms. Using Kounin's terminology, some teachers are more "with-it" than others. This finding indicates once again the necessity of multiple observers, especially in the case of teachers as observers. Purkey and his colleagues (Purkey et al., 1973) did not use multiple observers in their study and thus were unable to investigate the possible misinterpretations of their students made by teachers.

Despite these flaws, Purkey's (Purkey et al., 1973) approach to the assessing of affective characteristics in schools seems the only reasonable observational method available. Thus, from a totally practical point of view, self-report methods are more appealing than observational methods.

What about considerations from more theoretical perspectives? What approach seems more aligned with the general conceptualization of affective characteristics? There are two related answers to this question. First, we side with Gehman (1957), who stated that "the writer does not know the source of a more accurate statement of [a person's] likes and prefer-

TABLE 3.4

Problems Inherent in Methods for Gathering Information about Affective Characteristics and Solution Strategies for Each Problem

Method for Gathering Affective Information	Potential Problems in Using the Methods to Gather Affective Information	Possible Solution Strategies
Observational methods	1. Inferring affective characteristics from overt behaviors	1. Make multiple observations in a variety of situations.
	2. Observing relevant behaviors	2a. Have clear operational definitions. 2b. Use carefully trained observers.
	3. Misinterpretation of behavior by observer	3a. Use carefully trained observers. 3b. Use multiple observers.
Self-report methods	1. Social desirability	1. Attempt to control by • using appropriate administrative conditions and procedures, or • insuring anonymity of respondents or confidentiality of responses. 2. Attempt to extimate by • using judges to rate statements as to their social desirability, • administering a social desirability instrument, or • examining the empirical validity of the affective insturment.
	2. Acquiescence	1. Attempt to control by • having an equal number of "positive" and "negative" items, • randomly ordering items on instrument, or • keeping instrument short. 2. Attempt to estimate by • examining the number of responses changed (e.g., erasures.)

69

ences than those given by the [person], regardless of the motives operating" (p. 69). It seems reasonable that people will express themselves verbally more readily than they will behaviorally. A classic study (LaPiere, 1934) lends support to this supposition. Wicker (1969) presented a concise summary of LaPiere's study:

> In the 1930's when, according to studies of social distance, there was much anti-Chinese sentiment in the United States, LaPiere (1934) took several extensive automobile trips with a Chinese couple. Unknown to his companions, he took notes of how the travellers were treated, and he kept a list of hotels and restaurants where they were served. Only once were they denied service, and LaPiere judged their treatment to be above average in 40% of the restaurants visited. Later, LaPiere wrote to the 250 hotels and restaurants on his list, asking if they would accept Chinese guests. Over 90% of the 128 proprieters responding indicated they would not serve Chinese, in spite of the fact that all had previously accommodated LaPiere's companions. (p. 42)

The study is usually cited as evidence of the lack of relation between attitude and behavior. However, a more interesting perspective is possible. One question that must be raised in this example is: What actually is the socially-desirable response? At first it appears that some moral or ethical principle (e.g., love your neighbor as yourself) underlies the socially desirable response. Or perhaps a legal principle (e.g., discrimination against members of any ethnic group is forbidden) defines the socially desirable response. In either case, the socially desirable response would be to indicate (either behaviorally or verbally) an acceptance of the Chinese people.

What if, however, we were to conceptualize the socially desirable response as the one that is in harmony with the general sentiment of society at that time, namely, an anti-Chinese sentiment? In this case the socially desirable response would be to indicate a rejection of the Chinese people.

If the first interpretation of social desirability is used, the behavioral expression actually was influenced more by social desirability than the verbal expression. On the other hand, if the second interpretation of social desirability is used, the verbal expression was influenced more by social desirability than the behavioral expression.

This study, then, illustrates two points. First, behavioral expressions (as shown earlier in this chapter) can be influenced by social desirability at least as much as can verbal expressions. Second, what is actually socially desirable depends to a great extent on the person's point of reference. What is acceptable according to moral or ethical principles may not be acceptable according to the legal principles of a given state or country. Furthermore, what is acceptable according to the legal principles of a given state or country may not be acceptable to a subgroup or subculture of that state or country.

In the LaPiere (1934) example, it is likely that the moral-ethical-legal interpretation of social desirability is applicable. If so, the LaPiere study illustrates a situation in which behavioral expressions are more influenced by social desirability than are verbal expressions.

There is a second answer to the question of whether observational or self-report methods are more aligned with the concept of what affective characteristics are. This answer leads us to consider whether the more appropriate perspective is that of the observer or that of the participant. It could reasonably be argued that the observer provides a more objective[6] view of the situation than could be provided by the participant. However, it is not an objective view of the situation that is important given that we are concerned with assessing the affective characteristics of the participants. It is the subjective view of the participant that is important, even if this view differs from a more impartial observer's view, if we are interested in assessing how he or she feels. Conceptually, then, we should not try to eliminate the subjectivity inherent in self-report measures of affect. This would be akin to throwing the baby out with the bathwater.

In view of the previous discussion, we conclude that self report methods are more compatible with the conceptualization of the affective domain than are observational methods. Based on both theoretical and practical considerations, then, self-report instruments seem to be more appropriate than observational methods for the assessment of affective characteristics.

AN INTRODUCTION TO SOME TECHNICAL AND TERMINOLOGY ISSUES

This chapter comes to a close with a consideration of three issues. Although they are addressed in greater detail in subsequent chapters, the applicability of these issues for both approaches to assessing affective characteristics suggests that an initial discussion should take place here.

The Stability of Affective Assessment Data

Because of our focus on assessing affective characteristics, our affective assessment instruments should provide data that are stable over some reasonable period of time. The key question is "What is a reasonable period of time?" If responses to items are not at all consistent across situations and over time, we can have no confidence in the information we collect. However, stability is a two-edged sword. In addition to being stable (i.e., reliable),

---

[6]We use the term *objective* here in the sense of being emotionally detached from the situation. Herein lies the rub. What information can someone who is emotionally detached from a situation provide about the emotions of people in that situation?

affective instruments must also be sensitive to change over time, whether intended or otherwise, and to vastly different situations (e.g., two classrooms arranged and taught in completely different ways). That is, data obtained from affective instruments ought not to be stable when individuals change their views or when situations in which individuals find themselves are different in a way that may be reflected in the affect being assessed.

There is a problem of balance here. We seem to be saying, "Give us stability, but not too much." A partial solution to this dilemma is to focus attention more on another measure of reliability: internal consistency. Estimates of internal consistency require multiple assessments of the same affective characteristic, generally in one setting and one point in time. This typically is achieved by obtaining a series of responses about different aspects of the particular affect being assessed. For example, in a self-report instrument assessing students' general attitudes toward their school, different items focus on how students feel about each of the following: going to school each day, what they do in school, simply being in school, and being proud to be a student there (Ainley & Bourke, 1992). Each of these items would give rise to a slightly different feeling, but all would be concerned with the students' general attitude toward their school.

One primary benefit of internal consistency reliability is that there are guidelines for interpreting the magnitude of the reliability estimates (e.g., Robinson et al., 1991). These guidelines can be applied to all self-report instruments and all affective characteristics. In contrast, as mentioned earlier, an estimate of stability requires that those interpreting the estimate have a rather thorough knowledge of the affective characteristic being assessed, the extent to which that characteristic can be expected to remain constant over time, and any efforts being made to change the characteristic.

Single Instruments and Multiple Scales

It has become commonplace to design self-report instruments that are intended to assess multiple affective characteristics and multiple targets. By doing this, information on multiple characteristics and multiple targets can be obtained during a single administration of a single instrument. For example, if we include two affective characteristics (e.g., attitudes and values) and two targets (e.g., school and studying) on the same instruments, we can conceivably obtain four pieces of information: attitude toward school, the value of school, attitude toward studying, and the value of studying.

Each of these would be termed an affective scale. Thus, in this example, we would have one instrument and four scales. For each affect–target combination, a scale score could be calculated for each student. Each scale score would be derived from the student's responses to all of the items pertaining to that specific affect–target combination. (How scales are formed and how individual students receive scale scores are described in chap. 6, this volume.)

Multiple Meanings of the Term "Scale"

In the previous section, we used the term "scale" to refer to a set of items related to a single affect–target combination. We must point out, however, that this is not the only way in which the term "scale" is used by people working in affective assessment. The response categories included on an instrument to prompt students, and to standardize the coding of their responses are sometimes referred to as scales. The traditional 5-point Likert scale is an example (e.g., *Strongly Agree, Agree, Undecided, Disagree,* and *Strongly Disagree*). To avoid confusion, we reserve our use of scale to refer to the set of items themselves. We refer to the response categories simply as response categories or response options.

SUMMARY OF MAJOR POINTS

1. In a very general sense, there are only two ways in which we gather information about human characteristics: We look (observational method), and we ask and listen (self-report method).
2. The observation method can yield bad information if the person gathering the information
   • fails to observe the relevant characteristic or relevant indicator of that characteristic, or
   • misinterprets what he or she observes.
3. The self-report method can yield bad information if
   • the person gathering the information asks the wrong question, or
   • the person providing the information intentionally or accidentally misinforms the person gathering the information.
4. Affective characteristics can be inferred from overt behavior if
   • the behavioral indicators of the affective characteristics are clearly specified,
   • at least two carefully trained observers observe and similarly interpret the behaviors,
   • the behavior is observed across a variety of settings or across a fairly extended time period, and
   • the behavior is found to be fairly consistent across settings or time.
5. Affective characteristics can be inferred from self-reports if
   • socially desirable responses are minimized or estimated, and

- acquiescence or similar response styles are minimized or estimated.

6. There is some evidence to suggest that observational and self-report methods purporting to assess the same affective characteristic do not provide very similar information about that characteristic.

7. The extent to which acquiescence is a factor influencing a person's responses to a self-report instrument depends on the nature and purpose of the instrument. Social desirability tends to be a major factor when
   - extremely personal questions are being asked,
   - the information is to be used to make selection or placement decisions (e.g., placement in a program, selection for a college), and
   - individuals differ widely in their tendency to respond in a socially desirable manner.

8. The problem of social desirability can be dealt with either by minimizing or estimating its effect. The most preferable approach to solving the social-desirability problem is a combined approach of
   - the use of appropriate administrative conditions and procedures (which *minimize* the social-desirability factor),
   - an examination of the empirical validity of the instrument (which estimates the social desirability factor), and
   - assuring confidentiality of responses.

9. The extent to which acquiescence is a factor influencing a person's responses to a self-report instrument depends on
   - the extent to which a person understands and has some feeling about the affective target, and
   - the length of the scale.

10. The problem of acquiescence and other related response styles can be dealt with by
    - constructing an instrument with an equal number of positively and negatively worded items,
    - randomly placing the items on the instrument, and
    - keeping the instrument relatively short.

11. Within the context of the schools, self-report methods appear superior to observational methods for assessing affective characteristics. From a practical perspective, the difficulties associated with self-report methods are more easily overcome than are those associated with observational methods. From a theoretical perspective, it seems reasonable to assume that people express themselves more readily verbally than they do behaviorally.

12. The discussion in this chapter is not meant to be a blanket endorsement of self-report instruments or a blanket rejection of observational

methods. The quality of instruments within each category varies greatly. Rather, the discussion is intended to lay the groundwork for focusing the remainder of the volume on self-report instruments because they tend to be more theoretically and practically sound despite their flaws.

13. For assessing affect in the schools, questionnaires are generally preferred to interviews as providing greater standardization of questions and coding of responses

14. Both the stability of affective data and the sensitivity of affective data to change must be considered when interpreting affective data. Although these may well be in conflict, in different ways both are important. Internal-consistency estimates of reliability are more interpretable across affective characteristics and affective assessment instruments.

15. Self-report instruments often include assessments of multiple affective characteristics and their targets. Each affect–target combination included on an instrument is called a scale. Unfortunately, the term "scale" has multiple meanings, also referring to the response categories on most self-report instruments. We use the term scale to refer to a set of items pertaining to a single affect–target combination. Response categories are called response categories or response options.

4

Affective Instruments: What is Important and What do They Look Like?

In this chapter, described are the qualities of a good self-report instrument or questionnaire[1] that has been designed for the purpose of assessing one or more affective characteristics. Five qualities must be present at satisfactory levels if a self-report instrument is to provide accurate, precise, and usable information. They are: communication value, objectivity, validity, reliability, and interpretability. Although it is possible for all of the items included on an instrument to be associated with a single affect–target combination (e.g., attitude toward school) and thus have only one affective scale (see our discussion in chap. 3, this volume), the tendency is for most instruments to consist of multiple sets of items, each pertaining a single affect–target combination, and thus include multiple scales.

There are many different strategies used to construct self-report instruments for the general purpose of assessing affective characteristics (e.g., Guttman, 1944; Likert, 1932; Thurstone & Chave, 1992; Semantic Differential in Osgood, Suci, & Tannenbaum, 1957). Each strategy is based

---

[1]Throughout this chapter we use the terms "self-report instrument" and "questionnaire" interchangeably.

on somewhat different assumptions and gives rise to different types of statements and different sets of response categories or options. In this chapter, described in some detail is the strategy most frequently used to design affective self-report instruments, namely, Likert scaling. Other strategies for preparing affective scales (e.g., Thurstone, Guttman, Semantic Differential) are described in some detail in Appendix A.[2]

Before we begin, let us discuss briefly our use of three related, but quite distinct, terms: instrument, questionnaire, and scale. An instrument is the most general of the three and is used to describe a method of gathering information (e.g., a test, a questionnaire, an observation, an interview). A questionnaire is defined as a collection of questions, statements, or tasks placed on the same instrument for some reason. For example, they all may pertain to a particular topic, related set of topics, or a specific purpose for which the data are being collected. We use the terms "questionnaire" and "self-report instrument" synonymously. A questionnaire may consist of one or more scales. A scale, the most specific of the three terms, is a set of related statements, related in the sense that the responses to them provide information about a single affect–target combination (e.g., the value of education, text anxiety, academic self-esteem). There is a critical distinction between a scale and a mere collection of statements. A scale must be comprised of *related* statements as defined previously.

QUALITIES OF AFFECTIVE INSTRUMENTS AND THEIR SCALES

Before a questionnaire can be used to gather information about any affective characteristic or set of characteristics, a careful examination of the questionnaire is necessary. This examination should focus on at least the five important qualities mentioned previously: communication value, objectivity, validity, reliability, and interpretability.

Communication Value

Communication value is concerned with the extent to which a questionnaire can be understood by the person responding to it. Questions pertaining to communication value include the following: Does the person understand the task at hand? That is, does the respondent know what to do? Is the person able to understand the task well enough in order to be able to actually perform it? That is, does he or she know how to do it? Without an adequate level of communication the responses to the questionnaire are likely to be meaningless. With this in mind, we turn our attention

---

[2]Appendix A also includes a step-by-step procedure for designing a Likert scale. The discussion of Likert scaling in this chapter is more conceptual than procedural.

to two particular aspects of questionnaires, the instructions and the reading level required of respondents.

Questionnaire Instructions.   In ensuring that a person knows what to do in responding to a questionnaire, the key is to provide comprehensive and clear instructions at the beginning of the instrument. Having good instructions is always important, but it is absolutely essential when the questionnaire is sent out by mail and the person responding to it does not have ready access to advice from a person who is familiar with the questionnaire and its purpose.

After reading the instructions and any accompanying information sheet, those responding to the questionnaire should understand the conditions under which they are responding and the general purpose for which the information is being gathered. At a mechanical level, the instructions should also help to ensure that a respondent knows how to answer a questionnaire (e.g., to circle the letter corresponding to their choice). Quite typically the instructions also inform respondents that they are not being tested in the usual sense and, therefore, that there are no right and wrong answers to any questions. The instructions should also clarify the meaning of the affective target, if this is necessary, to ensure that all respondents are reacting to the same conception of the target (e.g., school; see chap. 2, this volume).

Two fairly typical sets of instructions follow (Fig. 4.1 and 4.2). In the first example, the instructions are for a questionnaire about how students feel about school and include a practice item. The inclusion of practice items is advised when some of the students may be unfamiliar with the type of questionnaire being used.

The second example is in the same area of school-related affect. These instructions are taken from the Quality of School Life questionnaire which is used extensively as a model for data analysis in chapter 6 of this volume. This questionnaire does not include an *Uncertain* response category, and the example states how respondents who cannot decide about a particular statement should deal with it.

Reading Level of the Questionnaire.   In ensuring that a person knows how to complete and is able to complete a questionnaire, there is a prime requirement that he or she can read it. It is the match between the students' literacy levels (i.e., their reading ability) and the difficulty and complexity of the written material (i.e., its readability) that is important. The first requirement, then, is to know something about the literacy level of the students. In general, it is not desirable to give questionnaires to students younger than about 9 or 10 years of age.[3] By restricting the administration of question-

---

[3]If a questionnaire is administered to younger students, then reading the questionnaire to them is highly recommended (see McKenna & Kear, 1990, for an example).

HOW YOU FEEL ABOUT SCHOOL

This is not a test. There are no "right" and "wrong" answer to any of the questions. Just answer as honestly as you can.

The statements ask you to say how you feel about school and learning in school. You should respond to each statement by circling one of the five ways given beneath the statement.

Here is a practice statement:

> Example 0:   School is boring.
> A. Strongly agree
> B. Agree
> C. Can't decide
> D. Disagree
> E. Strongly disagree

Which of the five ways tells best how *you* feel about the statement: A, or B, or C, or D, or E? Circle your choice.

Please work *carefuly* and *quickly*. Do not spend a long time on any one statement. Please respond to *each* statement and circle only *one* response to each.

FIG. 4.1.   Sample instructions—"How You Feel About School."

naires in this way we believe there is a strong probability that the students will be able to read and comprehend a carefully designed questionnaire. This restriction should also assist in ensuring that students have the level of maturity they need to have developed a capacity to think about the issue being dealt with and give their own perspective.

We do not mean to suggest that it is impossible to give any questionnaire to younger students. In fact, we offer some examples later. Rather, it is to suggest that, as a general rule, there is a lower age limit for the productive use of questionnaires. On the other hand, it would be foolish to claim that all mature adults are sufficiently literate to be able to read the type of written material required for responding to a questionnaire. In summary, we need to keep the capacities of students in mind when designing self-report instruments.

If, for the moment, we can assume at least an adequate level of literacy of our intended student population, then written material that is *easy to read* and comprehend is said to have high readability, whereas material

SCHOOL LIFE

We would like to know how you feel about your life in school. This is not a test, and there are no right or wrong answers. What we want is youropinion, so try to answer what you think about your school life. Your answers will not be seen by anyone else.

First of all, would you please answer these questions:

Name of Your School?_____

Your Class?_____ Boy or Girl?_____

Each statement on the next two pages starts with MY SCHOOL IS A PLACE WHERE ... some particular thing happens to you or you feel a particular way. You should give your opinion by ticking one of the boxes in each line to show that you **Agree, Mostly Agree, Mostly Disagree**, or **Disagree** with the statement.

Try to give an answer to every statement but, if you really cannot decide, leave that one out.

Don't forget that you have to think of **My School is a Place Where ...** before each item for it to make sense, for example, **My School is a Place Where ... I feel important.**

FIG. 4.2.   Sample instructions—"School Life."

that is difficult to read and comprehend is said to have low readability. The paper-and-pencil nature of questionnaires coupled with the possibility that they may be completed in isolation makes the issue of readability critical.

The best initial practice in this regard is to keep the material as easy to read as possible, consistent with the complexity of the concepts being addressed. A preliminary trial of an unfamiliar instrument or a new instrument with a small group of persons selected from the intended student population is also important. This preliminary trial is often called a *pilot test*. During this pilot test, simply asking students to complete the questionnaire and then examining their responses is insufficient for the purpose of judging whether they were able to understand what they were required to do and what they were being asked. Observing students during the pilot test is very important. Difficulties with instructions, for example, can often be seen by watching the students as they begin the questionnaire. It is also highly desirable to talk to the pilot-test group after they have completed the questionnaire, asking them about any difficulties they may have had. In addition, a handful of students can be queried individually about what they understood about some of the more complex or dubious items or parts of the instructions. Greater care and effort expended at this early trial stage will pay dividends later in a more trouble-free administration and interpretation of the questionnaire results.

Objectivity

Objectivity is concerned with the degree to which the scoring (or coding) of the responses made to an instrument is free from scorer (or coder) bias or error. If two different scorers arrive at very different total scores for the same person on the same questionnaire, a lack of objectivity is evident. When this is the case, the person's total score depends more on the scorer than on the person's responses to the questionnaire. Certainly, this is not a desirable state of affairs. Without an adequate level of objectivity, then, responses to an instrument are likely to be less meaningful (or, perhaps more accurately, the meaning depends more on who does the scoring). The objectivity of a questionnaire can range from a little to a lot. It is not a dichotomous quality (i.e., it is not all–none, either–or). Rather, we talk of a high degree of objectivity, of a moderate degree of objectivity, and so on.

For most structured, affective questionnaires loss of objectivity arising from bias should not be a major problem. The scoring (coding) rules are normally such that they remove the need for a great deal of human judgment. Point values are assigned to the response categories according to predetermined rules. For the four traditional response categories of Likert scales, for example, we could assign the following point values: "4" for *Strongly Agree*, "3" for *Agree*, "2" for *Disagree*, and "1" for *Strongly Disagree*. For each item, each student is given a score that corresponds to the point value assigned to the response category that he or she selects. These item scores can then be summed for all items included in a particular scale to yield a total-scale score for each student. Alternatively, this total-scale score can be divided by the number of items included in the scale or the number of items to which the student responded and a new total-scale score is produced (see chap. 6, this volume).

There may be a greater concern for loss of objectivity owing to error in using the coding rules. If there is a mix of positively and negatively worded statements making up a scale, it is essential that the coding of responses to the negative statements be reversed before the responses are added to give a scale score. In the previous example, strongly disagreeing with a negatively worded statement would yield 4 points. This transformation can be done at the point of *keying-in* questionnaire responses or subsequently by a command to the computer program being used to create the scale scores.

The latter method is preferred because the keying-in of responses becomes an automatic, clerical procedure, which makes it too easy for the person doing this work to forget which statements are worded negatively and, therefore, require reverse coding.

Errors of this type may be easy to detect when computing scale scores for individuals, but because forgetting tends to be somewhat random, it is almost impossible to correct all of these errors without a complete recoding of the questionnaire responses. This can be an expensive process as well as a time-consuming one. Of course, it is also possible to forget to reverse the coding for a negatively worded statement when instructing the computer to create total-scale scores. In this case, however, the error is consistently applied across individual students and, generally, it is easy to detect and correct.

Validity

In general terms, *validity* is the extent to which the data from an instrument enable you to accomplishes the purpose for which the instrument was designed. If, for example, an instrument is designed to predict future behavior or status, then validity has to do with the accuracy of the prediction made based on the data obtained from the instrument. This is *predictive validity*. In the case of affective assessment instruments, we are most often interested in how well data from an instrument describes the characteristic being assessed. Thus within the affective realm, validity generally refers to the extent to which an instrument provides information about the characteristic it was designed to assess. To put it another way, does the instrument really assess what is was intended to assess?

One cannot use a speedometer to measure distance traveled. This would be a mismatch between the instrument (a measure of speed) and the characteristic (distance). A speedometer would be an invalid instrument for the purpose of measuring distance. The meaning of validity as it applies to affective assessment instruments is very clear with physical examples such as this one.

Within an educational context, the question of validity is normally not as clear. Consider, for example, an arithmetic test that includes mostly word problems. Suppose the reading level required by the word problems is fairly high, so high in fact that the reading component is more difficult than the arithmetic required. In this example, the validity of the test for its intended purpose, testing students' knowledge and use of arithmetic concepts and skills, would be lowered because of the reading problem, even though the content of the word problems consists of the arithmetic knowledge and skills students have been taught. As was the case for objectivity, the validity of assessment instruments is not dichotomous; it would be inappropriate to refer to an instrument simply as valid or invalid. The validity of a scale is a matter of degree.

Methods of examining validity fall into two general categories. One category contains methods that examine the instrument itself. This category is concerned with *judgmental validity* (e.g., *face* validity, and *content* validity). The second category contains empirical methods that examine the nature of the responses made to the instrument. This category is concerned with *concurrent validity*, *predictive validity*, and *construct validity*. The methods in the first category are used to determine the extent to which an instrument will be *likely* to assess one or more affective characteristics. On the other hand, the methods in the second category are used to determine the extent to which responses made by students provide evidence that the instrument, in fact, *does* assess the affective characteristics.

Very concise descriptions of these different types of validity were provided by Zeller (1994). However, a few additional comments on construct validity seem appropriate at this time. There are two methods that can be used to examine the construct validity of affective scales. The first pertains to a single scale on a single instrument; the second is more appropriate for a number of scales on a single instrument. We consider the single-scale situation first.

Establishing construct validity for a specific affective scale requires that you see the affective characteristic assessed by the scale in a larger context. This context is often referred to as a conceptual framework. The conceptual framework includes the affective characteristic, characteristics (both affective and other) with which the affective characteristic should be related, characteristics (both affective and other) with which the affective characteristic should not be related, and groups that should and should not differ on the affective characteristic. This conceptual framework is used to generate hypotheses. Construct validity, then, is determined by the number of hypotheses supported by the data from the assessment instrument.

Suppose, for example, we are interested in designing a scale that assesses stress in middle-school students. Based on our conceptual framework that prominently includes stress, we formulate the following hypotheses:

- Children for whom academic success is important but who fail to achieve success should have higher levels of stress than those who believe that academic success is not important or those who achieve academic success on a regular basis.

- Children with observable indicators of stress (e.g., nervous ticks, panic attacks) should have higher scores on the instrument than those with no observable indicators of stress.
- Children with higher scores on a measure of anxiety should have higher stress levels, and vice versa (Anderson, 1992).

We use the data gathered from the stress scale to test these hypotheses. In general, the more hypotheses confirmed by the data, the greater the construct validity of the scale.

When a number of scales are included on a single instrument (e.g., attitude toward mathematics, mathematics anxiety, interest in mathematics as a career), it is important from a construct validity perspective that the scales are clearly differentiated. If the affect–target combinations truly are conceptually distinct, the responses to the set of items making up each scale should have a greater coherence than the responses to items making up the different scales. The most common method of assessing the relative coherence and differentiability of items on a multiscale instrument is factor analysis (see chap. 6, this volume).

If you are selecting a self-report instrument, you should look for evidence of as many aspects of validity as available. The needed evidence may be found in a technical report prepared in conjunction with a research study, a technical manual that should accompany a published instrument, or in the appendix to a thesis or dissertation. If, on the other hand, you are developing a new self-report instrument, you should be prepared to provide as much evidence as you can about the validity of the instrument. Examples of information that can be useful in establishing or estimating the validity of a self-report instrument are given in Table 4.1.

In looking back over these aspects of validity, the reader should be aware that two sets of evidence are important. One is the expectations we have for a questionnaire and the reasons for the expectations (judgmental validity). The other is the degree to which the responses conform to these expectations (empirical validity). Without both sets, the validity puzzle cannot be solved.

Finally, the reader concerned with selecting a self-report instrument is warned that the designer or publisher of the instrument is not likely to present evidence relevant to all of the aspects of validity discussed here. Rather, and hopefully, evidence relevant to at least some of these concerns will be presented by the author in support of the questionnaire. As usual, a single piece of information is better than none. Again, as usual, if none of the concerns has been addressed adequately, the validity of the instrument should be treated as suspect. In this latter situation, the potential user of the questionnaire could either use it tentatively, making his or her own estimates of validity, or discard it, at least temporarily.

Whether you are selecting or designing a questionnaire, the same qualities are desirable. The more validity information you can find or provide the more useful the instrument is likely to be.

TABLE 4.1

Evidence Pertaining to Various Types of Validity

For judgmental validity, you should look for or provide:

1. Clear definitions of the affective characteristics and the affective targets;

2. Clear descriptions of the overall process of designing the questionnaire and the steps used in writing the items;

3. An indication of the appropriateness of the judges (including students) who were used to examine the items in relation to the underlying affective characteristics; and,

4. A description of the process of selecting, revising, and discarding items for the final form of the questionnaire. (Some information used in this process is included in the following set of validity evidence.)

For empirical validity, you should look for or provide:

1. A clear labelling and description of the scale or scales included in the questionnaire, plus a rationale for each scale. (Some statistical evidence would be appropriate here, see chap. 6, this volume).

2. Evidence of empirical relations of the scales with other instruments, particularly other affective scales. Two different sets of "other instruments" should be selected. The first consists of instruments with which the scale or scales should be related (convergent validity). The second consists of instruments with which the scale or scales should not be related (divergent validity). The rationale for the expected relations should be specified.

3. If the instrument includes more than one scale, relationships between and among the scales should be examined. Factor analytic statistical techniques are generally used for this purpose. Some discussion of the meaning of relations found would be useful.

4. Evidence of the ability of the scales to differentiate between or among groups of people who are known or suspected to differ or are suspected of differing on the affective characteristics (known groups validity) For example, students enrolled in an elective, but not-for-credit mathematics course score might be expected to score higher on a mathematics interest scale than students currently enrolled in no mathematics courses. Do they? Reasons for suspecting that differences should exist would also be helpful.

Reliability

Reliability is the consistency of the information obtained from an instrument. Some writers equate reliability with dependability, which conjures up a common-sense meaning of the term. A reliable person is dependable, that is, someone who can be counted on (or relied on) in a variety of situations and at various times. Similarly, a reliable instrument is one that can be counted on to provide similar information in a variety of situations and at various times. In assessment terms, dependability and consistency are synonyms. Thus, a reliable instrument yields consistent information about one or more affective characteristics.

Like objectivity and validity, reliability is not a dichotomy; rather, it lies on a numerical continuum that ranges from zero to one. Reliability is strongly related to some of the empirical aspects of validity discussed above, particularly predictive and construct validity. In fact, the reliability of an instrument places an upper limit on empirical estimates of validity.

We cannot look at an instrument or a scale on that instrument and estimate its reliability. Reliability requires that the responses to the questionnaire items be examined. Technically, then, it is not the instrument that possesses reliability; rather, it is the data obtained through administering the instrument that possesses a certain degree of reliability. Because this is the case, if you select an instrument that has already been designed and used previously, you must be concerned with how closely the students in your population match those to whom the instrument was administered in previous research.

Similarly, if you are designing an instrument, the information needed to estimate reliability should be collected from students who are as much like the students for whom the instrument is designed as possible. The importance of pilot testing questionnaires is discussed in chapter 5 of this volume.

There are three common forms of reliability: *internal consistency, stability*, and *equivalence*. Each are touched on briefly here and then expanded on in chapter 6 of this volume.

Internal Consistency.   Internal consistency is probably the most commonly used form of reliability. It refers to the extent to which responses to items on the *same scale* are consistent. Notice the emphasis on "same scale." If multiple scales are included on a single instrument, you would have multiple estimates of internal consistency reliability, one for each scale. (Because of this distinction we shall use the term "scale" rather than "instrument" in the remainder of the discussion of reliability.)

Several coefficients are available for estimating internal consistency. The most frequently used in conjunction with affective assessment instruments is Cronbach's (1951) alpha coefficient. Other estimates include split-half correlation coefficients and two Kuder-Richardson (KR) coefficients (See Cronbach, 1951).[4] It is not possible to specify a generally required level of reliability, this depending on circumstances, although some guidelines are offered in chapter 5 of this volume (see also Robinson, Shaver, & Wrightsman, 1991). Suffice it to say that, all things being equal, higher numerical estimates of reliability are preferable to lower estimates. Furthermore, internal consistency estimates of reliability are the minimum acceptable evidence of reliability for affective scales.

Stability. The second form of reliability, stability, is perhaps the easiest to comprehend. Stability implies consistency over time. Hence, stability as a form of reliability refers to the extent to which the scores on a scale remain consistent over some time period. In order to estimate stability, the scale is administered at different times and the comparability of the scale scores on the two occasions are examined, typically using correlation coefficients. The higher the correlation coefficient, the higher the reliability (stability) of the scale.

For each affective scale there would be an optimal length of time between administrations that provides the best estimate of stability. One consideration is that the second administration is sufficiently distant in terms of time that the students will not remember the responses they gave during the first administration. A second consideration pertains to the affective characteristic being assessed. From a theoretical perspective, or from the results of prior studies of the characteristic, how stable should the characteristic being over how long a time period? Attitude toward school, for example, should be stable for a month, but is probably not stable from the beginning to the end of a school year. A final consideration is an awareness of significant events between the two administrations that could likely effect the affective characteristic being assessed. If a significant event happened in the interim, the results of the assessment would say at least as much about the effect of the intervention as it would about the stability of the scale. Based on our examination of stability estimates for several scales, from 3 to 6 weeks between administrations would seem reasonable.

Equivalence. Equivalence refers to the extent to which responses made to two scales, intended to assess the same affective characteristic, are similar. In one sense, then, equivalence is concerned with the extent to which the information gathered about the affective characteristic is "instrument free."

---

[4]For a summary of reliability concepts and formulas, see Thorndike & Thorndike (1994). Recently another index of reliability, known as the coefficient of determination, has become more prominent in use with attitude scales. This measure is particularly appropriate for ordinal data, as opposed to interval data. We recommend Holmes-Smith and Rowe (1994) to the interested

The simplest and most common method of estimating equivalence is to compute a correlation coefficient between the scores obtained on the two scales. The problem is to find another measure that assesses the same thing.

To the degree that this is a useful quality of affective information and an alternative instrument is available, equivalence of scales is a convenient form of reliability to estimate. For the reader who is a potential scale developer, a relevant question is, if a scale measuring the affect of interest already exists, why do you want to develop another?[5]

Summary of Reliability Estimates.   Whether an instrument is designed or selected, some estimate of reliability is essential. Which estimation procedure is used (internal consistency, stability, or stability) or whether a combination of procedures should be used depends on the type of reliability desired by the designer or the user of the scale. The very nature of an affective scale, however, would suggest that some index of internal consistency is necessary in all cases. When a number of scales are present, reliability should be calculated for each scale independently. Stability estimates are useful if you are concerned that the affect being assessed may not be, in fact, a characteristic; rather, it may turn out to be no more than a passing phase without conceptual substance. (See Table 4.2 for a summary of issues that should help the reader examine the reliability of affective scales.)

TABLE 4.2

A Summary of Issues Pertaining to the Examination of Affective Scale Reliability

1. Reliability estimates are highly dependent on the sample of students who are assessed. The original sample (whether it be that of the original designer of the scale or your own pilot test group) should be comparable with the intended sample if the estimates obtained are to be taken as a useful guide for your purposes.

2. The internal consistency of each scale must be reported and should be of a satisfactory level (see chap. 5, this volume). Multiple internal consistency estimates are needed when instruments include multiple affective scales.

3. Because they are assessing affective characteristics, affective scales require a degree of stability. At the same time, we need to be aware that scores on affective scales are susceptible to changes in the environment and over time.

4. Whether selecting or developing a scale, whether equivalence is important or relevant should be determined based on your particular purposes.

---

[5]A complete answer to this question is not attempted here. Although an existing scale may not be precisely what was wanted for the current research, it may be similar enough to be useful for checking the reliability of a new scale in this way.

Interpretability

Interpretability refers to the extent to which an instrument provides information that can be understood by interested parties. That is to say, the information must be meaningful to the people for whom it was being gathered. In actuality there is a parallel between interpretability and communication value. The major difference between these two qualities lies in the referent or audience. Whereas communication value is concerned with the match between the instrument and respondent, interpretability deals with the match between the results of the instrument and the audience (i.e., the person or persons for whom the assessment is being conducted). We say more about this aspect of quality in chapter 7.

A SUMMARY OF SCALE QUALITY

Before moving to a discussion of Likert scales, we believe it is useful to summarize the questions we would ask ourselves as we examine existing affective instruments or begin designing a new affective instrument. This summary is presented in Figure 4.3. Although few self-report instruments meet all of these requirements, the more that are met, the greater the confidence we have in the instrument.

Before a scale can be used to gather information about individuals, groups, or both, it must possess satisfactory levels of communication value, objectivity and validity, with reliability and interpretability coming later from the responses. What constitutes satisfactory levels? Let us suggest a few guiding principles.

Communication value is a matter of judgment, based initially on a consideration of both the literacy and maturity of the students to whom the instrument will be administered. Additionally, the reading difficulty (i.e., readability) of the instrument is considered. The instructions provided at the beginning of the questionnaire are crucial for communicating what is required and how responses should be made by the students. The judgment made by the designer of the scale on these matters should be supplemented by judgments made by other experts and by the results of pilot tests conducted with students like those ultimately being assessed. Observations of and discussions with these students are also helpful.

The objectivity of all structured questionnaires should be high. The scoring system does not normally leave room for judgment and, hence, possible misinterpretation of responses. But, like everything else, there is room for error. Forgetting to recode negative items in mixed scales was identified as a common source of error. Carelessness in coding any response, such as coding a 4 when 3 was intended, may also be a problem if coders are inex-

Communication value
1. Do the instructions clearly specify the nature of the task? That is, will the respondent know what to do and how to do it after reading the instructions?
2. Do the instructions clearly specify the general purpose of the questionnaire?
3. Do the instructions clearly indicate that there are no right and wrong answers?
4. Do the instructions contain a definition of the affective target? That is, do the instructions try to ensure that all respondents will be reacting to the same meaning of the target?
5. What is the likely reading level of the intended respondents for whom the questionnaire was designed? How does this compare with the readability level of the instructions and of the items? Will the respondents be able to read it?

Objectivity
1. Are the scoring or coding rules clearly specified? How objective are they?
2. Are there indications of qualifications of scorers or coders?
3. Is there a recognition of potential sources of error in coding?

Validity
1. Is the procedure used for constructing the items clearly stated? Do the steps appear to be logically related to one another and to the definition on which each scale is based? What subsequent steps were taken to revise and refine items and scales?
2. Is there more than one scale in the questionnaire? If so, is the item composition of each scale clearly set out? To what extent is evidence, either statistical or otherwise, offered for the existence of the hypothesized scales?
3. With what other measures are scores on the affective scale related? Is a rationale given for suspecting that the relationships exist?
4. Do the scores on the affective scale differentiate among groups of people who are known or suspected to be different in terms of the affective characteristic? Are reasons given for suspecting that the differences will exist?

Reliability
1. Are estimates of scale reliability available? Is there information about he sample used to estimate scale reliability? Is the sample comparable to the group to whom you intend to administer the scale?
2. To what extent does the scale have a satisfactory degree of internal consistency?
3. To what extent does the scale have a satisfactory degree of stability? How long was the time period between administrations?

FIG. 4.3. A listing of questions to be asked when searching for or developing a good affective scale.

perienced or disinterested in the task. One possible solution to using unsatisfactory coders is to code the data yourself (assuming that you are interested in your own research and will soon become experienced). If, however, your data set is too large for you to do it all, and your budget allows it, you should employ the best coders you can find, and check their error rates progressively. Training of coders is also essential, with accuracy rates checked on a fairly regular basis. Determination of the actual error rate is normally done by sampling a small number of coded questionnaires and recoding them yourself. Conventional wisdom is that, in general, if there is a coding error in fewer than 10% of the sample of cases, the coding accuracy of the scale is satisfactory.

With respect to validity, the issues are not quite so clear. The larger the correlation coefficients between the scale scores and measures of other characteristics thought to be related to the affective characteristics assessed by the scale, the more satisfactory the validity. Similarly, evidence that the scale scores are not correlated with measures of others characteristics with which they should not be corrected also strengthens validity. Finally, the larger the differences between groups that should differ on the characteristic, the more satisfactory the validity. In general, however, we must be satisfied with two or three pieces of information on these aspects of validity, as seen in the next chapter. Thus the best advice that can be offered is as follows: Do what you can. If two or three pieces of information relevant to the validity of the scale are offered and if these pieces support the validity of the scale, we believe there is satisfactory evidence of validity.

Turning to reliability, the task becomes somewhat easier. Internal consistency estimates higher than 0.80 are considered very satisfactory for affective measures. Scales with internal consistency estimates of less than 0.70 should not be used, certainly not when gathering information about individual students. This leaves a gray area between 0.70 and 0.80. In this area, scales should be used with caution. Estimates of stability and equivalence can be expected to be somewhat lower, with coefficients as low as 0.60 being seen as satisfactory in some situations. Under no circumstances should scales with reliability estimates lower than 0.60 be used.

LIKERT SCALING AND LIKERT SCALES

Developed by Renis Likert (1932), Likert scaling is by far the most frequently used strategy for designing affective self-report instruments. The scales derived from this strategy may take on a number of forms. The traditional form is to write a series of statements about a particular affect–target combination (e.g., the value of education) and then ask the students to indicate the extent of their agreement or disagreement with the position taken or point of view expressed in each statement. Ideally, all of the statements are short and to the point. We first describe the traditional form and then consider, briefly, some modifications.

Consider, for example, the following set of four statements:

1. I like working with numbers.
2. Mathematics problems are fascinating.
3. I detest mathematics.
4. If I had the choice, I would take additional mathematics courses.

All four statements are about some aspect of mathematics. Furthermore, all are related to our earlier definition of attitude (see chap. 2, this volume).

The response categories typically used with items like these are: *Strongly Agree, Agree, Undecided, Disagree* and *Strongly Disagree*.[6] Thus, Likert scaling allows individuals to respond to each statement in terms of both direction (positive and negative) and intensity (strength of agreement or disagreement).[7] The five categories would normally be given numerical codes from 5 to 1 so that a high score indicated a more positive affect.

In the previous example, three of the items (1, 2, and 4) are expressions of positive affect. For these items, *Strongly Agree* would be assigned 5 points, *Agree*, 4 points, and so on. In contrast, item 3 is an expression of negative affect. Before being combined into a scale, then, the numerical codes for this item must be reversed (i.e., *Strongly Disagree* would be assigned 5 points, *Disagree*, 4 points, etc.). After this reversal, the points assigned to all four items for a particular student can be summed to arrive at a total score. A higher total score would represent a more positive attitude toward mathematics. Conversely, a lower total score would represented a more negative attitude toward mathematics.

Despite the relative simplicity of Likert scales, there are several matters that need to be addressed. Chief among them are the scale length, the number and strength of response categories, and proper modifications of Likert scales. Each is discussed in some detail in the sections that follow.

---

[6]Although this five-category set of responses is the most common, it is not necessarily the best choice. More is said about that subsequently in this chapter.

[7]There is a problem with the measure of intensity because two persons may get different scores simply because one person tends to respond in a more extreme (i.e., overly intense) manner to everything. Thus, for a few individuals, the response alternatives offered might measure extremism as much as differences in strength of affect. This is only a problem when interpretations are made in terms of absolute comparisons; interpretations made on the basis of relative comparisons are minimally affected (see chap. 7, this volume).

Scale Length

Likert scales vary considerably in their length, ranging from as few as four items, like the last example, to as many as 20 or more items measuring the same affect–target combination. A sufficient number of items is needed to provide reliable information (more about this later) but not so many as to bore or otherwise deter students from giving thoughtful and accurate responses. The appropriate number of items is best guided by the level of generality or specificity of the affective characteristic being assessed and the overall length of the questionnaire. The latter issue is related in part to the number of characteristics assessed on a single questionnaire (i.e., the number of scales included on it).

The more general the affective characteristic being assessed, the more items that are needed to provide reasonable information about its different aspects. The four items about mathematics in the previous example would be unlikely to provide a good (i.e., reliable) measure of attitude toward mathematics. Mathematics is much broader concept than can be covered by any four items, including as it does arithmetic, algebra, geometry, measurement, numbers, word problems, and the like. Furthermore, student views about mathematics are commonly broken into a number of separate scales assessing different, but related, affective characteristics: attitude, interest, value, anxiety, and so on. Each of these possible affect–target combinations (e.g., attitude–arithmetic, interest–numbers, value–geometry, anxiety–word problems) are themselves scales that might well consist of four or five items for each scale. Thus, a questionnaire containing even six scales easily balloons to a length of 24 to 30 items.

The overall length of a questionnaire is a potential problem because of the time needed to complete it. What is an appropriate length in terms of time is related to the age, sophistication, and interest in the particular topic of the students. In general, young children should not be expected to spend more than 20 minutes completing a questionnaire; other students should spend perhaps no more than twice that time. Even mature adults may not be prepared to sustain their concentration over more time than young children if they are relatively unused to reading and writing, or if they are not particularly interested in the subject matter of the questionnaire. If, however, you have a topic that is of keen interest to a particular group of respondents, you might be able to persuade them to spend up to an hour. Obviously, these are only general guidelines based on experience, but you need to be aware that your students may not be able to concentrate for as long as you would wish or not always be as interested in your topic as you are.

Number and Strength of Response Categories

Four response categories would be a suitable number for relatively young students, who may be confused by too many choices; however, this number may well be ample for others as well. The four categories would normally range in strength from *Strongly Agree*, to *Agree, to Disagree*, and finally to *Strongly Disagree*. However, when students are able to make finer distinctions between and among response categories, it may be better (i.e., it may increase scale reliability) to have more categories, perhaps six (Bourke & Frampton, 1992; Masters, 1974). The six categories could be *Strongly Agree, Agree, Tend to Agree, Tend to Disagree, Disagree*, and *Strongly Disagree*, or a similar combination of categories giving three levels each of agreement and disagreement. Other commonly used categories for different scales are *Definitely Agree, Mostly Agree, Slightly Agree*, and their opposites. On the other hand, having fewer than four categories would likely reduce scale reliability.

Should there be an even or odd number of response categories? There is clear and increasing evidence that having an even number of categories produces a more reliable scale than having an odd number (Andrich & Masters, 1988; Bourke & Frampton, 1992). That is, having four or six response categories is better than having three or five. The reason for this phenomenon is probably that the middle (odd) category, being normally designated as *Uncertain, Not Sure*, or *Do Not Know*, is selected not only by those who genuinely are uncertain, but also by those who may have an definite opinion but do not want to express it. Also attracted by the middle or neutral category are those who do have a slight opinion one way or the other (but not a definite one) and who would give that opinion if the neutral option were not there. In artificially reducing the need to make clear decisions, the introduction of a neutral category lowers scale reliability through reducing variability.

Some readers will express concern about our argument. Their very reasonable point is probably something like this: What about the person who genuinely is uncertain about a particular statement? What should this person do when confronted with a forced choice he or she cannot honestly make? We accept that this might be the case, although we would suggest it applies very infrequently. If the questionnaire is written for and given to an appropriate group, students would normally have an opinion about each item, even if their opinion is not a strong one.

In light of this argument, however, it is advisable to make provision for the person who is genuinely uncertain. There are at least two ways this can be done. First, you can provide a *cannot decide* or *no opinion* box at the side of the questionnaire, removed from the main response categories. Second, you can invite people to omit an item when they definitely cannot decide. The effect of both of these strategies is to reduce the incidence of uncertain or omitted responses. Both strategies make it clear that those taking the option are making a positive choice not to complete the item in the usual way but to go outside the normal range of the response categories. (As a consequence of using these strategies, it is necessary to consider what can be done with what, effectively, is now missing data when scales are being developed. This issue is taken up in chap. 6, this volume)

In addition to the number of response categories, there is the matter of the strength of the categories.[8] To illustrate, take the simple case of four categories. The two positive categories could be selected from among a fairly wide range of alternatives: *Strongly Agree, Agree, Tend to Agree, Slightly Agree, Mostly Agree, or Agree Somewhat*. (Obviously, the disagree categories would mirror the positive ones.) The choice of the most appropriate categories should depend on the likely intensity of the affect students direct toward the target. If intensity is strong, it is both feasible and advisable to provide a *Strongly Agree* category; if not, such a category would generally not be used. If used, the items would effectively have two fewer categories than they appear to have on paper. With this reduction in categories would come a concomitant reduction in scale reliability. Consequently, we suggest that the relatively weaker categories (e.g., *Tend to Agree, Agree Somewhat*) be used when strong views are not commonly held by the students. The use of these weaker categories also has the advantage of attracting some students who otherwise would prefer to answer that they were undecided. (To some extent, strength of opinion about a topic can be determined by preliminary interviews or discussions with students, but trying out this aspect of a new questionnaire with a proper student sample is essential.)

When is a Likert Scale a Likert Scale?

Thus far we have focused our discussion on the traditional form of Likert scales. Various modifications of this traditional form have been made and are available. Fortunately, much of what has been said already applies equally to these alternate forms of Likert scales.

Using a Common Stem for Items. Reading time can be reduced and consistency of understanding increased by using a common stem for all items on a scale. For example, a 40-item questionnaire concerning students' perspectives on the quality of school life contains seven scales. Each

---

[8]The strength inherent in the response categories is related to the intensity of the affective characteristic. A decision as to which response categories to use, therefore, should take into consideration the range of intensity in the student population. If few if any students are believed to be passionate about the affect–target combination being assessed, then the use of "strongly agree" and "strongly disagree" would be ill advised.

item is structured so that the incomplete statement or stem, My school is a place where ... , is followed by the a clause that completes the statement. (The instructions for this instrument were used as an illustration earlier in this chapter.) Students are instructed to think of the stem as they read and respond to each of the clauses. To illustrate, a few items from different scales on this questionnaire follow:

	Agree	Mostly Agree	Mostly Disagree	Disagree
My school is a place where ...				
I really like to go each day.	[ ]	[ ]	[ ]	[ ]
Other students are very friendly.	[ ]	[ ]	[ ]	[ ]
My teacher is fair to me.	[ ]	[ ]	[ ]	[ ]

Obviously when using this modified form, you must be careful that every clause flows grammatically from the stem. You also need to emphasize in the instructions that the stem should be placed (i.e., read) before every clause.

Other Response Categories. Different response categories have been used with modified Likert scales. Unlike the traditional bipolar response options, these response categories commonly tap into unipolar dimensions such as *importance* or *frequency*. For example, students may be asked to indicate how important a particular affect–target combination is. The response categories may be *Extremely Important, Very Important, Important, Fairly Important, Of Minor Importance,* and *Not at all Important.* Similarly, students may be asked to indicate how frequently they participate in some event or activity (assuming the target is an event or activity). In this case, the response categories may be *Always or Almost Always, Often, Sometimes, Rarely,* and *Almost Never or Never.* An example of a questionnaire concerning high-school students' stress that uses both the frequency with which stress is experienced and the intensity of the stress when experienced as response categories for the same set of items is shown in Fig 4.4.[9]

Use of Paired Statements. A variant of the single statement format is to include two opposing statements for each item and ask the student to choose between them. In this format, the student will always be agreeing with one of the statements. A slight change from an earlier example could result in the following item:

[9]We are grateful to a doctoral candidate, Robert McAlpine, for permission to use the instructions for these, as yet unpublished, scales. The instructions and scales have been extensively tried out with secondary students.

I love mathematics....
(Strongly Agree, Agree / Agree, Strongly Agree)
... I hate mathematics.

This format minimizes the problem of acquiescence (see chap. 3, this volume) because students are placed in the position of always agreeing with one of the statements. Despite this advantage, there are some problems with this format. The three most frequently mentioned are increased amount of reading, increased time needed to respond to each item, and increased difficulty of writing the items. The reading component of each item, being roughly doubled, may constitute a problem for young and less-literate students. This additional reading burden means that students can respond to fewer items in a given time period that has an effect on the maximum possible length of the instrument. Finally, although *love* and *hate* in the previous example are clear opposites, it is sometimes difficult to find a pair of statements that would be understood by all students as being precisely opposite.

Use of Multiple Scales on a Single Self-Report Instrument. As mentioned earlier, it has become quite common for affective questionnaires to include

SENIOR SECONDARY STUDENT STRESS QUESTIONNAIRE

The following 60 statements have been collected from senior secondary students as answers to the question: "*What effects does stress have on you?*". Please read each statement carefully.

If you have experienced any of these effects in the last month or so, please indicate (1) how often it has happened (*Frequency*), and (2) how strong or intense the experience has been (*Intensity*) by circling the appropriate numbers, as shown below.

Frequency:		*Intensity:*	
	0 - Never happens to me		0 - Never happens
	1 - Less than once a week		1 - Low intensity
	2 - Once or twice a week		2 - Medium intensity
	3 - Most days		3 - High intensity
	4 - At least every day		4 - Almost unbearable intensity

Practice statement

	Frequency	Intensity
Butterflies in the stomach	0 1 2 3 4	0 1 2 3 4

FIG. 4.4   Sample instructions—"Senior Secondary School Stress Questionnaire."

several scales. One reason for this practice is a greater awareness that rarely does a single affective characteristics or a single target provide the necessary information about a person's affect. Because education is important in the lives of most people, affective instruments pertaining to education are particularly susceptible to finely grained distinctions being made by those responding to a given questionnaire. Take the attitudes to mathematics scales referred to earlier. It is almost certain that most students will not have a single, general attitude toward all of mathematics.

Furthermore, we may be interested in more than their attitudes. We may wish to know how interested they are in mathematics, how important they see mathematics as being, and how good of a mathematics student they see themselves as being. Thus, multiple targets and multiple affective characteristics tend to wind up on the same instrument. Hence, we have multiple scales. These multiple scales provide a richer understanding of students' math affect.

If a decision is made to have multiple scales on a questionnaire, it is desirable to mix the items throughout the questionnaire. This has the double benefit of ensuring that respondents are equally fresh when responding to items on the different scales and reducing the possibility that respondents will assume a response set, thereby providing less thoughtful and artificially similar responses for any particular set of items belonging to the same scale.

SUMMARY OF MAJOR POINTS

1. There are five qualities required of a good affective scale: communication value, objectivity, validity, reliability, and interpretability.
2. *Communication value* is concerned with the extent to which the questionnaire can be understood by the respondent. It is related to the reading ability of the respondent, and to the readability of the instructions and the items themselves.
3. *Objectivity* is concerned with the extent to which the scoring or coding of the responses is free from scorer or coder bias or error. For structured questionnaires, bias is not normally a problem, but error may be an issue, particularly when there is a mix of positively and negatively worded items in the scale.
4. *Validity* refers to the extent to which an instrument actually measures what it was intended to measure. Validity is not a dichotomous variable but is continuous, with scales being more or less valid.

5. There are a number of approaches to establishing validity, some based on human judgment and others on empirical measures. Both are important when examining the validity of scales.

6. *Reliability* refers to the consistency of the information obtained from the instrument. Three types of reliability estimates are traditionally used: internal consistency (inter-item measures, most frequently Cronbach's alpha), stability (based on consistency over time), and equivalence (based on relations between at least two measures of the same affective characteristics or affect–target combination).

7. Technically, it is the set of responses to the scale items, not the scale itself, that possesses a degree of reliability. Like validity, reliability estimates lie on a continuum that ranges from zero to one.

8. *Interpretability* refers to the extent to which the instrument provides information that can be understood by the persons for whom the affective characteristic was assessed. This quality is more a function of the use and reporting of the results obtained from the instrument than its development and, therefore, is discussed in chap. 7, this volume.

9. The checklist displayed in Fig. 4.1 contains the questions that should be asked when evaluating the technical qualities of affective instruments.

10. Before an affective instrument can be used to gather information about individuals, groups, or both, it should possess satisfactory technical quality. If it does not, the instrument should not be used.

11. Likert scaling is by far the most frequently used method of assessing affective characteristics. Although it can take many forms, in its simplest form a Likert scale consists of a series of statements to which respondents are asked to agree or disagree using a set of response categories provided.

12. Likert scales vary considerably in length, most commonly having from 4 to 20 or more items. The length of a scale is largely determined by the specificity or generality of the affect–target combination being assessed. More general affect–target combination normally require more items. However, the trend is to shorter, more specific scales.

13. The most common number of response categories used with Likert scaling is five, the middle category being neutral. However, an even number of categories, without a neutral category, tends to provide better scale reliability. Either four or six categories is recommended, the choice depending on the maturity and sophistication of the students.

14. The strength of response categories used with a Likert scale may vary, and should reflect the anticipated intensity of affect–target combination being assessed.

15. A minor, but useful, variation of the Likert-scaling approach is to use a common stem for all items in a questionnaire. This practice reduces reading time and provides a consistency in context for respondents.

16. An alternative to using bipolar response categories with Likert scales is to use unipolar categories of importance or frequency when these are more appropriate.

17. Another variant of Likert scaling is to use paired, opposing statements for each item. This practice effectively reduces the problem of acquiescence but increases the time required to respond to a set of items.

18. It is common practice to include multiple scales, normally assessing different affect–target combinations, on the same questionnaire. In these cases, items from the different scales should be interspersed throughout the questionnaire.

19. There are several other scaling methods, including the Thurstone (Thurstone & Chave, 1929), Guttman (1944), and Semantic Differential (Osgood, Suci, & Tannenbaum, 1957). These are described in some detail in Appendix A. Thurstone and Guttman scales tend to be more time consuming and difficult to develop.

20. All affective self-report instruments should be subjected to a critical examination in terms of the qualities required of good scales identified in this chapter before they are used.

5

Selecting and Designing Affective Instruments: How Do I Avoid Selecting a "Lemon" or Designing a "Dud?"

In the previous chapter we discussed affective instruments in general. This chapter includes a three-phase procedure for moving from conceptualization, through selection or design, to the administration of a specific affective instrument. Each phase contains a series of steps. These steps are best seen as guidelines, rather than as prescriptions to be followed rigidly and unthinkingly.

PHASE I: DEFINITIONAL ISSUES

The first phase consists of three steps: determining and describing the purpose for the assessment, identifying and describing the population of students you intend to assess, and identifying and defining the relevant affective characteristics and their targets.

Step 1: Determining and Describing the Purpose for the Assessment

There are many reasons to assess students' affective characteristics. In general, these purposes can be placed into four categories: enhancing student learning, improving the quality of educational programs, evaluating the quality of educational programs, and conforming to administrative or legislative mandates (e.g., school accountability and teacher evaluation). The major difference between the first two purposes is that the first, enhancing student learning, focuses on individual students, whereas the second, improving the quality of educational programs, focuses on groups of students (e.g., classes, schools). The major difference between the second and third purposes is that the second is concerned with what has been termed formative evaluation, whereas the third, evaluating programs, is concerned with summative evaluation (Bloom et al., 1971). Briefly, formative evaluation is intended to provide information that can be used for improvement purposes. In contrast, summative evaluation is used to make a more or less terminal judgment concerning overall effectiveness.

When the purpose is enhancing student learning, data from affective instruments can be used to identify affective characteristics that impede or otherwise interfere with learning and achievement. In the first edition of this book, this was referred to as the "diagnostic value of affective assessment." In diagnosis, one is looking for the causes of the problem. The core question is "Why is this student not learning?" Is it because he or she, for example: Is not interested?; Does not believe he or she can learn?; Does not see what is being learned as being of particular value? In combination, the second and third questions form the basis for the *expectancy x value* theory of motivation (Feather, 1982). (More is said about this theory in chap. 8, this volume.)

If these are the three most plausible reasons, then three affective characteristics are involved: interest, self-efficacy, and value. Several targets seem reasonable: school, subject matter, and specific topics or tasks within the subject matter. There are nine possible affect–target combinations; hence, nine scales. If each scale consists of five items, the complete instrument would contain 45 items.

When the purpose is improving the quality of educational programs, affective assessment generally focuses on students' feelings or beliefs about the curriculum they are being taught and the instruction they are receiving. Such affective instruments may address subject-specific targets: science (e.g., Germann, 1988), mathematics (e.g., Kloosterman & Stage, 1992), reading (e.g., McKenna & Kear, 1990), English (e.g., Morrison et al., 1993), and second language learning (e.g., Gardner & MacIntyre, 1993). In addition, they may include a variety of affective characteristics: mathematics anxiety (e.g., Hadfield, Martin, & Wooden, 1992), attitude toward science (e.g., Simpson & Troost, 1982), mathematics interest (e.g., Schiefele & Csikszentmihayli, 1995), and the value of science (e.g., Bateson, 1990). Instruments that focus on students' perceptions of their classrooms are also useful in this regard (e.g., Bolte, 1994; Fraser, Anderson, & Walberg, 1982; Fraser, Giddings, & McRobbie, 1995). (More is said about creating effective classroom-learning environments in chap. 8, this volume.)

When the purpose is program evaluation, instruments, whether they are selected or designed, must be aligned with the program goals. One of the goals of a program providing students with laptop computers, for example, was to improve students' attitudes toward studying (Morrison et al., 1993). Consequently, the affective instrument developed as part of the evaluation was a measure of students' attitudes toward studying.

Similarly, the goals of the Just Community Program (Higgins-D'Alessandro & Sadh, 1998) included improved relationships between students and teachers and among students themselves (i.e., a sense of community), decreases in unethical behavior (e.g., "There is very little stealing here"), and increases in perceived educational opportunity (e.g., "I can get a good education here"). The School Culture Scale (SCS) was designed, in part, to reflect these goals. Specifically, the SCS contains four scales: normative expectations, student–teacher–school relationships, student relationships, and educational opportunities. (More is said in chap. 8, this volume, about programs intent on building character.)

Even when the primary goals of a program are cognitive or psychomotor rather than affective, concerns are often voiced for what may be termed unintended outcomes of the program. When these unintended outcomes fall into the affective realm, we refer to them as affective consequences. Bateson (1990), for example, was interested in determining whether science achievement was greater in semester courses or all-year courses. Although his primary outcome was science achievement, he also included a measure of attitude toward science. He wanted to see whether or not differences in course length affected attitude toward science regardless of its effect on science achievement. In this case, attitude toward science is an affective consequence. (More is said about the importance of considering affective consequences in chap. 8, this volume.)

When the purposes are school accountability or teacher evaluation, instruments focusing on students' perceptions of their schools are useful. Examples include the Quality of School Life questionnaire (Ainley & Bourke, 1992), the NASSP School Climate Survey (Halderson et al., 1989), and the School Culture Scale (Higgins-D'Allesandro & Sadh, 1998). Most of these instruments contain multiple scales (see chap. 4, this volume). The NASSP School Climate Survey, for example, contains 10 scales: teacher–student relationships, security and maintenance, administration, student academic orientation, student behavioral values, guidance, student–peer relationships, parent and community–school relationships, instructional management, and student activities. The entire set of scales would be appropriate for school accountability purposes, whereas selected scales would be more appropriate for teacher evaluation (e.g., teacher–student relationships, student academic orientation, instructional management). At present, teacher evaluation instruments are far more common in higher education than in elementary and secondary education (e.g., Marsh, 1994).

We believe that school accountability may in fact be a new, potentially rich area for affective assessment. Accountability legislation has been enacted in many states in the United States; accountability expectations exist in numerous countries throughout the world. In most cases, neither educators nor the public seem to want accountability programs that rely exclusively on standardized academic achievement tests. Good, solid affective assessment instruments have the potential to provide data that can be incorporated into more broadly conceptualized school accountability programs.

Step 2: Identifying and Describing the Population of Students

Who are the students you want to assess? The answer to this question lies at the heart of the second step. Why is this step so important? At least two reasons can be given. First, as pointed out in chapter 4, it is important that both the affective characteristics and their targets be appropriate for the intended student population. In this regard, it is instructive that Bills (1975) stopped trying to assess the self-esteem of 6- and 7-year-old children when he found that children at these ages could not provide him with attributes that could be used to assess their self-esteem. Rather than words such as smart, lovable, and good, these children would mention words such as hair, shoes, tall (or short), and girl (or boy).

Second, it is important that the instructions and items are written in such a way that those being assessed can read them, understand them, and respond to them in an appropriate manner (see chap. 4, this volume). So having knowledge about students' ages, reading levels, and, particularly for older populations, education levels is important in designing or selecting appropriate affective instruments. If there are doubts that students possess the reading level required by an instrument (as is the case of younger students), the instrument can be read to the students (e.g., see McKenna & Kear, 1990). The issue of responding in an appropriate manner is generally dealt with by varying the number of response categories (i.e., fewer for younger students) or using smiley faces or cartoon characters rather than words in the response categories themselves (e.g., see McKenna & Kear, 1990).

Step 3: Identifying and Defining the Relevant Affective Characteristics and Targets

Conceptual definitions of eight specific affective characteristics were given in chapter 2. For affective characteristics not defined in chaper 2, definitions are quite often available in theoretical pieces or research studies pertaining to those characteristics.

Equal attention should be paid to defining the targets. For example, Morrison, Gardner, Reilly, & McNally (1993) included five targets in their study of the impact of portable computers on student attitudes: attitude toward teaching and learning in each of the core disciplines (i.e., mathematics, science, English, and social studies) and attitude toward school life in general. Similarly, Gardner and MacIntyre (1993) included several targets in their study, including interest in foreign languages, desire to learn French, and attitude toward the learning situation (i.e., the situation in which French was learned). Note that Gardner and MacIntyre varied both target and affective characteristic, thus producing several affect–target combinations. Finally, the Elementary Reading Attitude Survey (ERAS; McKenna & Kear, 1990) has two targets: recreational reading and academic reading. All targets need to be defined.

In many cases, targets can be defined by example, using portions of the items that address them. On ERAS, for example, one of the items assessing recreational reading is, "How do you feel when you read a book on a rainy Saturday?" "Reading a book on a rainy Saturday" is an example of recreational reading. A second question asks students, "How do you feel when the teacher asks you questions about what you read?" "Teachers asking questions about what is read" suggests academic reading. In most cases, however, at least a brief written definition of the target is extremely useful. For example, recreational reading may be defined as reading done for pleasure and which is unrelated to assigned school work, whereas academic reading may defined as reading related to one or more school subjects that is assigned by the teacher.

PHASE II: SELECTING OR DESIGNING INSTRUMENTS

Now that the definitional issues have been addressed, a decision must be made. Should I select an existing instrument or design my own? Furthermore, if I select an existing instrument should I use it "as is" or do I need to make modifications in it to suit my purpose?

In general, we suggest that, all things being equal, the selection of an existing instrument is preferable. However, this recommendation implies:

- An instrument appropriate for your purpose, student population, affective characteristics, and targets is available;
- There is sufficient information about the development, structure, and format of the instrument;
- The instrument provides data of sufficient technical quality (e.g., reliability, validity, interpretability); and,
- The instrument can be modified if modifications are needed.

We suggest selection over design because of the time, expertise, and, possibly, expense involved in the development of a new instrument. However, when the conditions listed above are not met, there is no choice but to design an instrument.

In light of our recommendation and the related considerations, we now turn to the steps involved in the selection of an instrument (Phase IIA) and those involved in the design of a new instrument (Phase IIB).

PHASE IIA: SELECTING AN AFFECTIVE ASSESSMENT INSTRUMENT

This phase consists of four steps: locating instruments, reviewing instruments, comparing instruments, and making a choice from among available instruments.

Step 1: Locating Instruments

In preparation for this step you will have dealt with all the definitional concerns in Phase I. That it, you have determined your purpose, identified your student population, and defined your affective characteristics and their targets. How do you find appropriate instruments? We tend to rely on five sources: electronic databases, commercial publishers, professional associations, research institutes or laboratories, and compendiums of instruments.

One of the popular on-line databases is the Educational Resources Information Center (ERIC). ERIC, like all electronic databases, has a search engine and operates using key words.[1] You go to the appropriate address on the World Wide Web to access the ERIC database. The internet address for the ERIC database is http://www.askeric.org/eric/. Once you have access to the database, you type in the words or phrases that focus your search and press the Enter key on the keyboard. The secret to successful

---

[1]Although the phrase *key word* is used, words or short phrases can be entered. Throughout this discussion we use the phrase *key word*.

searches lies in the choice of key words. If your key word is associated with too large a category (e.g., affect), hundreds of entries will be retrieved, most of which will be either unrelated or tangentially related to what you are seeking.

In searching electronic databases, we would suggest the following. First, familiarize yourself with the key words used by the designers of the database. ERIC, for example, has a thesaurus of its key words. To the extent possible, use these key words. Second, enter multiple key words. One key word usually produces a fairly global set of entries. With respect to searching for affective assessment instruments, we suggest one key word pertaining to the affective characteristic (e.g., *attitude*), one key word pertaining to the target (e.g., *mathematics*), and one key word pertaining to either assessment (e.g., *measures, instruments, scales*) or the age or school level of the students (e.g., *elementary, Grade 8*).

A second source of affective assessment instruments is commercial publishing houses. Commercial publishing houses that publish affective assessment instruments include the Consulting Psychologists Press in Palo Alto, California, EdITS in San Diego, California, Psychological Assessment Resources in Odessa, Florida, and Western Psychological Services in Los Angeles, California.

Professional associations, particularly those whose membership includes educational practitioners (e.g., principals, curriculum coordinators, test coordinators, teachers), are a third source of affective assessment instruments. For example, the Comprehensive Assessment of School Environments (CASE) battery of instruments is available from the National Association of Secondary School Principals (NASSP) in Reston, Virginia. The Association of Supervision and Curriculum Development (ASCD), also in Reston, Virginia, publishes product catalogues on a regular basis. These catalogs may include affective assessment instruments or books on the affective domain with references to affective assessment instruments.

Research institutes and laboratories are a fourth source of affective assessment instruments. Examples include the Australian Council for Educational Research (ACER) in Melbourne, Australia, the National Foundation for Educational Research (NFER) in London, England, and the Northwest Regional Educational Laboratory (NWREL) in Portland, Oregon.

Finally, there are a few compendiums of affective assessment instruments available. In the first edition (p. 116), we listed several compendiums. Most of these have not been updated so the instruments included in them are likely to be dated. We know of two compendiums that have been updated. *The Eighth Mental Measurement Yearbook* was published in 1992 (Kramer & Conoley, 1992). In addition, Robinson, Shaver, and

Wrightsman (1991) published an updated version of *Measures of Personality and Social Psychological Attitudes.* A search of university library holdings may yield additional compendiums.

Step 2: Reviewing Instruments

Once instruments have been located, they should be reviewed carefully. In reviewing instruments, we use the form shown in Table 5.1. The left-hand column of Table 5.1 contains the information needed to make a thorough

TABLE 5.1

Summary Form for Examining Existing Affective Instruments

Component	Description
Title/Source	
Definitions	
Number of Scale/Items	
School Level	
Directions	
Sample Items	
Reliability	
Validity	
Comments	

review of existing instruments. We begin by writing the name of the instrument and its source (e.g., journal, book, commercial publishing house). Next, we attend to the definitional matters: affective characteristics, targets, scales, and the school level of the students. Our attention then shifts to the elements of the instrument. We write the directions and examples of the items (including the response categories). We summarize the evidence (if any) provided about the reliability and validity of the instrument. Finally, there is space for any additional comments we want to make. A copy of a completed review form is shown in Table 5.2.

As mentioned earlier, there will likely be gaps in the information provided by many authors. Of 56 attitude instruments reviewed by Germann (1988), for example, the authors and users of 21 of them (almost 38%) did not report any reliability estimates. No validity evidence was provided for 18 of the instruments (almost one third). For an additional nine instruments, the authors and users relied exclusively on a panel of judges with no empirical evidence of validity provided. In contrast, for only seven of the instruments (12.5%) did the developers report validity evidence derived from multiple empirical methods (e.g., factor analysis, known group comparisons).

Step 3: Comparing Instruments

After the instruments have been located and reviewed, the instruments can be compared with one another and with your needs and purpose. The tables prepared in Step 2 provide the basis for the comparison. When multiple instruments have been located, an overall comparison of the instruments can be made quite easily by focusing on the completeness of the available information included in the tables. In general, the more complete the information, the higher the quality of the instrument. At the very least, unacceptable instruments can be eliminated.

Armed with the best instrument, a few acceptable instruments, or perhaps the only instrument, individual rows of the table can then be examined. For example, the results of completing Phase I (discussed earlier) can be compared with the relevant information contained in rows 2 through 4 of the table (definitions of affective characteristics and their targets, the scales, and the school level). Are the definitions the same or sufficiently similar? Do the scales seem reasonable? Are the number of items sufficient? Are there too many items in light of the student population? Is the student population the same or sufficiently similar?

Considering the student population, do the directions and sample items seem appropriate in terms of both content and readability (rows 5 and 6)? Is there any evidence that any check on readability was conducted? Are the results of any trials of the instrument with similar student populations presented?

TABLE 5.2

Sample Completed Summary Form

Component	Description
Title/Source	Elementary Reading Attitude Survey (ERAS) McKenna, M. C. & Kear, D. J. (1990). Measuring attitude toward reading: A new tool for teachers. Reading Teacher, 43, 626–639.
Definitions	Attitude toward reading defined as how students feel about reading. Two types of reading, academic and recreational. Academic reading is related to school subjects, generally assigned by teacher. Recreational reading is reading done by students as a matter of choice and on their own time.
Number of Scales/Items	Two scales: academic reading with 15 items and recreational reading with 24 items.
School Level	Elementary.
Directions	(Said by teacher) Begin by telling students that you wish to find out how they feel about reading. Emphasize that this is not a test and that there are no "right" answers. Encourage sincerity.
Sample Items	Each item worded with a uniform beginning: "How do you feel ..." • when you read a book on a rainy Saturday? (Recreational) • when the teacher asks you questions about what you read? (Academic) The response options are in a pictorial format taken from Garfield (the cat) comic strip. There are four pictures of Garfield: one with big smile, one with slight smile, one with slight frown, one with big frown.
Reliability	Alpha coefficients across grade levels and scales range from 0.74 to 0.89; early grades lower than later grades.
Validity	Careful detail given to instrument development. Students with public library cards had higher scores than those without. Students who had checked books out of library had higher scores than those who did not. Attitude scores significantly correlated with reading achievement. Results of factor analysis support presence of two scales.
Comments	Teacher reads each item aloud twice as students mark their responses.

Do the sample items measure up in terms of the item writing and editing guidelines included in chapter 3?

Finally, attention turns to the reliability and validity data (rows 7 and 8). Robinson, Shaver, and Wrightsman (1991) prepared a set of standards for examining alpha reliability estimates. They are:

- Exemplary; 0.80 or higher;
- Extensive; 0.70 to 0.79;
- Moderate; 0.60 to 0.69;
- Minimal; < 0.60; and
- None; no data reported.

Stability data, when available, should also be examined, but its interpretation (as discussed in chap. 4) will depend on the length of time between administrations and the degree of stability that can be expected of the affective characteristics over that time period.

In terms of validity, the stronger the empirical evidence that supports the construct validity of the instrument (i.e., the confirmation of hypotheses derived from theory, prior research, or practical experience) and the structure of the instrument (when it is multidimensional), the higher the quality of the instrument. In this regard, the following standards are recommended for examining the validity data:

- Exemplary; multiple methods of empirical validation, with strong statistical support (e.g., statistically significant results). Careful attention paid to instrument development and judgmental validity;
- Extensive; multiple methods of empirical validation with some statistical support (e.g., differences and–or correlations in right direction); Some attention paid to instrument development and judgmental validity;
- Moderate; at least one method of empirical validation with strong statistical support; Some attention paid to instrument development and judgment validity.
- Minimal; no empirical validity data. Only information about instrument development and judgmental validity is presented; and
- None; no data presented.

Step 4: Making a Choice

On the basis of this rather comprehensive examination, a decision can now be made. If the best instrument seems very strong, we suggest that it be chosen. If, on the other hand, an instrument is fairly strong but some questions remain, modifications may be needed. The nature, possibility, and feasibility of the modifications must be considered.[2] Finally, the end result of this analysis may be that no existing instrument fills the bill. In this case, a new instrument must be designed and we move to Phase IIB.

---

[2]If the modifications include preparing new items or revising existing items, then that portion of the instrument is best considered a new instrument. Consequently, you would then move on to Phase IIB.

PHASE IIB: DESIGNING AN AFFECTIVE ASSESSMENT INSTRUMENT

This phase consists of six steps: preparing a blueprint, writing the items, writing directions, having the draft instrument reviewed, pilot testing the instrument, and readying the instrument for administration.

Step 1: Preparing a Blueprint

A blueprint is the master plan for the instrument. What scaling method will be used? What will the response categories be? How many scales will it include? How many items will there be for each scale? These are the questions that must be answered to prepare a blueprint. In the previous chapters we have provided the information needed to help you answer these questions in light of your purpose, your affective characteristics and targets, and your student population.

For most purposes, we recommend the use of Likert scales with either four or six response categories depending on the age and sophistication of the intended student population. The labeling of the response categories should depend on the likely range of views of the intended student population. For practical reasons the number of scales in a questionnaire and the number of items per scale are linked. Although the overall questionnaire should not be too long, there should be no fewer than four items per scale.

It also is worth mentioning here that, when initially designing a questionnaire, you need to plan to write many more items than you eventually will include on the final form of the instrument. During the review and pilot testing phases of instrument development many items will be found to be inadequate and either need to be discarded or rewritten substantially.

Step 2: Writing the items

This step has two parts. Both were discussed in chapter 2, this volume. The first is to decide on a general approach to generating items that are clearly related to the affect–target combinations that you wish to include on your instrument. The two approaches described in chapter 2 were the mapping-sentence approach and the domain-referenced approach. If these are thought to be too rationale or sterile, you could simply bring together a group of people for a brainstorming session for the purpose of generating items. If this alternative is selected, you would be wise to include some students in the session.

Regardless of the approach used to generate items, it is important to get as wide a range of item content as possible, given the affect–target combination you are attempting to assess. Also regardless of the approach used, the items must be carefully edited. Eight editing guidelines were presented in chapter 2. Because of their importance in this step, they are reproduced as Table 5.3.

Step 3: Writing Directions

This is an important, yet often neglected step. As discussed earlier, the directions should:

- communicate the general purpose for which the information is being gathered;
- describe the conditions under which the students are responding (e.g., they are not forced to complete the instrument);
- indicate how to respond to each statement (e.g., to circle the letters that best expressed their feeling about the statement);
- clarify the meaning of the affective target, if this is necessary; and
- inform respondents that there are no right and wrong answers—their candid opinion is being sought.

It is very important that written directions are included on the instrument. If necessary (because of age or literacy issues), they also can be read.

Step 4: Having the Draft Instrument Reviewed

At least two groups should be involved in the review of the draft instrument. The first group consists of those who possess knowledge of the affective characteristics and their targets. To a lesser extent, these individuals should have some knowledge of the scaling method used to prepare the instru-

TABLE 5.3
Guidelines for Editing Statements

1. Write statements that cover the entire range of the affective characteristic (Plus its target).
2. Ensure that each item involves feeling and affect and not a statement of Fact (or a statement that can be interpreted as factual).
3. Keep the language of the statements simple, clear, and direct.
4. Write statements in present tense.
5. Each statement should contain only one complete thought.
6. Avoid statements likely to be endorsed by everyone or almost no one
7. Avoid words that are vague modifiers or words that may not be understood by those who are asked to respond to the scale.
8. Avoid statements that involve double negatives.

ment. Members of this group would be asked to focus on the relationship between the items included on the instrument and the affective characteristics and targets being assessed. Are there items that are unrelated to what is being assessed? Are there items that are so similar that they might be redundant? Are there items that should be included on the instrument but are not? These are the types of questions to which this group should attend.

The second review group is composed of students similar to those for whom the instrument is intended. Members of this group should be asked to focus on the wording of the directions and the individual items. Is the language used appropriate? Is the meaning clear? What changes should be made to make the instrument more appropriate and meaningful? Questions such as these should be asked of the second review group. Revisions of the draft questionnaire may need to be undertaken after both reviews.

Step 5: Pilot Testing the Instrument

The importance of language in the design of affective assessment instruments is nicely illustrated by the verbal summary of this step. This book was written by two authors—one American and one Australian. The verbal summary, "Pilot Testing the Instrument," was written by the American. If the Australian had his way, it would have read something like "Trialing the Instrument." Whatever it is called, trying out the instrument with at least a small sample of the student population is very important.

As mentioned in chapter 4, it is not sufficient just to let these students complete the instrument. This is not to suggest that just having students complete the instrument is not a good source of information. Watching students as they complete the draft instrument can be very informative (e.g., do they understand the instructions at all?). Rather, it is to suggest that more can be learned by talking with students after they have completed the instrument. What did they not understand? What changes could be made to make the instructions and individual items more clear? These are the questions that are likely to provide the needed information. Once again, the questionnaire will likely require further revision at this point in its development.

If time and resources permit you to pilot test the questionnaire with a larger sample of students, this would provide valuable additional information. The more information available to you as a result of the pilot testing step, the fewer problems that should arise when the questionnaire is actually used for real (e.g., in your research, in your school assessment program).

Step 6: Readying the Instrument for Administration

Once changes have been made based on the results of the field test, a final form of the instrument must be prepared. This final form should possess at least two qualities. First, it should look as professional as possible. Stated simply, it should look as if it were prepared by someone who really cared about how students felt. Indicators of professional preparation include the quality of paper, the absence of typographical errors, and even the font used in preparing the instrument. Second, it should be as short as possible. Instruments that are 10 or 12 pages long are intimidating. Questionnaires of one or two pages (even if printed back-to-front) are much more likely to elicit response.

PHASE III: ADMINISTERING THE INSTRUMENT

Once a final draft of the instrument has been prepared, the instrument must be administered to a fairly large sample of students. Depending on how extensive and through the pilot testing was, this new administration may be considered another trial of the questionnaire. In that case, it would be advisable if you were to retain a few more items than essential, to allow for further item attrition.

Prior to this administration, at least three questions must be addressed. How large a sample is needed? What other information do you need from these students? What are the practical considerations in administering self-report instruments?

Sample Size

A general rule of thumb is that the sample size should be at least 10 times the number of items. If the instrument contains 45 items, then, the sample should contain at least 450 students. Sample sizes this large tend to produce sufficiently reliable data on the technical quality of the instrument (i.e., reliability, empirical validity). If, however, you are unable to achieve the appropriate sample size, the guideline must be to obtain as large and as representative a sample as possible given your resources. In these circumstances the stability of the affective data may be less than you would like and the comparisons between and among groups (see the following) may need to be restricted.

This minimal sample size may need to be increased depending on what types of validity evidence you intend to gather and what kinds of data summaries you intend to produce. If, for example, you intend to examine differences among several known groups, then each group must include a sufficient number of students to enable you to make meaningful comparisons. Furthermore, if statistical procedures are used to test the significance of the differences, then the group sizes must be large enough so the statistical test has sufficient power to detect group differences when they, in fact, exist (Anderson & Finn, 1996). Similarly, if you intend to summarize the data at each grade level (e.g., Grades 3 through 6), then the sample at each grade level must be sufficiently large to provide reliable summaries (e.g., mean scale scores).

Additional Information

In almost all cases, additional information is needed to examine the empirical validity of an instrument. If group comparisons are to be made, then you need to know which students belong in which groups. If associations between scale scores and other measures (e.g., grades, test scores, scores on other affective instruments, overt behaviors) are to be examined, then some means of obtaining the information on these other measures is needed.

One way to determine what other information is needed for validity purposes is to establish a series of hypotheses as illustrated in chapter 4. We suggest beginning with the following question: If this scale really assesses the affect–target combination I think it does, then what predictions can I make about relation of the scale scores with other information and measures? Subsequent questions may include: What differences between or among groups do I expect? What correlations do I expect and do I not expect with other measures?

The point here is that you must plan to gather the additional information you need so you can plan how you are going to get it. It is a sad situation to go through all the time and effort to design an affective assessment instrument only to find you do not have sufficient additional information to begin to establish its validity.[3]

Practical Administrative Concerns

There are two major concerns here. The first is obtaining approval to administer the questionnaire; the second is the actual process of administering it. In most school systems, it is necessary to obtain approval to administer a questionnaire to students (or teachers). Parental approval may also be required. In many institutions, approval by an ethics committee is required. In any case, you should find out what the requirements are in your area and follow them.

In some cases the "gatekeepers" will want to see your completed questionnaire before giving approval. If the questionnaire is part of a larger research project, they may want to see a complete research proposal in

---

[3]The word *begin* is important. No one study establishes the validity of an instrument. Multiple studies over a fairly lengthy time period are needed. In this regard, it is instructive to note that Robert Bills (1975) worked on his "System for Assessing Affectivity" for about 25 years.

which the use of the questionnaire data is explained. Any research plan and timetable must allow for possible delays in obtaining approval to administer your questionnaire.

Those who have been involved in the administration of achievement batteries are aware of the careful administrative policies and procedures recommended by the authors or publishers of the batteries.[4] One of the most important principles governing the administration of affective assessment instruments is that the conditions under which students respond to the instrument should be conducive to honest responses. If possible, then,

- the person administering the self-report instrument should establish rapport with the students to whom the instrument is being administered;
- the person administering the instrument should be independent of the power structure in the school or school district (e.g., this person should ideally be an outsider such as a university researcher or research assistant rather than a teacher at the school or the school principal);
- if it is not possible for an outsider to administer the instrument, then at the very least someone other than the students' teachers should administer it. This is particularly important when any of the items pertain to the actions of or relationships with the classroom teacher;
- the person administering the instrument should inform the students of the purpose and importance of the information being gathered; and,
- the administrative conditions should be as relaxed and comfortable as possible.

SUMMARY OF MAJOR POINTS

1. The first phase in deciding whether to select or design a self-report instrument requires establishing clear parameters and definitions. The purpose of the assessment, the population of students, and the relevant affective characteristics and their targets must be described.
2. Purposes of affective assessment generally fall into four categories: enhancing student learning, improving the quality of educational programs, evaluating the quality of educational programs, and conforming to administrative or legislative mandates.
3. All things being equal, we recommend selecting an instrument over designing one. The primary reason is the time, expertise, and, possibly, expense involving in the development of a new instrument.

---

[4]The word *recommended* is used here because both authors have been in testing situations in which recommendations were not followed. As a consequence, the data gathered were not worth examining.

4. Selecting an instrument requires the completion of four steps: locating instruments, reviewing instruments, comparing instruments, and making a choice from among available instruments.
5. There are five possible sources of affective assessment instruments: electronic databases, commercial publishing houses, professional associations, research institutes and laboratories, and compendiums.
6. A systematic review of existing instruments may be aided by the use of tables such as the one shown in Table 5.1. A general comparison is usually sufficient to eliminate instruments from consideration. A more detailed comparison is likely needed to make defensible choices among the primary contenders.
7. Standards are available for judging the adequacy of alpha reliability coefficients: Exemplary, 0.80 and higher; Extensive, 0.70 to 0.79; Moderate, 0.60 to 0.69; Minimal, below 0.60; and None.
8. Standards are available for judging the validity evidence provided along with the instrument. They are: Exemplary, multiple methods of empirical validation with strong statistical support; Extensive, multiple methods of empirical validation with some statistical support; Moderate, at least one method of empirical validation with strong statistical support; Minimal, only information about instrument design and judgmental validity provided; and None.
9. Designing an instrument requires the completion of six steps: (1) preparing a blueprint, (2) writing the items, (3) writing directions, (4) having the draft instrument reviewed, (5) pilot testing the instrument, and (6) readying the instrument for administration.
10. The blueprint establish the basic parameters: scaling method, response categories, number of scales, and number of items per scale.
11. Writing items involves generating items that are consistent with your definitions and them editing them for clarity.
12. Having experts and students review the draft instrument, making revisions, and then subjecting the instrument to a pilot test are key aspects of producing a quality self-report instrument.
13. The final form of the instrument should be professional in appearance and as short as possible.
14. Prior to administering the final form, attention should be paid to: the size of the sample, additional information needed for the purpose of examining empirical validity, and practical administrative considerations (e.g., the physical environment in which the instrument is completed).

6

Treating and Analyzing Affective Data: What Do I Do With All The Numbers?

Whether a self-report instrument is selected or designed, once it is administered it yields data. If the questionnaire is quite lengthy or the sample is quite large, it is very easy to be swamped by the data. In this chapter, we describe and illustrate one way of organizing and summarizing the data.

A single data set is used throughout the chapter. The data were obtained from administrations of the Quality of School Life (QSL) questionnaire (Ainley & Bourke, 1992). The QSL contains 40 items divided into seven scales, two general (General Satisfaction and Negative Affect) and five specific (Social Integration, Opportunity, Teacher, Adventure, and Achievement).

Because this data set is used in this chapter and the next, the QSL questionnaire is reproduced in Appendix B, together with a description of the seven scales. By using this data set, this chapter has an operational focus, rather than a conceptual one (although a number of conceptual issues are addressed in passing).

There are five steps involved in producing scale scores: (1) coding, entering and checking data; (2) dealing with missing data; (3) recoding items; (4) estimating scale validity and reliability, and (5) calculating and reporting the scale scores. These steps are detailed in this chapter using the simplest acceptable methods. More advanced approaches to scale development and analysis can be found in Jöreskog and Aish, (1993), Jöreskog and Sörbom (1993a, 1993b, 1993c), and Holmes-Smith and Rowe (1994).[1]

Where it is desirable to make reference to a specific process, we elected to use the Statistical Package for the Social Sciences (SPSS). We chose SPSS for several reasons. First, it is by far the most available statistical software for social science students, including education students. Second, its syntax is more readily understar.dable than many other statistical packages. Third, it is a reasonably powerful and comprehensive package.

DATA CODING, ENTRY, AND CHECKING

The first step is r.ɔt very different from any other situation where data are entered for subsequent computer analysis. Consequently, the reader more experienced with computer data analysis may elect to move quickly through this section.

Deciding on a Coding Scheme

As discussed in chapter 4, this volume, the most common type of questionnaire used in assessing affective characteristics consists of a series of Likert-type items, each normally with four, five, or six response categories. The QSL, for example, has four response categories: *Agree, Mostly Agree, Mostly Disagree, and Disagree.* Those responding to the QSL are asked to indicate which response category best captures their feelings about each item by checking or ticking the corresponding box.

The simplest way of coding the responses, then, is to assign 4 to the first category (in this case, *Agree*), 3 to the second category (*Mostly Agree*), 2 to the third category (*Most Disagree*), and 1 to the fourth category (*Disagree*).[2] If a student has failed to respond to an item, has made more than one response to it, or has responded in any other way that makes it impossible to assign a definite single number, the data relating to the item for that

---

[1] The more advanced methods recognize that the items making up a scale are ordinal variables and, thus, use a polychoric rather than a Pearson product-moment correlation matrix in the analysis. The item weightings subsequently used in calculating scale scores for individual students are then the proportionally weighted factor score regression coefficients of the one-factor congeneric measurement model.

[2] Generally, more positive response categories are assigned higher numerical codes. This is because most items are written in a positive way. Thus, agreeing with a positively worded item receives more score points When item codes are summed to produce a scale score, higher scale scores indicate more positive affect. Of course, there is the problem of negatively worded items. In this case, the codes are reversed later on using the SPSS program.

person are considered to be missing. (More about that shortly.) To clearly distinguish missing data from acceptable codes, missing data are normally coded as 9, although zero, −1, or any other unused code could indicate that information is missing.[3]

Although we suggested using the numerals 1 to 4 (or 1 to 5, or 1 to 6, depending on the number of response categories) to code responses, we are aware that Likert-type response categories form an ordinal rather than an interval scale. Strictly speaking, the response category codes should really be 1st, 2nd, 3rd, 4th, and so on, rather than 1, 2, 3, and 4. What we have suggested, however, is simply a device to enable us to achieve the objective of calculating scale scores, which can subsequently be treated as interval data (as seen later in this chapter).

Data Entry

To enter the questionnaire data, you can choose to use a word processing program, a spreadsheet, or a data entry program attached to a statistical analysis package, as you wish. Because of their power to find specific sequences of data and their flexibility in making large-scale changes to data sets, when required, we prefer to use one of the word processing programs. The files created are raw data files of numerals and, when complete, are saved as text files (e.g., qsl.txt). This is an option with all word processing packages. These text files are then read into SPSS.

Data are normally entered student by student, using a new row for each student. You will want an identification code for each student so that you can check the data at some later time or make comparisons with any other data gathered on that student. As well as recording the identification code in the data file, the identification number should be written on the top of each questionnaire. Although the coded responses for individual students can be entered in the data file in any order, it is convenient for later checking if natural groupings of data are entered together (e.g., students in the same grade level, students at the same school). At the same time as the questionnaire responses are coded, it is often convenient to place in the data file other relevant information about the students (e.g., school, gender, grade level).

The instructions for coding a set of data used for the QSL is shown in Fig. 6.1. Of course, any other nonambiguous coding scheme would be acceptable. Coding males as 1 and females as 2 (as done in the example), for example is simply a convention; any other convention could be substituted for it.

---

[3]Of course it would be possible to use a different missing data code for different categories of missing data. Suppose, for example, one wished to distinguish between an item being omitted and an item for which two responses have been given. For most purposes, however, the reason data are coded as missing is irrelevant, and the same missing data code is used for all.

There are three phases to this task: (1) Identify each student   (2) Code the QSL questionnaire   (3) Check the coding and data entry.**The coding may be done using any PC word processor package which can save text (ASCII) files.**

1. IDENTIFICATION

List the schools and classes involved in the study. Each school must have a unique number, each class within each school has a different number, and each student within each class will have a different number. This is done as follows:

Schools	Codes	Classes	Codes
First school	01	First Year 5 class in each school	051
Second school	02, etc	Second Year 5 class in each school	052, etc
		First Year 6 class in each school	061
		Second Year 6 class in each school	062, etc

Students
Simply number from 01 to 35 (or whatever the number in the class). The identification number should be written on the top of the front page of each questionnaire, thus: 1806209 meaning the 18th school, the 2nd Year 6 class in the school, 9th student in that class.

Gender
Finally (in column 8) add a 1 if the student is male, a 2 if female, and the total identification for this particular male student would then be: 18062091.

2. CODING THE QSL QUESTIONNAIRE

Each questionnaire is coded on a single line. The 8-digit identification number for each questionnaire is coded in the first 8 columns, leave a space (column 9), then from column 10 begin coding the QSL data in groups of 5 items (with a space between each group of 5), as follows:

Response	Code	Response	Code
Agree	4		
Mostly Agree	3	Item is omitted, or	
Mostly Disagree	2	two responses, or	
Disagree	1	indecipherable	9

Thus a line of data would look like this:
18062091 12332 43223 22339 23332 11142 22233 33311 22244
where the student missed one item (Item 15 is coded 9).

3. CHECKING THE CODING

It will be necessary at your end to have the questionnaires bundled by class and school ready to find individual forms when possible errors detected during the analyses need checking.

FIG. 6.1.   Instructions for coding the school life questionnaire.

To illustrate the coding of items for relationships of students with items and scales in a set of data, Table 6.1 has been designed to show data from two of the QSL scales, Social Integration and Achievement, for a total of 52 students in two classes at one school. Class 1 has 24 students; Class 2 has 28. The order of the items is not the same as on the QSL (see Appendix B). Rather, we have rearranged the order to group them according to their scales for convenient viewing. As mentioned earlier, each row represents the responses of one student and the students have been grouped by class. Data from other schools and classes would be added to the file in the same way.

Examining the columns of the table, we see, after the three identification columns, that each column represents the responses of all students to one item. Thus, it is examine the data in two ways: horizontally (where the focus in on the students) and vertically (where the focus is on the items). Students can be grouped into classes and then into schools. Items can be grouped into scales. More is said in chapter 7, this volume, about the use of individual student data and group data.

Two final points should be made about the actual codes entered in Table 6.1. First, for each student, each item is generally coded from 1 to 4. Second, there are a few cases where an item is coded as 9 (Item 26 for Students 12 and 27, in School 2, and Item 36 for Student 21, also in School 2). As mentioned earlier, 9 is used as the code for missing data.

Data Checking

As much as we might regret it, there are always inaccurate and inappropriate codes in any set of data. These arise from many sources including simple typing mistakes by those coding the data, a lack of clarity or other ambiguity in instructions to students or coders, and a lack of care (or malice) on the part of students responding to the items. Lack of clarity in instructions to students has been discussed in chapter 4, this volume. We shall briefly consider the others.

Typing mistakes, being random, are the most difficult to detect unless they result in a code that is not possible under the coding scheme (e.g., finding a 6 when the only possible codes are 1 to 4, and 9). Because typing errors are random, however, they are the least damaging to the data set because they do not introduce a systematic bias. Coding data twice and identifying the differences in the data sets would be possible, but the time and expense necessary to do this normally preclude such a practice.

A more common practice is to check the coding of a sample of the questionnaires (perhaps 10% of the total). It would be necessary to engage in more comprehensive checking only if a high proportion of the rechecked questionnaires were found to have errors. This checking procedure is nec-

TABLE 6.1

Student by Item Data for One School

			Two Sets of Items From The QSL Instrument												
			Social Integration Items								Achievement Items				
Identification (N = 52)															
School Number	Class Number	Student Number	Q3	Q6	Q20	Q24	Q29	Q30	Q35	Q36	Q4	Q7	Q16	Q26	Q40
1	1	01	3	1	2	1	1	1	2	3	3	3	3	3	3
1	1	02	4	4	4	4	4	4	4	4	4	3	3	4	4
1	1	03	4	4	2	1	1	2	4	1	3	3	1	2	1
1	1	04	4	4	3	2	4	4	3	4	3	4	4	4	4
1	1	05	4	4	4	3	1	2	2	4	2	2	2	4	4
1	1	06	3	4	4	4	1	4	3	4	3	3	3	3	4
1	1	07	4	4	4	1	4	3	2	2	3	3	2	3	4
1	1	08	4	4	2	4	1	2	4	1	3	3	1	1	1
1	1	09	4	4	4	4	2	3	3	3	3	3	3	3	3
1	1	10	4	4	4	4	2	3	3	4	2	3	3	3	3
1	1	11	4	4	3	4	3	4	3	4	3	4	4	4	4
1	1	12	1	4	4	1	1	3	3	2	4	1	1	1	1
1	1	13	4	4	4	4	4	4	4	4	3	4	3	3	3
1	1	14	2	2	3	3	3	2	3	1	1	3	2	3	1
1	1	15	4	4	3	4	3	4	3	4	4	4	4	4	3
1	1	16	4	4	4	4	1	4	4	4	4	4	3	4	4

V1	V2	V3	V4	V5	V6	V7	V8	V9	V10	V11	V12	V13	ID	G1	G2
4	4	4	4	4	2	4	3	4	4	4	4	3	17	1	1
4	4	3	3	3	3	3	4	3	2	3	2	3	18	1	1
3	3	2	3	1	2	1	3	1	2	2	4	4	19	1	1
1	3	3	4	2	3	2	2	2	2	2	3	3	20	1	1
1	4	4	1	3	2	1	4	4	4	1	4	4	21	1	1
4	3	1	2	2	1	1	4	1	3	1	3	4	22	1	1
3	3	2	3	4	2	2	2	4	4	4	4	4	23	1	1
4	2	1	4	4	4	1	1	4	4	4	4	4	24	1	1
3	4	1	3	4	4	1	1	1	3	4	1	4	01	2	1
4	3	3	4	4	4	4	1	3	2	2	4	3	02	2	1
3	3	4	3	3	3	2	4	2	3	3	3	4	03	2	1
4	3	4	4	4	4	4	2	4	4	4	4	4	04	2	1
4	4	2	4	4	4	3	4	4	4	1	4	4	05	2	1
3	3	3	3	2	2	3	4	1	2	4	3	4	06	2	1
4	1	3	3	2	4	3	4	4	3	4	3	4	07	2	1
4	3	3	3	3	4	3	4	3	3	3	2	4	08	2	1
4	4	4	4	4	3	4	4	4	4	4	4	4	09	2	1
4	4	3	4	4	4	4	3	4	4	3	4	2	10	2	1
4	4	3	2	4	4	3	3	3	4	4	3	4	11	2	1
3	9	4	2	2	3	1	4	3	3	2	3	3	12	2	1

continued on next page

School Number	Class Number	Student Number	Q3	Q6	Q20	Q24	Q29	Q30	Q35	Q36	Q4	Q7	Q16	Q26	Q40
1	2	13	3	3	3	4	1	4	3	4	3	4	2	3	2
1	2	14	3	3	3	2	1	3	4	3	3	4	2	3	3
1	2	15	3	3	3	3	2	3	2	2	3	4	3	3	3
1	2	16	4	4	4	3	2	4	3	4	3	4	3	4	4
1	2	17	3	4	3	3	3	3	3	3	3	3	3	3	3
1	2	18	4	4	4	3	2	4	3	3	4	3	3	3	4
1	2	19	4	4	4	4	4	4	4	4	3	4	3	4	4
1	2	20	4	4	3	3	1	4	3	3	4	4	3	3	4
1	2	21	3	4	3	3	3	4	3	9	4	4	3	3	4
1	2	22	4	3	4	3	1	3	2	3	3	3	3	2	4
1	2	23	4	3	3	1	4	3	4	3	4	4	4	3	3
1	2	24	3	4	4	3	2	3	3	3	4	4	4	4	4
1	2	25	3	3	4	4	2	3	2	3	4	3	4	4	4
1	2	26	4	3	3	1	2	3	3	3	4	4	4	3	4
1	2	27	3	2	1	4	2	3	2	3	4	3	3	9	1
1	2	28	3	4	4	4	3	4	4	4	4	4	3	3	4

essary to detect errors that result in wrong codes, but possible ones (e.g., a code of 3 instead of 4).

Perhaps the most economical method of detecting impossible (or unlikely) codes in a large set of data is to obtain a frequency distribution for each item. For items in the questionnaire described previously, if numbers other than 1, 2, 3, 4, or 9 show up in the frequency distribution, these are errors . If such numbers are discovered, say two students have a 5 entered for Question 6, the identification numbers of these respondents can be found using the Select Cases command in the Data menu of SPSS. The command would take the following form: SELECT IF Q6 = 5. Then the Case Summaries command in the Summarize option of the Statistics menu can be used to list the identification numbers of the selected cases. Once the identification of the cases with errors are detected, it will normally be necessary to go back to the original questionnaires to make the corrections.

A potentially more difficult and contentious issue is detecting and deciding what to do about responses resulting from a lack of care (or perhaps an inability to read) by some students. There usually is a small number of respondents who, without reading the item, will always mark the first or last box in any column, may respond in a pattern (e.g., 1, 2, 3, 4, 3, 2, 1, 2, 3, 4, 3, 2, etc.), or may simply answer at random. What should we do here?

Consistent, but nonsensical, responses (e.g., a complete row of 1s) are relatively easy to detect simply by glancing over pages of data; however, pattern responding is more difficult to detect and random responding is impossible to detect in this way. These three types of false or misleading data can often be identified by checking individual responses to items where one could reasonably expect a very similar or a very different response. Responses to two opposing items (e.g., *My school is a place where I really like to go, My school is a place where I feel unhappy*) would be expected to be in opposite response categories (e.g., *Agree* and *Disagree*). Where data for a student showed 4 (i.e., *Agree*) to both items we would have identified a problem with that student's data. To do this, we may select the SPSS command syntax, SELECT IF Q1 = 1 AND Q5 = 1, to identify if any such cases exist, and then list the identification numbers of any selected cases, as described previously.

Of course random responding will not be so consistently detected by this method, but if there are a number of opposing item pairs in a questionnaire, the chances are that most cases of random responding can be detected by careful cross-checking of answers. Some instrument designers have a practice of including opposing items specifically for this purpose; however, increasing the length of a questionnaire in this way creates its own problems. It is probably better to rely on naturally occurring near-opposite items.

Once we are relatively certain that a particular student's data are false or misleading, we are faced with the decision of whether to delete that student's data (known in SPSS lingo as a case) in whole or in part. The safe way is to delete all the data obtained from that student, although there may be circumstances where it is preferable not to do that. For example, it may be that the respondent has answered, apparently thoughtfully, most items on the questionnaire and then, perhaps because of fatigue, a lack of interest, or time pressure, responded with a set of 1s to the remainder. Depending on the size of the sample to which the instrument was administered, we may prefer to delete only the data where we are sure items were not responded to with some care. In this situation we would recode only the items providing the clearly faulty data as missing (i.e., 9) for this student.

It is, however, not only an issue of sample size that might indicate we should make the decision not to exclude the student from the data set entirely. It is likely that many of the students who tend to provide false data for at least part of a questionnaire are different from the other students with respect to the affective characteristics being assessed. If so, excluding them entirely would have the undesirable effect of biasing the sample toward those who were more enthused about the affect–target combination being assessed and those who were more compliant.

DEALING WITH MISSING DATA

Some aspects related to treatment of missing data should already have been considered in the design of the self-report instrument. For example, the selection of response categories and the instructions given for those unable to respond to an item for any reason are relevant as to what constitutes missing data and what can be done with it. Regardless of why data are missing, however, a very practical issue is the magnitude of the missing data problem. If there is little missing data, the issue is less pressing and we can consider the consequences of including in the data set only those students who responded to each item. However, the caution given concerning potential sample bias related to false data, previously mentioned, also has relevance here so we might not want to exclude these possibly atypical students.

The larger data set from which the data in Table 6.1 were selected included 3,062 students at 34 elementary schools in a particular district. The amount of missing data was quite small. Overall, 84% of the elementary students responded to every item. Only 9% failed to respond to only one item; only 1% failed to respond to more than four items.[4] Summaries of missing data such as these can be obtained from SPSS using the Count command (within the Transform menu). The Count command can provide the missing data codes across all items on the questionnaire or for sets of items forming a scale (see the following).

More often with affective questionnaires there is a moderate amount of missing data, with perhaps as many as 5% of students failing to respond to any single given item. Overall, there are indications that as many as 25% of a sample might fail to respond to at least one item in a 40-item questionnaire. This generally is far too many cases (i.e., students) to eliminate from the effective sample without reducing sample sizes to unacceptable levels and possibly introducing sample bias. Consequently, we need to consider missing data substitutions that will permit at least those students with relatively small amount of missing data to be included in the data set.

What is the most appropriate method of assigning a numerical value to a nonresponse? Consider a student who does not respond to Item 5 *(My school is a place where I feel unhappy)*, an item of the Negative Affect (NA) scale. We have two options: First, we can base the numerical value we assign on the student's responses to the other items on the NA scale. Second, we can base it on the responses to Item 5 given by a group of students.

Missing Data Substitution Based on Other Items

It can be argued that the student's responses to other items on the Negative Affect scale are the best guide as to how he or she would have responded to Item 5. After all, this set of items was written to provide data on a single affective characteristic, negative affect. If this option is chosen, the mean score for the other scale items to which the student responded is assigned to the item with missing data.

This argument is sound unless there is a wide discrepancy in the overall tendency to agree or disagree with Item 5 in comparison with the other items on the scale. If this is the case, the NA scale score would be inflated or deflated for that student proportionally to the difference between Item 5 and the other items. Shorter scales would be influenced in this regard more than longer ones because the influence of any one item on the mean score is greater for shorter scales.

Sometimes, of course, a student will omit more than one item in any given scale. What is the limit to the number of items where information is

---

[4]We note here in passing that elementary school students are often more careful in responding to questionnaires than are secondary students or teachers at either level.

missing before we declare that the score for that scale is missing?[5] To the extent that we can assume that the students' responses to the missing items are not very different from responses to other items belonging to the same scale, up to one half of the items could be missing, and the scale score could still be calculated and used. If more than one half of the items for a particular scale were missing for a student, that respondent should receive a missing value for the entire scale.

The method for carrying out this type of missing data substitution using SPSS is linked with the development of scale scores, discussed in a subsequent section of this chapter. Because of its importance for dealing with missing data, the method is illustrated and explained in Fig. 6.2 for the QSL questionnaire (made up of items Q1 to Q40) in which five items (Q5, Q14, Q18, Q28, and Q37) formed the NA scale. The same would be done to permit missing data substitutions for items in each of the other scales.

Missing Data Substitution Based on Other Students

An alternative is to use the responses of other students to the same item rather than responses of the same student to other items in the scale. If this alternative is chosen, the first question to be asked is which group should be used as the reference group. The most obvious choice is the total group of students. That is, the mean score on Item 5 calculated from the responses of all those students who responded to the item would be used as the substitute value. This procedure effectively removes any differences among the students with missing data for that item, but does not bias the NA scale score if Item 5 happens to be an extreme item in terms of agreement or disagreement.

If the total group is not used, an alternative is to use a group that has some affiliation with the student who did not respond to the item. Choices here include students at the same school, students of the same gender, and students who gave the same response to another item on the scale. Selection of the appropriate group could be broad or narrow, depending on the strength of relationships between group membership and the responses to the item. If male and female students tended to give very different answers to Item 5, for example, it would be more accurate to substitute the mean value for the appropriate gender group than for the total group.[6]

---

[5]Note that we are recommending that this decision be made on a scale-by-scale basis, rather than declaring data for the whole questionnaire as missing.

[6]A method that is used by the preliminary PRELIS program of the structural equation modelling program LISREL (Jöreskog & Sörbom, 1993c) uses a sophisticated combination of the item and group methods. It can be used to select the group of items making up the Negative Affect scale with Item 5 and to define the reference group as students who gave the same answers to the other items. The response most frequently given to Item 5 by that specially defined group is then substituted for the missing value.

COMMAND	EXPLANATION
COUNT MDNA = Q5 Q14 Q18 Q28 Q37 (9).	Count the number of items missing for the NA scale for each respondent.
FREQUENCIES MDNA.	Examine the extent of missing data.
RECODE Q1 TO Q40 (9 = 0).	Remove missing data from additions.
COMPUTE NA (Q5+Q14+Q18+Q28+Q37)/(5-MDNA).	Calculate the scale score (NA) by dividing the total by the items which were not missing.
FREQUENCIES NA/ STAT ALL.	Obtain the frequency distribution for the scale score, NA.
RECODE Q1 TO Q40 (0 = 9).	Return the items to their original codes.

Note. The SPSS syntax for these commands is shown here to explain the process. With the exception of the COMPUTE command, all commands could be selected from the SPSS Windows menus.

FIG 6.2. Dealing with Missing Data.

Dealing With Missing Data: A Summary

It is probably desirable to first consider the extent of missing data before deciding how to deal with it. The magnitude of the problem determines how much time and effort should go into missing data substitutions. As indicated previously, in most circumstances we recommend the substitution of the mean score for that student on the other items comprising the same scale as the item with a missing value. Once a method is decided on, however, it is essential that a clear set of rules is set down and clarified. This is useful for you as well as for anyone with whom you will communicate, particularly in writing.

RECODING ITEMS

If item recoding is required, it must be done before scale scores are computed. There are two different situations where recoding items on a questionnaire is necessary. The first is where there is a mixture of positively and negatively worded items on a single scale. Clearly, recoding is necessary before these items are added to form the scale score. Because this is not the situation with the QSL, two other items are used to illustrate this type of recoding.

Suppose the two items are *I hate school* and *I enjoy school*. A student who liked school a lot would be expected to disagree (which was assigned code of 1) with the former and agree (which was assigned a code of 4) with the latter. It would make no sense at all to add the codes assigned to these two items as they stand, so one needs to be reverse recoded. Typically, it is the negatively worded item that is recoded. In this way, higher scores reflect more positive affect.

In reverse coding, a code of 1 becomes 4, 2 becomes 3, 3 becomes 2, and 4 becomes 1. The SPSS command syntax for this recoding is as follows: RECODE Q45 $(1 = 4)(2 = 3)(3 = 2)(4 = 1)$ where Q45 is the item to be recoded. Once this recoding has been completed, the codes assigned to the two items can then be added with consistency of meaning.

The second situation is one where recoding is suggested of whole sets of items comprising a scale to assist understanding of scale scores. In general, it makes sense that higher values on a scale indicate more positive affect. Suppose instead of initially coding *Agree* as a 4, *Mostly Agree* as a 3, and so on, *Agree* was coded as a 1, *Mostly Agree* as a 2, and so on. This might be done if the left-to-right increasing number values are believed to be easier to type or believed to result in fewer typographical errors being made. In this situation (assuming all items are worded positively), all items would be recoded.

ESTIMATING SCALE VALIDITY AND RELIABILITY

As pointed out in chapter 4, this volume, there are several types or forms of validity and of reliability. When an instrument contains multiple scales, some evidence of the validity of the scales comes from their interrelations. In this section we examine the relations among the QSL scales. Furthermore, the items included on each scale are meant to elicit similar responses from the students. Thus, internal consistency reliability is at issue and is examined in this section as well.

As mentioned earlier, the QSL has 40 items organized into seven scales, two general and five specific. For simplicity of explanation, however, only the 29 items connected to the five specific scales are discussed.

Estimating and Improving the Validity of Scales

The cohesion of items on a single scale and the relative distinctiveness of items belonging to different scales in the same questionnaire are indicators of scale validity.[7] Both can be examined by obtaining a correlation matrix

---

[7]The reader will note that the "cohesion of items" is a hallmark of internal consistency reliability. Thus, as mentioned in chapter 4, this volume, reliability is a necessary condition for empirical validity. Stated in the opposite, low reliability restricts the level of empirical validity that is possible.

of responses to all the items. Items belonging to the same scale should have correlation coefficients that are higher with each other than they are with items from different scales. To the extent that this pattern is not the case, it is likely that some work will be required to improve the validity of the scales. The routine use of such a cumbersome method involving the inspection of a large number of correlation coefficients, however, is impractical. A more functional method, namely factor analysis, is required.

Within the range of factor analytic techniques, we are faced with a choice between relatively simple methods that yield approximations and more complex methods that yield more precise estimates. In addition, a choice must be made between exploratory and confirmatory analyses. With respect to the second issue, our decision is straightforward. Because we are concerned with a questionnaire that was designed to include five specific, separate scales, we are setting out to confirm the existence of these scales. With respect to the first issue, we opt for the most simple method, a principal component factor analysis followed by a Varimax rotation.[8] The scales under consideration are labelled *Teacher*, *Social Integration*, *Achievement*, *Opportunity*, and *Adventure* (see Appendix B). Factor analysis may be accessed in SPSS by selecting *Data Reduction*, then *Factor* under the Statistics menu.

Figure 6.3 shows the factor loadings for the 29 items making up these five scales.[9] The items have been grouped around the five logically derived scales. In presenting factor loadings, it is common practice to show only those of 0.30 or higher. In this example, however, the lower limit has been set at 0.25 so that we include those loadings near the typical cut off.[10]

As you examine Fig. 6.3, two things should be noted. First, all items load on the factor associated with the intended scale, with only two of the Social Integration items loading less than 0.60. Second, there is only one item in which the loading on a scale other than the one to which it was assigned is greater than 0.30. Specifically, one of the Adventure items also loads on the Social Integration factor. There are three other items that have cross-loadings between 0.25 and 0.30, two from the Adventure scale and one from the Opportunity scale. Note, however, that for each of these

---

[8]In making this choice we are aware of the limitations of this method, particularly that it is not designed to cope with the ordinal variables that make up item responses. However, the factor loadings obtained from use of this method are good approximations of those that are obtained from the use of polychoric correlation matrix designed for ordinal measures.

[9]Conceptually speaking, a factor loading is a correlation between an item and each hypothetical factor. Because there are five hypothesized scales, there are five hypothetical factors. If the logically derived, hypothesized scales were identical to the empirically derived hypothetical factors, the factor loadings would be identical to the item-scale correlations.

[10]Selection of a cut off and the ordering of items may be done within the SPSS Options that are available for factor analysis. A Varimax rotation is selected under Rotation on the same screen.

Item		Scale & Loading			
My school is a place where ...	S.I.	Opp.	Tch.	Adv.	Ach.
I am popular with other students.	.694				
I get on well with others.	.691				
I know people think a lot of me.	.666				
Others accept me as I am.	.665				
Other students are very friendly.	.641				
People trust me.	.612				
People can depend on me.	.574				
I learn to get along with others.	.495				
what I learn will be useful.		.783			
things I learn will help in secondary school.		.755			
I learn what I need to know.		.652			
work is a good preparation for my future.		.644	.272		
things I learn are important.		.615			
my teacher treats me fairly in class.			.770		
the teacher helps me with my work.			.733		
the teacher listens to what I say.			.730		
my teacher is fair to me.			.724		
the teacher takes an interest in my work.			.718		
I get excited about the work we do.				.749	
learning is fun.					.734
I like to do extra work.				.681	.281
the work we do is interesting.				.267	.654
I get enjoyment from being there.	.320			.615	
I am good at school work.					.709
I know how to cope with school work.				.700	
I can keep up with the work.					.687
I am a success as a student.					.657
I achieve a satisfactory standard in my work.		.621			

Where the scale codes are as follows: S.I. = Social Integration, Opp = Opportunity, Tch = Teacher, Adv = Adventure, Ach = Achievement. Only factor loadings greater than 0.250 are shown after a Varimax rotation. Number of students

FIG. 6.3.   Results of the rotated factor matrix.

items, the loading on the intended factor is much higher than its unintended cross-loading on another factor.

In this case, we would make a decision not to exclude any of the items when computing the scale scores. However, we should point out that the presence of either one of the following two circumstances could lead to a recommendation to delete an item from a scale. First, if an item's factor loading on an intended scale is less than 0.30 the item probably should be removed. Second, if an item's cross-loading is greater than 0.30 and–or the cross-loading is of similar magnitude to or higher than its loading on the intended factor, it probably should be removed.

At this point the more statistically minded reader might be thinking that we should be more definitive about whether items are excluded or not—that the rules should be set down and followed. We suggest, however, that hard and fast rules are not appropriate in this endeavor; rather, general guidelines are the best we can do. Making decisions such as these requires not only an understanding of the results of the factor analysis, it also requires an understanding of the affective characteristic or affect–target combination being assessed. In this regard, removing one or more items from a scale has the potential to change the nature of the very thing being assessed. Thus, a balance needs to be struck here between increasing empirical validity (by removing poor-loading items) at the cost of judgmental validity (omitting important aspects of the affective characteristic or affect–target combination). Finally, the total number of items remaining in a scale also needs to be considered when deciding whether to eliminate items. The total items on a scale influences the internal consistency reliability of that scale, an issue to which we now turn.

Estimating and Improving the Reliability of Scales

Examining the consistency of students' responses to a set of items comprising a scale is the most common method of determining scale reliability, especially for short scales consisting of few items. One way of determining response consistency is to calculate the correlation coefficients for each pairing of items comprising the scale. These are referred to as *interitem correlations*. Of course, there are many possible combinations of item pairs, and each pair would produce a different correlation coefficient. For the five items of the Negative Affect scale, for example, there are 10 item pairs (e.g., Q5 and Q14, Q5 and Q18, Q14 and Q18, and so on). For the sample of over 2,500 students, the interitem correlation coefficients for the Negative Affect scale ranged from 0.255 to 0.418, with a mean of 0.331.

The alpha reliability estimate, based on the mean of all possible interitem correlations, is 0.704.[11] The alpha is a thorough and conservative estimate of scale reliability (Cronbach, 1951).[12] Its calculation is provided

---

[11]This is the least reliable of the seven scales of the QSL questionnaire.

[12]Holmes-Smith and Rowe (1994) suggested using the coefficient of determination (R-squared) in lieu of the alpha. The alpha is a lower bound estimate of reliability. Furthermore, alpha is dependent on scale length regardless of shared variance. It also is based on Pearson product-moment correlation coefficients that, Holmes-Smith and Rowe asserted, are not appropriate for items with four to six response categories. The coefficient of determination is equivalent to the composite scale reliability coefficient for a one-factor solution and is calculated from maximally weighted factor score regression coefficients. For our purposes, however, the alpha is fairly useful, provided it is understood that it is a lower bound estimate of reliability.

by SPSS under the heading of *Scale* in the Statistics menu. One very useful option that can be selected in SPSS is a calculation of what the alpha reliability of the scale would be if each item was removed from the scale. In this way we can see immediately if any item is reducing the scale reliability.

As previously discussed in the section on validity, we may once again find ourselves in a position of considering an increase in reliability against a loss of the content covered by an item that is a candidate for removal. The decision to be made would need to balance the magnitude of the potential improvement to reliability (i.e., whether the improvement was substantial or marginal) against the residual composition of the scale, the latter depending on the content covered by the remaining items. Estimates of the alpha coefficients for the five specific QSL scales are shown in Fig. 6.4. Estimated coefficients for each scale if single items were deleted is also provided to illustrate the usefulness of this option. In Fig. 6.4, the first two columns, *scale mean* and *variance,* if each item was deleted, indicate the extent to which each item was atypical in terms of tendency of students to agree or disagree, and the spread of responses to the item was comparable to the responses made to other items on the scale. None of the items in Fig. 6.4 would seem to be atypical in either mean or variance. This result is perhaps not unexpected because the QSL questionnaire was carefully designed and tried out in many studies before being administered to this sample.

The final column in Fig. 6.4 shows the alpha reliability for the scale if each item was removed. In this case, no improvements to the existing reliability estimates would result from the removal of any item. Again, this is quite likely a result of extensive scale development that has taken place previously.

CALCULATING AND REPORTING SCALE SCORES

There are two more decisions to be made before undertaking the calculation and recording of scale scores. The first concerns whether to weight the items in calculating the scale scores. This decision requires that questions of simplicity, comparability and precision of measurement be addressed. The second concerns the proper metric for scale scores. This decision actually is a choice among options: the total score for the items comprising the scale, the mean score for these items, or some derivation.

Unweighted and Weighted Scale Scores

Thus far in our examples we have used unweighted scores. It is possible, however, to assign weights to each item response. Generally, the set of weights correspond with the factor loadings for the items on a particular scale. These weights would be multiplied by the numerical code assigned to each student's responses to the items before a scale score for the student was computed (e.g., $0.694 \times 3 + 0.571 \times 4$, etc.). These item weightings would reflect the different strengths of relations between the items and the scale, giving emphasis to stronger items at the expense of weaker ones.

Although such a procedure has an intrinsic appeal, the question is, should we develop weighted scores for scales? The answer depends on the major purpose in developing the scales and computing the scale scores. If the intention is to compare scale scores obtained from one administration to those from others, weighted scale scores should not be used. If they are, any differences found between samples could be due, in part or entirely, to differences in the weights assigned to the items. Unweighted scores also have the advantage of simplicity, especially if we have to deal with missing data (see the earlier discussion in this regard).

If, however, we are concerned with only one administration of the instrument and if increased precision is necessary because the examination of relatively weak relations is a critical part of our validity considerations, weighting the responses in the process of creating scale scores would be advisable. The scores obtained through the weighting process would be provide more accurate assessments than the simple, unweighted item scores.[13]

For the sake of simplicity, the remainder of the discussion assumes that unweighted scale scores are calculated. This assumption seems reasonable in light of the fact that scores on the QSL scales are commonly compared across different school districts and over time.

Deciding on a Metric for Scale Scores

The simplest method of creating scale scores is to add the numerical codes for all the items on a scale (after they have been recoded, if necessary). We, however, recommend the use of mean scores for scales. That is, a scale score is calculated by adding the numerical codes for all items for all students and dividing this sum by the number of total responses. We offer three main reasons for this recommendation: First, this method simplifies the treatment of missing data (as discussed earlier); second, the use of the mean provides comparability between scores on scales of different lengths; third, the creation of the mean score returns the scale score to the original metric inherent in the ordered response categories. This provides an anchor that assists in the interpretation of the scale scores.

---

[13]If item weights are to be used, we also recommend the use of polychoric correlation matrices in confirmatory factor analysis to determine the factor loadings or weights for each item (Jöreskog & Sörbom, 1993a), in place of the weights obtained from simple principal components factor analysis. Use of a polychoric matrix is a recognition of the ordinal nature of the response scales for items.

RELIABILITY ANALYSIS - SOCIAL INTEGRATION
Item-total Statistics

	Scale Mean if Item Deleted	Scale Variance if Item Deleted	Corrected Item-Total Correlation	Alpha if Item Deleted
Q3	22.3245	17.4339	.4222	.8180
Q6	22.5429	15.9465	.5240	.8059
Q20	22.5554	15.9492	.5680	.8001
Q24	22.8962	14.8014	.5776	.7992
Q29	23.1182	14.9542	.5749	.7993
Q30	22.4975	15.6008	.6133	.7939
Q35	22.5165	16.2304	.5276	.8054
Q36	22.6782	15.7292	.5593	.8010

N of Cases = 2573.0   N of Items = 8
Alpha = .8234

RELIABILITY ANALYSIS - OPPORTUNITY
Item-total Statistics

	Scale Mean if Item Deleted	Scale Variance if Item Deleted	Corrected Item-Total Correlation	Alpha if Item Deleted
Q9	18.2464	5.4431	.5516	.7989
Q12	18.2386	5.7230	.5360	.8009
Q15	18.1578	5.7130	.5330	.8015
Q25	18.1877	5.5787	.6006	.7877
Q31	18.1866	5.3820	.6283	.7812
Q39	18.1862	5.2542	.6592	.7741

N of Cases = 2573.0   N of Items = 6
Alpha = .8195

RELIABILITY ANALYSIS - TEACHER
Item-total Statistics

	Scale Mean if Item Deleted	Scale Variance if Item Deleted	Corrected Item-Total Correlation	Alpha if Item Deleted
Q2	13.6887	7.1017	.6254	.8453
Q19	13.7583	6.6484	.6589	.8369
Q22	13.8103	6.4282	.6841	.8307
Q34	13.7155	6.5753	.7120	.8238
Q38	13.8014	6.1320	.7203	.8214

N of Cases = 2573.0   N of Items = 5

Alpha = .8609
RELIABILITY ANALYSIS - ADVENTURE
Item-total Statistics

	Scale Mean if Item Deleted	Scale Variance if Item Deleted	Corrected Item- Total Correlation	Alpha if Item Deleted
Q10	11.5142	8.2297	.5416	.8069
Q13	10.9188	8.5731	.6616	.7654
Q23	10.7517	9.0942	.6195	.7795
Q27	11.4831	8.3657	.6116	.7795
Q32	10.8892	8.7292	.6329	.7737

N of Cases = 2573.0   N of Items = 5
Alpha = .8166

RELIABILITY ANALYSIS - ACHIEVEMENT
Item-total Statistics

	Scale Mean if Item Deleted	Scale Variance if Item Deleted	Corrected Item- Total Correlation	Alpha if Item Deleted
Q4	13.5717	4.8639	.5263	.7440
Q7	13.4279	5.0108	.5354	.7417
Q16	13.6549	4.6367	.5858	.7238
Q26	13.5461	4.4914	.5859	.7237
Q40	13.4823	4.8104	.5212	.7459

N of Cases = 2573.0   N of Items = 5
Alpha = .7771

FIG. 6.4.   Reliability analysis for the five specific QSL scales

One problem with the use of mean scale scores is that we need to use decimals in recording the scores. For example, we may arrive at a scale score of 3.05 that indicates very slightly more than *Mostly Agree* on the four-point continuum. A common approach, traditionally used in standardized achievement testing, is to multiply the score by 100 to remove the decimal entirely (i.e., 305). Although the original metric is lost, the obvious relation with the response categories is maintained (i.e., 100, 200, 300, and 400); thus it is still possible to consider the scale score in terms of the actual questionnaire responses.

Reporting Scale Scores

Despite scale scores being calculated by either summing or averaging numerical codes assigned to ordinal response categories, once created, the scores are normally treated as interval measures.[14] Thus, means and standard deviations are used to describe the distribution of the scale scores. We still must be concerned about the normality of the distribution before using the scale score. In this regard, it is important to check the skewness and the kurtosis [15] and, based on this examination, possibly recode or normalize the score. Estimates of skewness and kurtosis are available within the Frequencies menu of SPSS.

Once again, we can offer but brief guidelines for determining the significance of skew and kurtosis. Certainly if the skewness is more than three times its standard error some attention is required. If a highly skewed distribution is a result of a long tail with few cases, perhaps recoding to compress those few cases is the advisable course of action. If, however, there is no obvious tail but the skew is high, perhaps normalizing the scale is necessary.[16] For most purposes, departures of kurtosis from normality are less important, but at least should be noted. We offer these suggestions with the knowledge that some would suggest we are too liberal in our tolerance of departures from normality. We would counter that the advice we have given is based on considerable experience in designing and analyzing questionnaires. For other views and advice as to procedures for dealing with departures from normality, we suggest the interested reader should consult a statistics text.

The first stage in reporting the results of the administration of a self-report instrument to a sample of students is generally to construct a table. The initial table typically includes the means, standard deviations, and the numbers of students involved in the calculations for each scale. An example of such a table for the seven QSL scales is shown in Fig. 6.5.

Given that this questionnaire used a four-category response set that was coded 1 to 4, the midpoint of this range is 2.5. When scale scores are multiplied by 100 as previously suggested, this midpoint is recorded as 250 and

---

[14]The purist may object here that the scale score, a variable created out of a set of ordinal variables, remains ordinal. In recognition of this objection, of course it would be possible to use the median in place of the mean and a derivation of the interquartile range rather than the SD but, for most purposes, that is unnecessary and more complex.

[15]The reader should remember that a normal distribution is a bell-shaped curve. Both skewness and kurtosis are measures of deviations from normality. Skewness results when the curve has a long *tail*. That is, the distribution is unbalanced to one extreme or the other. Kurtosis indicated the *flatness* (too many students near or at the extremes) or *peakedness* (too many students near or at the mean).

[16]Normalizing involves a transformation of the scores in a way that the distribution resembles a normal curve. A variety of transformations can be used in this regard (e.g., logistic, arcsin).

indicates a neutral attitude to the aspect of schooling assessed by a scale that ranges from 100 to 400. (More will be said about the neutral point and its role in interpretation of scores in chap. 7, this volume.)

As mentioned earlier, higher numbers generally indicate more positive affect. Consequently, scores above 250 would indicate more favorable views of school; scores below 250 would indicate less favorable views. The exception here is the NA scale where higher scores (e.g., those above 250) indicate more negative affect. In this case, then, lower numbers indicate less dissatisfaction with school.

In Table 6.2 the mean scores on all scales indicate positive affect. That is, the mean score is higher than 250 for six scales and less than 250 for the NA scale. At 277, however, the mean for the Adventure scale is only slightly above the neutral point, 250.

With respect to spread of scores (i.e., the SD), the seven scales are quite different. The General Satisfaction scale, the Teacher scale, and particularly the Adventure scale, have the highest SDs. These results suggest that the views of students on these aspects of schooling are more different than their views on the other aspects. The NA, Social Integration, and Achievement scales have a moderate spread, whereas the Opportunity scale differentiates least among the students. The very high mean of the Opportunity scale (362 of 400) suggests that scores have been compressed at the higher end of this scale. A check of the distribution for this scale (i.e., skewness and kurtosis) would confirm this.

Following the initial reporting of the score distributions of the scales, a next step is often to compare mean scores for different groups of students. This may be done for validity purposes (see chap. 4, this volume) or for the

QSL SCALE	MEAN	SD	N
General Scales			
General Satisfaction	317	64.9	3054
Negative Affect	158	57.3	3055
Specific Scales			
Social Integration	322	56.8	3057
Opportunity	362	47.3	3051
Teacher	342	63.4	3055
Adventure	277	71.2	3054
Achievement	336	54.8	3052

The number of respondents varies because of differential incidence of missing data across scales. The total number of cases remaining if listwise deletion was used for missing data would be 3046.

FIG 6.5. Descriptive data for QSL scales.

purpose of addressing research questions or testing hypotheses. For example, it is often hypothesized that male and female students have different views of school and school life. This hypothesis can be tested by comparing the mean scale scores of male and female students. When this was done with the QSL data, the female students did have significantly more favorable views of school than their male counterparts (see, for example, Ainley & Bourke, 1992). Other possible group differences could include age or grade level, different schools, different school districts, and different regions of the country. Similarly, relations of the scale scores with other information can examined, either again as part of the validation process or to investigate questions of interest to the teacher, administrator, or researcher.

SUMMARY OF MAJOR POINTS

1. Recognition of the desirability of summarizing information when studying affective characteristics will often lead to the need to develop scales made up of a set of items to assess specific affective characteristics or affect–target combinations.
2. Five major steps are involved in developing and analyzing scale scores including: coding, entering and checking data; dealing with missing data; recoding items as necessary; checking scale validity and reliability; and, finally, creating and reporting scale scores.
3. Numeric codes are the most practical way of recording data obtained from responses to typical Likert-type questionnaires of four, five, or six categories.
4. Data may be entered into computer file by many alternative methods, but use of a word-processing package is recommended for its power and flexibility.
5. There are always errors in data sets. Thus, it is necessary to check for different types of faulty data at several stages of data entry and initial analyses. Faulty data may arise from one or more of the following: simple typing mistakes, ambiguous or inaccurate instructions to respondents or coders, and either lack of care or malice of those responding to the instrument.
6. Some duplication of coding is recommended as a check of random errors. However, other errors may be detected as impossible or unlikely codes, or combinations of codes. An example of the latter is a respondent agreeing with both positive and negative items about the same concept.
7. Faulty data must be found and corrected, if possible. When faulty data cannot be corrected, a decision must be made about the amount

of data to delete from the file. Because of loss of sample size and possible sample bias resulting from removing all information about a person with some faulty data, it is recommended that only that part of the information known to be faulty be recoded as missing data (see the following).

8. There is always a proportion of missing data in any set of data when someone omits an item or otherwise provides an uninterpretable response. Where possible, guidelines for the treatment of missing data should be established at the time the questionnaire is developed. As with faulty data, decisions will need to be made about the deletion or preservation of cases with missing data. Where possible, missing data substitutions should be undertaken to retain cases rather than to include only respondents with full sets of data in a study.

9. A range of methods of missing data substitution are available. When a response for an item in a particular scale is missing, the most commonly adopted method is to allocate the student's mean score for all other items comprising the scale to the missing item. There is a limit to the amount of missing data that should be substituted. Generally if more than half of the items comprising a scale are missing, the scale score should not be calculated and be declared as missing. There is still no requirement to delete the whole case from the data set.

10. It is essential that a clear set of guidelines for missing data substitution are set down and clarified.

11. Individual items and sets of items may need recoding before any scale scores are created. Recoding may be necessary because individual items belonging to a scale may be opposite in meaning to the other items in the scale (e.g., the item may be the only negative item in the scale). Alternatively, it may be desirable to recode all items in a scale to assist understanding. In this regard, it is normal for higher numbers in a scale to represent more positive affect. In certain cases, higher numbers may represent more of the characteristic being assessed even though it is negative (i.e., anxiety).

12. The empirical validity of a multiscale instrument is addressed, in part, using factor analysis. An example has been provided in the text and a relatively simple method involving principal component factor analysis has been described. Other, more complex methods involving structural equation modeling are referred to but are not pursued here. Guidelines for the exclusion of items from scales are suggested to improve scale validity.

13. Cronbach's alpha, a measure of internal consistency, is adopted as the appropriate and most common method of estimating scale reli-

ability. Again guidelines are suggested for excluding items, this time to improve the reliability of scales. Examples of scale reliability calculations and other associated statistics are given.

14. Should items be weighted by their factor loadings before being used in scale development? On the grounds of simplicity and of having comparable scale scores across studies and samples, a recommendation is made not to weight items for most studies. However, the greater measurement precision resulting from the use of weighted items is also a factor to be considered.

15. Alternative methods of scale score creation are canvassed, principally the use of total item scores or mean item scores. To provide comparable data for scales of different length and to accommodate some missing item data, mean scores are preferred. However, to make scale scores more readily interpretable as whole numbers, the mean scores are often multiplied by 100.

16. Scale scores, once created are usually treated as interval measures, with means and SDs being used to describe their distributions. The normality of distributions is considered through inspection of skewness and kurtosis. Guidelines are offered for recognizing substantial departures from normality.

17. Approaches to the initial reporting of scale scores are suggested. Means and SDs for the total group of respondents and the comparisons of means for particular groups are normally reported.

7

Interpreting Affective Data: What Do Those Numbers Mean?

In chapter 6 the concern is with the treatment, processing, and technical quality of the data obtained by administering affective instruments. In this chapter the focus is on making sense of these data.[1] Throughout the chapter we assume that the data have been collected using an affective instrument containing scales with sufficient technical quality.

How do we make sense of data? Simply stated, we make sense of data by comparing them with things we understand. Suppose, for example, you walk outside your house in the Southern United States and notice that it is a beautiful summer morning. You walk by a neighbor's house and notice a large outdoor digital thermometer. It reads 68°. That makes sense to you. Why? Because you have had a lot of experience with beautiful summer mornings, the Southern United States, temperature, and thermometers. Based on your composite experience, a temperature of 68° makes sense.

Suppose you continue your walk and see another digital thermometer on another neighbor's house. It reads 20°. You say to yourself, "That can't

---

[1]In the language of assessment, both cognitive and affective, the word "interpret" means to make sense of. Thus, making sense of data and interpreting data are synonymous.

be. It makes no sense. It's warmer than 20°." If you are curious you may try to explain the 20° reading. "It must be broken," you mutter. A few minutes, as you continue your walk, you stop suddenly. "Wait a minute. Isn't that the house that some Aussies just moved into?" you ask yourself. You retrace your steps; it is "20° Celsius!" you exclaim. "Now that makes sense!" "Australians" and "Celsius" have entered your consciousness. Now the 20° reading is compared with your knowledge of Australians and their use of the Celsius rather than the Fahrenheit scale. It does make sense.

How do we make sense of data collected from affective assessment instruments? Like all interpretations, we make comparisons with things we know and understand. When it comes to affective assessment instruments, we know and understand two things. First, we understand the nature of affective scales. For starters, we have defined the affective characteristics or affect–target combinations we are assessing, we know the endpoints of the affective scale, and we know the midpoint of the scale. We can use this knowledge to help us make sense of scale scores.

Second, we understand something about the students we are assessing. We know their ages, their genders, and, perhaps, their races, ethnic backgrounds, or social class memberships. We may know their achievement levels, their school attendance patterns, or the ratings their teachers give them on a variety of factors. We can use this knowledge to help us make sense of the scale scores.

Throughout this chapter we refer to comparisons of the scale scores of individual students or groups of students with the underlying affective scale as absolute comparisons. In contrast, we shall call comparisons of the scale scores of individual students or groups of students with the scale scores of other students relative comparisons.[2] Inherent in these definitions is the possibility of interpreting the scale scores of both individual students and groups. Thus, our possible interpretations of affective data can be conceptualized in the form of a two-dimensional table (see Table 7.1).

The framework in Table 7.1 is used to organize our discussion of the interpretation of affective data in this chapter. We begin with a discussion of absolute comparisons, first of individual student's scale scores, then of groups. We next move to a discussion of relative comparisons, again focusing first on individual student's scale scores, then groups. To aid in our discussion we use part of the Quality of School Life (QSL) data set that is included in chapter 6, this volume (see Table 7.2).

---

[2]Our distinction between absolute and relative corresponds with the distinction between criterion-referenced and norm-referenced interpretations in the achievement realm. Criterion-referenced interpretation (as the phrase was used by Glaser, 1963) means making sense of test scores by comparing them to some underlying continuum of achievement. In contrast, norm-referenced interpretation means making sense of test scores by comparing them with the test scores of other students (i.e., the normative sample or "norm group").

TABLE 7.1

A Framework for Making Sense of Affective Data

	Scale Scores Being Interpreted	
Type of Comparison	Individual Students	Groups of Students
Absolute		
Relative		

THE QSL DATA SET REVISITED

Table 7.2 summarizes the responses made by two classes of students to the items included on the Social Integration scale of the QSL. The Social Integration scale contains eight items (see Appendix B). It is the longest of the seven QSL scales, with an alpha reliability estimate of approximately 0.82 The eight Social Integration items contain the following phrases:

- get along with other people,
- students accept me as I am,
- people trust me,
- I am popular,
- people think a lot of me,
- I get on well with other students,
- people can depend on me, and
- other students are very friendly.

In combination, these items suggest that Social Integration scale assesses students' sense of school belonging (see chaps. 2 and 8, this volume); more specifically, a feeling of self-worth in the school and a perceived ability to get along with others.

As mentioned in chapter 6, students' responses to the items are coded on a 4- point scale: 4 for agree, 3 for mostly agree, 2 for mostly disagree, and 1 for disagree. Higher scores mean more positive affect. These numerical codes are shown in Table 7.2.

TABLE 7.2
Student by Item Data for Two Classes

	Identification		One Scale From The QSL Instrument									
				Social Integration Items								
School Number	Class Number	Student Number	Q3	Q6	Q20	Q24	Q29	Q30	Q35	Q36		Student Scale Score
1	1	01	3	1	2	1	1	1	2	3		175
1	1	02	4	4	4	4	4	4	4	4		400
1	1	03	4	4	2	1	1	2	4	1		238
1	1	04	4	4	3	2	4	4	3	4		350
1	1	05	4	4	4	3	1	2	2	4		300
1	1	06	3	4	4	4	1	4	3	4		338
1	1	07	4	4	4	1	4	3	2	2		300
1	1	08	4	4	2	4	1	2	4	1		275
1	1	09	4	4	4	4	2	3	3	3		338
1	1	10	4	4	4	4	2	3	3	4		350
1	1	11	4	4	3	4	3	4	3	4		363
1	1	12	1	4	4	1	1	3	3	2		238
1	1	13	4	4	4	4	4	4	4	4		400
1	1	14	2	2	3	3	3	2	3	1		238
1	1	15	4	4	3	4	3	4	3	4		363
1	1	16	4	4	4	4	1	4	4	4		363

Class	ID									Total
1	17	3	4	4	4	4	3	4	2	350
1	18	3	3	2	2	3	4	3	3	288
1	19	4	3	2	1	1	3	2	3	238
1	20	3	4	2	2	2	2	3	1	238
1	21	4	4	1	4	4	1	2	1	263
1	22	1	3	1	1	1	1	1	2	138
1	23	4	4	4	2	2	4	4	4	350
1	24	4	4	4	1	2	4	4	4	338
	Number of 1s	2	1	2	7	9	3	1	5	4301 (69)
	Class 1 Mean (SD) $n_1 = 2$									
2	01	4	1	1	1	1	4	4	4	250
2	02	4	4	4	4	1	4	3	4	350
2	03	3	3	3	2	2	2	2	3	250
2	04	4	4	4	4	4	4	4	4	400
2	05	4	4	4	4	4	4	4	3	388
2	06	4	2	3	1	1	3	2	3	238
2	07	4	4	3	4	4	4	4	4	388
2	08	4	3	2	4	3	4	4	3	338
2	09	4	4	4	3	3	4	3	3	350
2	10	2	4	4	4	4	4	4	4	375

continued on next page

School Number	Class Number	Student Number	Q3	Q6	Q20	Q24	Q29	Q30	Q35	Q36	Student Scale Score
1	2	11	4	4	4	3	3	4	3	3	350
1	2	12	3	2	3	3	4	1	4	3	288
1	2	13	3	3	3	4	1	4	3	4	313
1	2	14	3	3	3	2	1	3	4	3	275
1	2	15	3	3	3	3	2	3	2	2	263
1	2	16	4	4	4	3	2	4	3	4	350
1	2	17	3	4	3	3	3	3	3	3	313
1	2	18	4	4	4	3	2	4	3	3	338
1	2	19	4	4	4	4	4	4	4	4	400
1	2	20	4	4	3	3	1	4	3	3	313
1	2	21	3	4	3	3	3	4	3	9	329
1	2	22	4	3	4	3	1	3	2	3	288
1	2	23	4	3	3	1	4	3	4	3	313
1	2	24	3	4	4	3	2	3	3	3	313
1	2	25	3	3	4	4	2	3	2	3	300
1	2	26	4	3	3	1	2	3	3	3	275
1	2	27	3	2	1	4	2	3	2	3	250
1	2	28	3	4	4	4	3	4	4	4	375
Number of 1s			0	1	2	4	7	1	0	0	
Class 2 Mean (SD) $n_2 = 2$											320 (49)
Grand Mean (SD) $N = 52$											311 (59)

Reading across the columns, a scale score has been computed for each student. Each student's scale score is simply the sum of the numerical codes assigned to the responses to the eight items, divided by eight (the number of items), and then multiplied by 100 (to eliminate the decimal point). Thus, for the first student in school number 1 and class number 1, his or her scale score is:

$$[3+1+2+1+1+1 +2+3] / 8 \times 100, \text{ which is}$$
$$[14 / 8] \times 100, \text{ or } 1.75 \times 100, \text{ or } 175.$$

Reading down the *student scale score* column for each class, you will find the mean and SD for that class. For Class 1, the mean scale score is 301 with a SD of 69; for Class 2, the mean is 320 with a SD of 49. Finally, you will see what is called a *grand mean*. This is the mean for all 54 students regardless of class membership. Associated with the grand mean of 311 is a SD of 59.

So these are all the numbers? What do they mean?

INTERPRETING INDIVIDUAL STUDENT'S SCALE SCORES USING ABSOLUTE COMPARISONS

The continuum underlying the Social Integration scale ranges from 100 to 400, with a midpoint of 250. As mentioned in chapter 6, 250 represents the *neutral point* of the scale. That is, it is the point where negative becomes positive or where less becomes more (or vice versa). In the case of Social Integration, it is the point where students stop questioning their self-worth and ability to get along with others and start believing in them. Using the neutral point as a benchmark, then, students with scale scores above 250 tend to have a greater sense of school belonging, whereas those with scale scores below 250 tend to have less of a sense of school belonging.

What about students scoring exactly 250? They can be said to be neutral on the matter. Obviously, it is very difficult to score exactly at the neutral point. This leads to an interesting question; namely, how far from this neutral point can an individual student score and still really be considered to be neutral in terms of their perceptions of Social Integration? One answer to this question can be derived from the concept of standard error of measure.

In simplest terms, the standard error of measure is the amount of error made in assigning a particular scale score to an individual. Because no assessment is completely reliable, no individual can be assigned a scale score with perfect accuracy. That is, an individual student's scale score will deviate at least slightly from the true amount of the affective characteristic or affect–target combination he or she possesses. Stated somewhat differently, because of this imperfect reliability, an individual's scale score may vary somewhat if a few different items were included in the assessment or if the instrument was readministered at another time.

The standard error of measure is based on the reliability of the scale scores and, as such, permits us to estimate the amount of expected variability due to measurement error alone. The formula for the standard error of measure is as follows:

$$SEM = SD\sqrt{(1-r)}$$

where SEM = the standard error of measure;
SD = the standard deviation of the scale scores of a fairly large group; and
r = the reliability of the scale scores.

This formula can be applied to the QSL data set in Table 7.2. We mentioned earlier that the alpha reliability for the Social Integration scale was approximately 0.82. From Table 7.2, the SD associated with the grand mean (that is, the mean of all students) is 59. Substituting 0.82 for r and 59 for SD in the formula, we have:

$$SEM = 59\sqrt{(1-0.82)}$$

which is 59 × 0.425, or about 25.

In general, we would suggest that a student's scale score can be said to fall into the neutral range if it is less than one standard error of measure from the neutral point in either direction. The neutral range for the QSL Social Integration scale, then, would be from 225 to 275. Using the neutral range, students can be placed into one of three categories for the purpose of interpretation: those with a more negative sense of school belonging (those with scale scores less than 225), those with a more positive sense of school belonging (those with scale scores greater than 275), and those with ambivalent feelings about school belonging (those with scale scores between 225 and 275).[3]

---

[3]Joan Herman, a colleague who reviewed a draft of this manuscript, suggested that we were using a "very liberal definition" of what's positive in light of the "reality of socially desirable responses." She makes a good point. When socially desirability does influence students' responses to a particular affective instrument, it is possible that neutral is really negative. This is yet another reason why multiple perspectives and comparisons are needed if proper interpretations of affective assessment data are to be made.

Using these three categories, we can begin to make sense of the student scores in Table 7.2.[4] The first student in Class 1 has a negative sense of school belonging (scale score of 175). A more complete understanding is possible by looking at those items with which this student disagrees. He or she does not feel accepted by others (Q6), does not feel popular (Q24), does not believe people think a lot of him or her (Q29), and does not get along well with other students (Q30).

In contrast, the second student in Class 1 has a perfect score. This student agreed with all eight items. Assuming the scale scores are highly valid, we can say this student has a very positive sense of school belonging.

Finally, consider the third student in Class 1. His or her scale score is 238, which puts this student in the ambivalent category. The pattern of responses to the individual items supports this ambivalence. This student sees himself or herself as getting along with other students (Q3), being accepted by other students (Q6), and being dependable (Q35). At the same time, however, the student disagrees that he or she is popular (Q24), that people think a lot of him or her (Q29), and that other students are very friendly (Q36). From these responses, this student seems to believe he or she gets along with others, but does not have a good feeling about his or her self-worth. Because of this conflict the overall result is an ambivalent feeling in terms of a sense of school belonging.

Two points must be made at this time relative to interpreting individual student's scale scores in terms of the underlying affective scale. The first is that the two-step procedure of initially placing each student into one of the three categories and then examining individual item responses produces a reasonable degree of understanding. Thus, both overall scale scores and individual item responses are useful in facilitating this type of interpretation. (See Table 7.3 for a summary of the procedure.)

The second point to be made here is in response to the second student's perfect score. For the neutral-point interpretation to be meaningful, the empirical validity supporting the scale must be strong. As mentioned in chapter 3, socially desirable responses can also produce a perfect score (in either the positive or negative direction. If a high degree of empirical validity is present in the scale, it is unlikely that socially desirable responses are a major factor in the individual student's scale score. To summarize, to the extent that the scale score is empirically valid, the neutral-point interpretation of scales scores is likely to be valid.

---

[4]The classification of students can be done efficiently using SPSS. The initial command is *Recode* under the *Transform* menu. We suggest recoding into a different variable name. If, for example, the original label is SI for Social Integration, the recoded label might be SICAT for Social Integration Categories. Next, *Sort* by SICAT. Then you can print out the student numbers in each of the three categories.

TABLE 7.3
A Procedure for Absolute Interpretations of an Individual Student s Scale Score

Step 1.	Determine the scale score corresponding with the neutral point of the underlying affective continuum. Simply add the minimum possible scale score to the maximum possible scale score, and divided by two. Thus, if the affective continuum ranges from 100 to 700, the sum would be 800, which when divided by 2 would yield 400. This (400) would be the scale score corresponding with the neutral point.
Step 2.	Calculate the standard error of measure. The formula is: $SEM = SD \sqrt{(1-r)}$ where SEM is the standard error of measure, SD is the standard deviation associated with the grand mean, and r is the reliability estimate (most often the alpha coefficient).
Step 3.	Add one standard error to the neutral point. Subtract one standard error from the neutral point. This defines the neutral range.
Step 4.	Interpret individual students scale scores as follows. If the score is above the neutral range, the affective is positive (or more positive). If the score is below the neutral range, the affect is negative (or more negative).Finally, if the score falls within the neutral range, the student is neutral or ambivalent.
Step 5.	Use individual item responses, where necessary and appropriate, to aid in the interpretation. Remember, the goal of interpretation is understanding.
Step 6.	If group interpretation is desirable, compute the frequencies within each of the three categories. SPSS can be used to facilitate this computation. Look at the overall frequency distribution to make general statements about the students.
Step 7.	If group interpretation is desirable, look for items on the scale that have relatively large numbers of 1s coded. These items can give useful clues as to the basis for the more negative overall scale scores.

INTERPRETING GROUP SCALE SCORES USING ABSOLUTE COMPARISONS

Once each student has been assigned to the proper category (i.e., positive, negative, or neutral), the frequencies within each category can be calculated (see Table 7.3). To do this using SPSS, you would select *Summarize*, then *Frequencies* within the *Statistics* menu. You may wish to compute separate frequencies for each class. In this case, you would Sort by Class before requesting the frequencies.

Table 7.4 summarizes the frequencies for the two classes. Only two students have a negative sense of belonging, both in Class 1. The vast majority of students, 36 in all, have a positive sense of belonging. The remaining 14 students are neutral or ambivalent about their sense of belonging.

We refer the reader back to Table 7.2 for a moment. In addition to examining the rows of this table (i.e., the students), we also can examine the columns (i.e., the items). One easy way of doing this is to look for responses in each column that are coded 1 (i.e., disagree). We have summarized the number of 1s for each item for each class at the bottom of the respective class data (just above the class mean and SD).

There are two items that elicit a fairly large amount of disagreement: Q29 (with a total of 16 students disagreeing) and Q24 (with a total of 11 students disagreeing). Q29 states, "My school is a place where I know people think a lot of me;" Q24 reads, "I am popular with other students." Both of these seem to tap the self-worth component of school belonging.

So what can we say about these two classes of students? The vast majority (almost 70%) have a positive sense of school belonging. Only two (less than 5%) have a negative sense of school belonging. Furthermore, the issues that seem to contribute to a more negative sense of school belonging have to with perceived self-worth (e.g., being popular, being well thought of by others).

INTERPRETING INDIVIDUAL STUDENT'S SCALE SCORES USING RELATIVE COMPARISONS

As mentioned earlier, relative comparisons involve interpreting students' scale scores in terms of the scale scores of other students to whom an affective instrument was administered. These other students can either be a large number of unspecified students (generally referred to as a *normative sample*) or members of groups with known or suspected characteristics (generally referred to as *known groups*). Both types of relative comparisons are useful.

TABLE 7.4

Frequencies of Scale Scores in each of the Interpretation Categories

	Class Number		
Interpretation Category	*Class 1*	*Class 2*	*Total*
Positive	15	21	36
Neutral	7	7	14
Negative	2	0	2

Comparisons With Normative Samples

Continuing with our QSL example, the normative sample would include the 52 students who completed the QSL, regardless of the classroom in which they were enrolled. We begin by generating a stem-and-leaf diagram for this sample of students (see Table 7.5). The stem consists of scale scores counting backward by 10s (e.g., 400, 390, 380, 370, etc.) down to the lowest scale score in the sample. The leaves are formed by indicating a scale score for each student who falls within the 10-point range. Consider, for example, the leaf:

330 88888.

This means that there were five students who had scale scores of 338 (330 + 8).

One way of interpreting individual student's scores is to divide the normative sample into quarters. Because in our example there are 52 students, there would be 13 students in each quarter. In Table 7.5 we have used underlining to differentiate the quarters. The top quarter of the students has scale scores ranging from 350 to 400. The next quarter has scale scores ranging from 310 to 349. The next quarter has scale scores ranging from 270 to 309. The lowest quarter has scale scores ranging from 138 to 269.

Now suppose a student has a scale score of 288. This student would be in the second-to-the-lowest quarter. The interpretation, then, would be that the student has a sense of school belonging that places him or her slightly below the average (technically, the median) student in the normative sample. Furthermore, because a quarter of the students have lower scale scores than he or she does, this student is not among the lowest students in terms of their school belonging.

Quite obviously, this is a very small normative sample. As a consequence, the scores differentiating among the four quarters are not likely to be particularly stable over time. As other students are administered the instrument, we would suggest they be added to the normative sample. This will enhance the reliability of the "cut scores," thereby increasing the accuracy of the interpretation. (Table 7.6 outlines the steps involved in interpreting scale scores using normative samples.)

Comparisons With Known Groups

In contrast to a single heterogeneous sample of students, known group comparisons involve multiple, somewhat homogeneous groups. Gen-

TABLE 7.5

Stem-and-Leaf Diagram for Student's Scale Scores

400	0 0 0 0
390	
380	8 8
370	5 5
360	3 3 3
350	0̲0̲0 0 0 0 0 0
340	
330	8 8 8 8 8
320	9
310	3̲3 3 3 3
300	0 0 0
290	
280	8 8 8
270	5 5 5
260	3 3
250	0 0 0
240	
230	8 8 8 8 8 8
220	
210	
200	
190	
180	
170	5
160	
150	
140	
130	8

erally, we would expect these groups to emerge when the validity of the affective instrument was being investigated and established. In the development of an questionnaire assessing attitude toward mathematics, for example, we may have hypothesized that high school students enrolled in advanced mathematics courses (Advanced Group) would have a more positive attitude than high school students enrolled in regular mathematics courses (Regular Group) who, in turn, would have a more positive attitude

TABLE 7.6

A Procedure for Relative Interpretation of Individual Student's Scale Scores Using a Normative Sample

Step 1	Prepare a stem-and-leaf diagram. SPSS can be used to do this. Within the Statistics menu, select Summarize, then Explore, then Plots. On the Plots screen, make sure that stem-and-leaf is checked.
Step 2	Divide the normative sample into four quarters. Again, SPSS can be useful in this regard. On the Explore screen (see Step 1) select Statistics and make sure that percentiles is checked. The 75th percentile differentiates the top quarter from the second quarter. The 50th percentile differentiates the second quarter from the third quarter. Finally, the 25th percentile differentiates the third quarter from the lowest quarter.
Step 3	Use quarter membership to interpret individual student's scale scores.

that high school students not currently enrolled in any mathematics class (No Math Group). When we computed the mean scale scores for the three groups we obtained the results shown in Table 7.7.

At first glance, the results seem to support our hypothesis. The mean scale scores for the three groups are in descending order: Advanced Group, 320; Regular Group, 284; No Math Group, 221. If we assume the underlying continuum ranges from 100 to 400, with a midpoint range of 223 to 277, then the Advanced Group students, on average, have a positive attitude, the Regular Group students, on average, have a slightly positive attitude, and the No Math Group students, on average, have a slightly negative attitude.

As part of the validation process and in light of the fact that the differences among the groups are in the predicted direction, the magnitude of these differences would likely have been examined. The question here becomes whether these differences are sufficiently large to aid in interpretation. There are two ways of answering this question. The first involves the concept of effect size, the second, the concept of statistically significant difference.

The concept of effect size (Glass, 1976) is used to describe the magnitude of differences between pairs of groups using a standard metric, namely, standard deviation units. The effect size is computed by dividing the difference between the two means by the SD of the total sample. In Table 7.7 the SD of the total sample is the SD reported in the bottom row, namely, 56. Comparing the Advanced Group with the Regular Group, then, the effect size is (320 -284) / 56 or about 0.64. That is, the mean scale score of Advanced Group students is almost two thirds of a SD higher than the mean scale score

TABLE 7.7

**Attitude Toward Mathematics Scale Scores for Three Groups
of High School Students**

Group	n	Mean	SD
Advanced	63	320	48
Regular	154	284	65
No Math	117	221	59
Total	334	269	56

of the Regular Group students. Comparing the Regular Group with the No Math Group, the effect size is (284-221) / 56 or about 1.12. Here, the mean scale score of the Regular Group is over one SD higher than the mean scale score of the No Math Group. When the Advanced Group and No Math Group are compared, the effect size is a whopping 1.77. Along with Cohen (1977), we would argue that these differences are sufficiently large to allow meaningful comparisons to be made.[5]

Now that we know that groups are sufficiently different, how do we go about interpreting individual student's scale scores? Suppose a student, Benjamin, has a scale score of 290. His scale score is closest to the Regular Group mean than it is to the other two groups. Thus, Benjamin is considered to have an attitude toward mathematics similar to that of the members of the Regular Group. And, who are the members of this group? They are students who tend to enroll in regular mathematics courses in high school. So, Benjamin has an attitude toward mathematics similar to students who enroll in regular mathematics courses (as opposed to advanced mathematics courses or no mathematics courses) in high school.

We can interpret Benjamin's scale score in another way. In this case, we note that the mean scale score of the Regular Group is slightly positive; consequently, Benjamin has a slightly positive attitude toward mathematics. Notice that this more expanded interpretation is based on two pieces of information: Benjamin's placement into a group and the position of the group along the underlying affective continuum. More will be said about expanded interpretations later in this chapter. (Table 7.8 outlines the steps involved in interpreting scale scores using known groups.)

---

[5]You can also examine the statistical significance of the differences. SPSS makes this job quite easy. Within the *Statistics* menu, your first selection *Compare Means* and then *One-Way Anova*. If there are two groups, you can select *Independent Samples T-Test* instead of *One-Way Anova*. If *One-Way Anova* is selected, be sure you also select appropriate descriptive statistics on the *One-Way Anova* screen (e.g. means, SDs).

TABLE 7.8

A Procedure for Relative Interpretation of Individual Student's Scale Scores Using Known Groups

Step 1	Identify several groups whose members are believed to differ in terms of the affective characteristic or affect–target combination being assessed.
Step 2	Compute the mean scale scores and SDs for each group.
Step 3	Compare the mean scale scores among the groups using the concept of effect size or statistical significance.
Step 4	If the mean scores do not differ as expected, return to Step 1, and select new groups. If the mean scores do differ as expected, prepare a table like Table 7.7.
Step 5	Select the student whose scale score you wish to interpret. Assign that student to the group whose mean scale score is closest to his or hers.
Step 6	Interpret the student's score either by:
	a. Using the label assigned to the group (e.g., students who tend to enroll in regular mathematics courses, rather than advance mathematics courses or no mathematics courses at all); or
	b. indicating where the group to which the student is assigned falls on the underlying affective continuum (e.g., students who tend to have slightly positive attitudes toward mathematics).

INTERPRETING GROUP SCALE SCORES USING RELATIVE COMPARISONS

This will be a very short section because the procedures used to interpret group scale scores using relative comparisons are identical to those used to interpret individual student's scale scores. That is, the difference is not in the procedures; the difference is in what might be called the *unit of comparison*. To illustrate, we refer the reader back to Table 7.5. The data entered in this table are individual student's scale scores. In the case of interpreting group data, however, the data would be group mean scale scores.

As mentioned in chapter 6, for example, the QSL was administered to over 3,000 students at 34 elementary schools. Suppose we are interested in making sense of the students in Elementary School K; to see how they stack up against students in the other 33 elementary schools. We would calculate mean scale scores for all 34 elementary schools. Then we would place these mean scale scores (rather than individual student's scale scores) in a stem-and-leaf distribution. We would next separate the schools into (roughly) quarters based on their mean scale scores. For example, there might be eight in the top and bottom quarters and nine in the middle two quarters. Once done, the same interpretations can be made for schools as for individual students.

We could say, for example, that based on the mean scale score, Elementary School K is in the second-to-the-lowest quarter of all elementary schools in the district. That is, the students' sense of belonging in this school is slightly below the average of the other elementary schools in the district. However, because another quarter of the elementary schools have lower mean scale scores, this school is not among the lowest in terms of students' sense of school belonging.

The same reasoning can be applied to the interpretation of group data relative to known groups. For example, the students' sense of belonging in Elementary School K is similar to that found in other elementary schools serving the same socioeconomic population of students. Alternatively, the students' sense of belonging in Elementary School K is similar to that found in elementary schools in which students are actively engaged in out-of-school activities and have high levels of parental involvement in the schools.

THE BENEFITS OF MULTIPLE INTERPRETATIONS

The interpretations made on the basis of absolute and relative comparisons are likely to be somewhat different, largely because the comparisons themselves are different. Comparisons with the neutral point of the underlying affective continuum are not the same as comparisons involving a large heterogeneous group that, in turn, is not the same as comparisons involving multiple, homogeneous groups with known or suspected qualities or characteristics. Rather than this being a reason for concern, however, we view it as an opportunity for greater understanding.

Let us consider an example that emphasizes the importance of multiple comparisons in enhancing interpretation. Suppose a 15-item, traditional Likert scale is designed to assess the extent to which students value education. The responses to each statement are coded from 1 (strongly disagree) to 4 (strongly agree). Furthermore, suppose the instrument is administered to a sample of 2,000 young adults (ages 16–21). The total sample is divided into four known groups:

- High school dropouts (n = 150);
- Students still in high school (n = 1,350);
- Students who have graduated and are in the work force (n = 300); and
- Students who have graduated and are currently enrolled in college (n = 200).

The hypothesis, which is confirmed by the data collected, is that the scale scores will increase as we move from the high school dropouts (mean scale score = 180) to current high school students (mean scale score = 230) to currently employed high school graduates (mean scale score = 275) to current college enrollees (mean scale score = 330). Assume that the effect sizes are large and the differences between each pair of groups is statistically significant.

Now let us consider Jo Terry, a high school graduate who has a scale score of 267 (assuming minimum and maximum scale scores 100 and 400, respectively, and a neutral range from 220 to 270). We begin by comparing her scale score with the underlying affective continuum, an absolute comparison. Because her scale score lies in the neutral range, we would say she is somewhat ambivalent about the value of education.

When (relative) comparisons are made with the total sample, her scale score of 267 places her in the upper quarter (i.e., as one of the top 500 scores). Based on this comparison, we would say she values education quite a bit—certainly relatively more than the other young adults in the sample.

Turning our attention to the four groups, we note that her scale score is closest to the mean for the high school graduates currently in the workforce. So we can say that she values education as much as the typical high school graduate who is currently working.

So we have three somewhat different interpretations of how much value Jo Terry attaches to education. She is ambivalent about it; she attaches relatively more value to education than young adults her age; she attaches as much value to education as high school graduates who are not attending college and are currently working. Which is the real Jo Terry? They all are.

Consider, for example, there are 500 high school graduates in the total sample. Also, notice that because of the increase in scale scores across groups, these high school graduates, on average, have higher scale scores than the other two groups (i.e., those still in high school and those who have dropped out). Consider also that the normative sample is weighted toward students currently in high school. Thus, it is not surprising that her scale score is quite high relative to the normative sample. In fact, given the normative sample, this relative interpretation is probably an overestimate of the extent to which she values education.

The other two interpretations are actually quite consistent. Absolutely speaking, she falls within the neutral range, although near the upper end (267 vs. 270). Relatively speaking, the mean scale score of the group of "school graduates now working" lies just beyond the neutral range (275 vs. 270). When all is said and done, then, we conclude that Jo Terry is either ambivalent about the value of education or attaches a slightly positive value to education. This seems the most reasonable interpretation when all the information is considered.

In this example, then, the use of multiple comparisons produces a far better interpretation than would be possible making any one comparison. In fact, using multiple comparisons not only helps us better understand the extent to which Jo Terry values education, but also the extent to which the members of the entire normative sample and the various subgroups value education.

A CLOSING COMMENT

In this chapter we suggest that interpreting affective data involves making comparisons. We discuss several comparisons that can aid in interpreting the data, both individual and group, and we set out procedures for using each comparison to interpret the data. It is important to point out that these comparisons and procedures are simply interpretation aids. That is, they facilitate proper interpretation of affective data.

At the same time, however, we are quick to point out that it is people, not procedures, that make sense of data. As a consequence, a person can use a correct interpretative procedure and still make an incorrect interpretation. An appropriate interpretation becomes more likely, however, when multiple comparisons are made, and the person making the interpretation is well grounded in the affect–target combination being assessed and the instrument used to assess it.

SUMMARY OF MAJOR POINTS

1. Interpretation means making sense of the data or making the data meaningful. In general, data are made meaningful by comparing them with what we already know and understand.
2. Two types of comparisons can aid in the interpretation of affective data. The first comparisons based on the underlying affective continuum. These are referred to as absolute comparisons. The second are comparisons based on affective data obtained by administering the scale to groups of students. These are relative comparisons.
3. When making absolute comparisons, the neutral point of the affective continuum is identified, and a neutral range is established by taking into consideration the standard error of measure. Three categories of scales are thereby formed: one lying above the neutral range, one lying below the neutral range, and the other being the neutral range itself. These categories aid in interpretation (see Table 7.3).
4. There are two approaches used to make relative comparisons. The first involves a large, heterogeneous group of students (i.e., compari-

sons with a normative sample; see Table 7.6). The second involves a set of generally smaller, homogeneous groups that are believed to differ in their mean scale scores (i.e., comparisons with known groups; see Table 7.8).

5. There are problems inherent in the interpretations based on any single comparison. For example, the appropriateness of absolute comparisons depends in part on the meaning attached to the neutral point of the scale and the extent of the empirical validity of the scale. Similarly, the appropriateness of relative comparisons rests on the comprehensiveness of the normative sample, the accuracy of the beliefs held about the various known groups, and the extent to which the known groups have different scale scores.

6. Consequently, the interpretations derived from different comparisons are likely to be somewhat different because the comparisons themselves are different. Therefore, it is likely that the best interpretations will result when comparisons are made.

7. In interpreting data pertaining to groups of students, the same comparisons are appropriate. What changes is the unit of comparison. Units such as classrooms or schools replace the individual student.

8. The comparisons and procedures described in this chapter are best considered as interpretive aids. The quality of interpretation depends to a large extent on the person or persons making the interpretation: what that person or those persons know about the students, the affect–target combination, and the affective instrument being used.

8
Affective Assessment and School Improvement: So What?

This book begins with a rationale for considering and assessing affective characteristics. In chapters 2 through 7 the focus turns toward definitional concerns, the selection and design of good, affective instruments, and the analysis and interpretation of affective data. The purpose of this final chapter is to discuss the potential uses of affective information for school improvement. This chapter is divided into four major sections, each corresponding with a problem area in which the results of affective assessment can be used productively: motivating students, designing learning environments, building character, and considering affective consequences.

MOTIVATING STUDENTS

Motivation can be described, or motivation can be explained. Descriptively, motivation refers to the time and effort students are willing to spend learning or trying to learn. It is this definition of motivation that causes teachers to cry out, "My students aren't motivated!" That is, the teacher wonders why his or her students do not spend the time and effort they need to spend in order to learn or learn well. This is often followed by a second question, "Why?" The poser of the why question seeks an explanation for the perceived lack of motivation. "Aren't they interested? Don't they care?" The very nature of such why questions suggests the primary causes of poor motivation are affective (e.g., interest, attitude).

Several studies have confirmed the affect–motivation link that exists in teachers' minds. Keith, Wetherbee, and Kindzia (1995), for example, conducted a study of the way in which middle school teachers described motivated students. In general, the teachers perceived that students who were motivated believed that school was important (value), loved school and loved learning (attitude), and had high educational aspirations (value).

One of the most widely accepted theories of motivation, the *expectancy x value* theory (Feather, 1982), also affirms the affect-motivation connection. In simplest terms, the theory asserts that the amount of time and effort people will spend on a task (i.e., their degree of motivation) is a product of two factors. The first is the extent to which they **expect to be able to perform the task successfully** if they apply themselves; the second is the extent to which they **value participation** in the task itself or they **value the benefits or rewards** that successful task completion will bring to them. The first factor is known as *self-efficacy*, in the vernacular a "can do attitude." As defined by Weiner (1992) self-efficacy pertains to a "person's belief in his or her capability of performing a behavior required to reach a goal" (p. 861). Within the context of the expectancy × value theory, in order to motivate students to learn, "teachers must both help them to appreciate the value of academic activities and make sure they can achieve success on these activities if they apply reasonable effort" (Brophy, 1987, p. 41).

Consistent with this theory, Brophy (1987) developed a list of 33 principles that are related to motivating students to learn. These principles, listed in Table 8.1, are divided into five categories: essential preconditions, motivating by maintaining success expectations, motivating by supplying extrinsic incentives, motivating by capitalizing on students' intrinsic motivation, and stimulating student motivation to learn. We call the reader's attention to the fifth and final category. The majority of these principles incorporate affective characteristics.

With respect to the fourth category, motivating by capitalizing on students' intrinsic motivation, Brophy (1987) stated the following: "Intrinsic motivation usually refers to the affective aspects of motivation—liking for or enjoyment of an activity" (p. 41). Thus, the vast majority of the principles included in Table 8.1 either directly embody affective characteristics or are indirectly linked with the affective aspects of motivation.

Brophy (1987) referred to the principles in Table 8.1 as a "'starter set' of strategies to select from in planning motivation elements to include in instruction" (p. 48). The question facing teachers, then, is how to make proper selections. This is where we believe affective assessment enters the picture. In this regard, we would offer a six-step procedure (see Table 8.2). The procedure begins with the identification of unmotivated students, includes a relatively short instrument to collect data on four of the more promising affective characteristics, moves to the selection and implementation of one or more motivational principles based on the data, and ends with an evaluation of whether the motivational strategy was effective.

Understanding students' affective characteristics and using that understanding in modifying teaching practices can go along way toward motivating initially unmotivated students. In this regard, there is substantial evidence that motivation is an alterable, malleable characteristic of students, rather than a stable, static characteristic (Keller, 1994).

Before we move to the next section, a caveat is in order. Educators must avoid falling into two traps. The first is focusing on the affective aspects of motivation at the expense of learning. The second trap is believing that affect is a necessary condition for motivation.[1] Brophy (1987) summarized these pitfalls well:

> Intrinsic motivation, even for academic activities, does not necessarily imply motivation to learn. For example, students may enjoy participating in an educational game without trying to derive any academic benefit from it. Similarly, students can try to learn the knowledge or skills that an activity is designed to teach without enjoying the activity. (p. 41)

Motivating students requires that teachers use affective assessment data and make decisions. As Weiner (1992) pointed out: "Motivational research has been hindered because of an unrealistic expectation that a cookbook can be provided telling educators how to motivate their students. This is not possible; the equivalent of putting a 'man on the moon' for the field of motivation is not forthcoming" (p. 864).

DESIGNING CLASSROOM LEARNING ENVIRONMENTS

In the almost 20 years since the publication of the original edition of this book, a substantial body of research has been generated pertaining to effective classroom learning environments. Drawing largely from the theoetical

---

[1] There are cases, in fact, where educators have equated motivation with affect. An example can be found in Goodenow and Grady (1993) where the School Motivation Scale, consisting of four items, is defined in terms of school being satisfying, worthwhile, and important, rather than boring and irrelevant. This is particularly important because school motivation is the dependent variable of the study.

TABLE 8.1

A Summary of Principles Related to Motivating Students to Learn

Essential Preconditions
1. Supporting environment.
2. Appropriate level of challenge–difficulty.
3. Meaningful learning objectives.
4. Moderation/optimal use.

Motivating by Maintaining Success Expectations
5. Program for success.
6. Teach goal setting, performance appraisal, and self-reinforcement.
7. Help students to recognize linkages between effort and outcome.
8. Provide remedial socialization (to help overcome initial failure).

Motivating by Supplying Extrinsic Incentives
9. Offer rewards for good (or improved) performance.
10. Structure appropriate competition.
11. Call attention to the instrumental value of academic activities (i.e., utility).

Motivating by Capitalizing on Students' Intrinsic Motivation
12. Adapt tasks to students' interests.
13. Include novelty/variety elements.
14. Allow opportunities to make choices or autonomous decisions.
15. Provide opportunities for students to respond actively.
16. Provide immediate feedback to student responses.
17. Allow students to create finished products.
18. Include fantasy or simulation elements.
19. Incorporate game-like features.
20. Include higher level objectives and divergent questions.
21. Provide opportunities to interact with peers.
22. Model interest in learning and motivation to learn.
23. Communicate desirable expectations and attributions about students' motivation to learn.
24. Minimize students' performance anxiety during learning activities.
25. Project intensity.
26. Project enthusiasm.
27. Induce task interest or appreciation.
28. Induce curiosity or suspense.
29. Induce dissonance or cognitive conflict.
30. Make abstract content more personal, concrete, or familiar.
31. Induce students to generate their own motivation to learn.
32. State learning objectives and provide advance organizers.
33. Model task-related thinking and problem solving.

TABLE 8.2

A Procedure for Selecting Motivational Principles

Step 1   Identify the unmotivated students. This can be done through informal or systematic observation coupled with conversations with other teachers. The conversations with other teachers would help you determine whether the problem is situation specific (i.e., a state) or more general (i.e., a trait).

Step 2   Administer a relatively short affective instrument to the entire class*, finding a way to identify group membership (i.e., motivated vs. unmotivated) while ensuring students individual anonymity. Using different fonts or colors of paper may be one way to do this. The instrument should include separate scales for interest, expectations, attributions, and value. If the problem is situation specific the targets may be include the subject, the class, and–or the teacher. If the problem is more general, the targets must be more general (e.g., academic subjects, school, and–or teachers-in-general). With four affective characteristics and, say, three targets, the entire instrument should be no longer than 48 items (i.e., 12 scales × four items per scale).

Step 3   Compute scale means for the two groups. Compare these means looking for differences that are substantial, statistically different, or both. Substantial may mean a mean difference of at least one third of an aggregated SD. Statistically significant differences may be difficult to find with such small sample sizes.

Step 4   Once substantial or statistically significant differences are found, look through the principles in Table 8.2 to identify those more closely associated with the affective characteristic represented by the scale.

Step 5   Develop a strategy for implementing the principles with the entire class, focusing on the subgroup as necessary and appropriate. (Even the motivated students may benefit from the strategy.)

Step 6   After some period of time (e.g., 6 weeks, 9 weeks, one semester), re-administer the affective instrument, this time looking for substantial or statistically significant increases in scores of the originally unmotivated students.

*Multiple classes or an entire school can be used in place of a single class if the motivational problem extends beyond a single classroom.

and empirical work of Moos (1979) and Walberg (1968), Fraser and his colleagues (e.g., Fraser et al., 1995) argued that three general dimensions are sufficient to conceptualize all human environments. These dimensions are:

- Relationships (i.e., the nature and intensity of social relationships);
- System maintenance and system change (i.e., the extent to which the environment is orderly, clear in expectation, maintains control, and is responsive to change); and,
- Personal development (i.e., opportunities for personal growth and self-enhancement).

Fraser and his colleagues (Fraser et al., 1995) developed and validated several learning environment measures and conducted numerous large-scale studies using these instruments. Across these studies a set of four components of generally effective classroom learning environments have emerged: cohesiveness (the relationship dimension), goal direction and organization–rule clarity (the maintenance and change dimension), and satisfaction (the personal development dimension). (As an aside, it is striking how similar these components are to the qualities students have long associated with "good" teachers. As summarized by Klausmeier and Goodwin (1971), five adjectives are used consistently by students to describe their most admired and successful teachers. They are social, friendly, knowledgeable, businesslike, and enthusiastic.)

Cohesiveness refers to a feeling of togetherness among students in the classroom as well as between students and the teacher. Students believe that they genuinely care for one another and are willing to help one another as the need arises. Similarly, students believe the teacher is concerned about their welfare and their learning.

Goal Direction refers to the extent to which students believe that there is an academic purpose in their classroom and are aware that a large proportion of the classroom time is devoted to that purpose. *Clear academic focus* and *task orientation* are phrases often used to denote these two parts of goal direction. In combination with cohesiveness, goal direction produces classrooms that can be described as businesslike, yet warm and friendly (Anderson et al., 1989).

Organization–Rule Clarity refers to a perception on the part of students that the classroom is a structured learning environment. Structure is established through the establishment and communication of clear rules, and the use of procedures that routinize many of the classroom activities (e.g., taking roll, passing out and collecting materials, making transitions between activities). Classrooms with a structured organization are characterized by a large proportion of class time devoted to instruction and learning.

Satisfaction refers to the degree to which students are pleased with the classroom environment. More importantly, they enjoy being in the classroom and believe the time they spend there is worthwhile.

Operating from a different theoretical perspective, Finn (1989) posited an *identification-participation model* to account for school withdrawal among at-risk students. In essence, the model suggests that unless students identify with the school to at least some extent, feel they belong as part of the school, and believe themselves to be welcomed, respected, and valued by others, they may begin the gradual disengagement process of which officially dropping out is the final step. In simplest terms, all students, particularly those considered at-risk, need a sense of belonging. Although *sense of belonging* has been used primarily to refer to school membership (Wehlage, 1989), it seems equally applicable to the classroom.

At first blush, the applicability of these findings to the classroom seems quite straightforward. Teachers should create classrooms that are cohesive, are goal directed, are well organized with clear rules, and promote student satisfaction and a sense of belonging. Unfortunately, there are two problems with such direct application of these findings. The first is that these are students' perceptions of or beliefs about their classrooms. This is a reality that external observers, let alone teachers, cannot describe or document in objective terms. The second problem is related to the first. Because these are beliefs and perceptions, not all students see their classrooms in the same way. This second problem has been recognized only fairly recently by some researchers (e.g., see Fraser et al., 1995).

Hence, there is once again the need for affective assessment. Fortunately, there are several available instruments that can provide the needed information. The three "granddaddies" are the My Class Inventory (Fraser et al., 1982), the Learning Environment Inventory (Fraser et al., 1982), and the Classroom Environment Inventory (Moos & Trickett, 1987). In recent years, more focused instruments have become available (e.g., The Science Laboratory Environment Inventory; Fraser et al., 1993) as have instruments based on different philosophical assumptions about learning (e.g., The Constructivist Learning Environment Inventory; Taylor, Fraser, & Fisher, 1997). Also, the Psychological Sense of School Membership Scale (Goodenow & Grady, 1995) can be altered fairly easily to focus on the classroom rather than the school. The same is true of the QSL questionnaire described in chapter 6.

In light of the availability of appropriate and technically acceptable instruments, we suggest the following procedure for those educators interested in improving the quality of classroom learning environments (see Table 8.3). The procedure begins by assessing students' perceptions of their preferred learning environment and their beliefs about their current classroom environment using one of the existing instruments. Research studies increasingly suggest that students achieve more when there is a greater congruence between the actual classroom environment and that preferred by students (Fraser et al., 1995). The next step is to have the teacher complete the instrument, focusing on the current learning environment as he or she sees it. The third step is to compare these three sets of perceptions. The comparison between the students' preferred and actual learning environments provides data as to the fit between the environment and the student. The comparison of students' beliefs about the learning environment with the teacher's provides useful insights into the validity of the teacher's point of view. In other words, teachers benefit by looking at the classroom through the eyes of the students.

The availability of learning environment instruments makes it possible for teachers to obtain convenient, reliable information about their classrooms as perceived by their students. This information can be used by teachers as a basis for reflection upon, discussion of, and systematic attempts to improvement classroom environments (Fraser, Anderson, & Walberg, 1982).

TABLE 8.3

Procedure for Improving the Classroom Learning Environment

Step 1	Select an appropriate learning environment instrument and administer it to a class of students. If possible, find an instrument that requires students to express their opinions of both their preferred or ideal environment and the actual classroom learning environment.If such an instrument cannot be found, then administer the same instrument twice, changing the directions from the first time to the second.If the directions on the instrument pertain to the actual learning environment, modify them to refer to the preferred or ideal learning environment (and vice versa).
Step 2	As teacher, complete the actual learning environment (as opposed to the preferred or ideal) portion or form of the instrument.
Step 3	Compare students' actual and preferred or ideal perceptions, looking for discrepancies. Similarly, compare students' perceptions of the actual learning environment with teacher's perceptions of the actual learning environment, again looking for discrepancies.
Step 4	Based on these comparisons, identify those components or dimensions of the classroom learning environment that require change.
Step 5	Share the results of the study with the students, indicate the components that you (the teacher) believe need to be changed, and ask for their insights into the specific changes that need to be made.
Step 6	Decide on the changes that will be made and implement them.

BUILDING CHARACTER

Character is the "configuration of mental, moral, and emotional traits that make up the essence of who [we] are.... A person's character [consists of] the basic beliefs or moral values that guide decisions and action" (Schubert, 1997, p.17). "Qualities of *good* character are called virtues" (Lickona, 1997, p. 46; emphasis ours).

During the 1990s, there has been a renewed interest in the development of character in our students in our schools.[2] In response to this interest, a plethora of character education programs have been developed. Examples include the Center for the 4th and 5th Rs (Respect and Responsibility) Program (Lickona, 1997), the Child Development Project (Watson et al., 1998), the Just Community program (Power & Higgins, 1992), and Literature-Based Character Education (Gibbs & Earley, 1994; Steller & Lambert, 1996).

Although these programs have different emphases and different ways of teaching character, they share numerous qualities. Virtually all of the programs, for example,

- Focus on virtues or core values. Examples include compassion, fairness, honesty, loyalty, respect, and responsibility.
- Establish a caring classroom community. Virtues or core values are the operative norms within the classroom. It is up to the teacher to guide the formation of virtues or core values that are in harmony with those of the wider society. Students must be taught ways of resolving conflicts without resorting to force or intimidation.
- Expect teachers to be moral mentors. The teacher serves as a moral model. The teacher's authority does not come from his or her being an adult or holding an office; rather, the teacher's influence comes from the group itself.
- Operate on the basis of moral discipline. The collective norms represent the constraining force of discipline (Durkheim, 1925). Rules should be established in a way that enables students to see the values behind the rules. To the extent possible, authentic rather than contrived consequences should be used to enforce the rules. Students should learn to follow rules because "it's the right thing to do."
- Create a democratic classroom environment. Students are involved, consistent with their developmental level, in shared decision making

---

[2]Character education is quite different from other approaches to character development (e.g., values clarification, moral development) that were in vogue when the first edition of this book was published. "Values clarification and moral development approaches (promote) decision-making rather than good habits, autonomy rather than respect for authority, and relativism rather than the traditional values" (Power & Khmelkov, 1998, p. 539).

that increases their responsibility for making the classroom a good place to be.

- Help students engage in *ethical reflection*. Ethical reflection implies respecting the perspective of others, reasoning morally, and building a capacity for self-criticism. Many of the literature-based programs use literary works to help students in this endeavor.

Character education programs are consistent with the principles of social constructivist theory. According to social constructivist theory, the "best way to alter students' affect in the classroom is to alter the norms that prevail in the classroom.... Efforts aimed at individual students miss the point" (Prawat & Anderson, 1994, p. 213).

So how does affective assessment "fit into" programs intent on building character? The results of affective assessment can be used to evaluate the effectiveness of the programs in achieving their goals, and improve the programs by identifying weaknesses that subsequently can be strengthened. In this regard, we would offer the eight-step procedure shown in Table 8.4.

The first step is to define what is meant by a person of character. In developing their literature-based character education program, Steller and Lambert (1996) asked the question, "What is a moral person?" Their answer was as follows:

A morally mature person habitually respects human dignity, demonstrates active responsibility for the welfare of others, integrates individual interests and social responsibility, demonstrates integrity, applies moral responsibili-

TABLE 8.4

A Procedure for Using Affective Assessment with Attempts to Build Character

Step 1	Define a person of character (i.e., the desired end result).
Step 2	Select a program or develop a strategy that attempts to develop that type of person.
Step 3	Select or design an affective assessment instrument that is appropriate for evaluating the effectiveness of the program or strategy.
Step 4	Administer the affective assessment instrument prior to the start of program or strategy implementation.
Step 5	Implement the program or strategy.
Step 6	Re-administer the affective assessment instrument.
Step 7	Compare the results for Step 6 with those from Step 4, looking not only for overall changes but changes on specific aspects or components.
Step 8	Use the data from Step 7 to make revisions in the program or strategy.

ties when making choices and judgments, and seeks peaceful resolution of conflict. (p. 27)

The second step involves selecting or designing a program or strategy that seeks to develop that kind of person. The process of selecting a program has been made easier by the sheer increase in the number of programs that have been developed over the 1990s. Nonetheless, educators still might not find the program they are seeking. In describing their program, Steller and Lambert (1996), for example, advocated the development of a program unique to the needs of a school or district. "Though packaged character education programs do exist—and we have looked into them—our program is a collection of initiatives, some homegrown, that we've adopted over the years" (p. 25).

The third step calls for the selection or design of an affective assessment instrument. Unfortunately, but as might be expected, there seem to be far fewer affective assessment instruments focused on character development than there are character education programs. There are, however, a few affective assessment instruments that are worthy of a look. Among them are:

- *The Moral Development Test* (Ma, 1989). The Moral Orientation scale may be particularly relevant. It measures one's tendency to gratify psychological needs and to perform altruistic acts toward others.
- *The Moral Values Questionnaire* (Francis & Greer, 1992). The primary value of this instrument is in its ease of modification to include core values or virtues unique to particular programs.
- *The Defining Issues Test* (Rest, 1979). This is one of the older affective assessment instruments related to moral development. It focuses not only on what is believed to be the "right" thing to do but on the reasoning behind the decision made by the students.
- *Survey of Interpersonal Values* (Gordon, 1960). This instrument assesses the relative importance of six values: support, conformity, recognition, independence, benevolence, and leadership. These values are associated with the way in which people relate to one another.
- *Moral Judgment Test* (Lind & Wakenhut, 1985). This instrument has been used fairly extensively in international research studies. It yields a score of a student's moral competence.

The next three steps (4, 5, and 6) involve administering the affective assessment instrument, implementing the program, and re-administering the affective assessment instrument. Step 7 requires a comparison to be made between the data obtained from the two administrations. This comparison should focus both on an overall comparison (i.e., total scale score) as well as individual virtues or core values (if the chosen affective instrument provides such data). The final step (8) involves using the data from Step 7 to make revisions in the program, either its design or its implementation.

There are some educators who believe that building character is not a goal of schooling and, further, that it should not be goal. These educators would argue that consensus on values prohibits it from being so. To address these concerns, we end this section with two quotations. This pertains to the issue of *is*; the second, to that of *should be*.

> There are numerous examples of values that are more or less uniformly imparted by way of general public and professional consensus. Schools teach that work and effort are good.... Students are urged to be polite, respectful, and obedient to adults in general and school personnel in particular. They are taught.... that those who flaunt the rules and expectations deserve to be punished.... Schools teach that time is valuable; tardiness, absences, and missed deadlines are considered offenses. Students are taught to do things they may not wish to do and are taught that this is a good thing. (Purpel, 1997, p. 145)

> Whenever community is emphasized, character education will be important. As Philip Selznick puts it, "we look to virtue and character as the foundations of morality (Selznick, 1992, p. 34)." (Noddings, 1997, p. 8)

AFFECTIVE CONSEQUENCES

> I would like to see teachers set forth several important affective objectives each year and, having done so, deliberately devote a modest amount of instructional time to the pursuit of those outcomes. Affective goals should not simply be endorsed verbally by school officials at a start-of-school orientation for educators and then be forgotten about. Deliberate instructional efforts should be focused on the attainment of affective goals." (Popham, 1994, p. 408)

Although we agree wholeheartedly with Popham's sentiments, we believe that teachers also must be cognizant of unintended affective outcomes—what we refer to as affective consequences. Most educators agree that the cognitive–affective separation is somewhat contrived. As illustrated throughout this book, there are cognitive elements inherent in affective definitions and instruments. Similarly, there are affective consequences of cognitive learning, in particular, and schooling, in general.

This assertion is quite easy to support. Few teachers would be pleased if their students learned to read, but hated reading as a result of the reading material assigned or the way in which reading was taught. Similar examples can be given in virtually all subject matters at virtually every grade or school level. There are two areas in which concerns for affective consequences are particularly important: the promotion of self-esteem and the influence of the latent curriculum.

The Enhancement of Self Esteem

Self-esteem has become a "favorite son" among many educators, including those working in the area of affective assessment. Messick (1979), for example, wrote:

> Attitudes toward the self, especially the self as a learner, are important educationally as both instrumental and outcome variables and have been widely examined under the rubric of self-concept or academic self-concept…. The enhancement of self-concept is generally viewed as a central educational objective, especially for the disadvantaged. (p. 285)

Popham (1994) was even more enthusiastic in his endorsement:

> For me, one of the most important affective goals is the promotion of students' positive self-esteem. If our schools were to do a dazzling job in all cognitive realms, yet allow students to regard themselves as unworthy, I think the schools would have failed. A person's self-esteem is such a potent determinant of that individual's future happiness, it is a variable I would like to see educators tackle with fervor. (p. 407)

We too believe that self-esteem is important. However, we would temper our enthusiasm with the caveat that self-esteem is best seen as an affective consequence, rather than an affective goal. In our terminology, an affective goal is something teachers work toward directly. Building character is a worthy, affective goal. In contrast, an affective consequence is something that one attempts to influence indirectly. It occurs as a result of the attainment of a related goal, one that teachers address directly. Academic self-esteem occurs as the result of academic success (i.e., cognitive learning). Stated somewhat differently, academically successful students tend to develop more positive academic self-esteem, whereas academically unsuccessful students tend to develop less positive academic self-esteem (e.g., see Kifer, 1975). Furthermore, because success is actually perceived success, students must be aware of their attainment of success and must be helped to achieve success. Thus, any instructional program that increases the frequency with which students achieve academic success and makes students aware of what constitutes real success is likely to contribute to the development of positive academic self-esteem in students.

Working toward the raising of academic self-esteem independent of having students achieve academic success is likely to lead to an interesting paradox, one nicely illustrated by the results of the Third International

Mathematics and Science Study (TIMSS). At the majority of tested grade levels, the U.S. students scored in the middle of the pack or lower. At the same time, the attitudes toward mathematics of the U.S. students at these same grade levels ranked near the top of the countries that participated in the studies. One of the weekly news magazines in the United States summarized the results with the following headline: "Feeling good about doing bad."

We must teach our children well, not help them feel better about learning poorly. Such is the danger of seeing self-esteem as an affective goal.

The Effect of the Latent Curriculum

For the past 25 years, sociologists (e.g., Dreeben, 1968; Overly, 1970) have differentiated between the stated goals and the implicit goals of a curriculum. The term *manifest curriculum* has been used to refer to the stated goals, whereas the term *latent curriculum* has been used to refer to the implicit goals.

What are some of these implicit goals? In a discussion of the manifest and latent curricula Bloom (1981) suggested the following implicit goals:

> Schools teach much about time, order, neatness, promptness, and docility in this latent curriculum. Students learn to value each other and themselves in terms of the answers they give and the products they produce in school. Students learn how to compete with their age mates in school and the consequences of an academic and social pecking order. (p.343)

And what does the latent curriculum have to do with affective assessment? Bloom continued:

> Schools can and do have considerable effects on both the cognitive and affective aspects of the manifest curriculum. But to judge the effects of schools only in terms of the manifest curriculum is to ignore a great range of other influences resulting from the ways in which we have organized and the processes involved in schooling. (p. 344)

We should examine the consequences of the latent curriculum. And, because the majority of these consequences are affective in nature, affective assessment should contribute to that examination. Why is this assessment so crucial? "Where the manifest and the latent curricula are in conflict, one would expect the latent curricula to become dominant. It is not what we talk about but what we do that becomes important" (Bloom, 1981, p. 343). If the two curricula are in conflict and we assess only the manifest curriculum, we are missing a large portion of the impact of schools on students.

As described by Bloom (1981), most of the affective characteristics associated with the latent curriculum are values. Thus, instruments assessing values are the most relevant. Existing instruments assessing values tend to focus on values that are goals of schools, rather than consequences (e.g., Eccles, Adler, & Moore, 1984). The format of these instruments, however, is quite reasonable; modifications in the content of the items can be made to reflect values inherent in the latent curriculum. For example, one of the items on the instrument used in the Eccles et al. study asked, "How valuable do you think your education will be in getting the job you want?" For neatness, the item can be worded, "How important do you think it is to keep your desk and work area clean and tidy?"

CONCLUSION

In this chapter, we have addressed the "so what?" question. That is, even if we can, in fact, assess affective characteristics, why would we want to do that? In response to that question we have argued that affective characteristics hold the key to solving some of the major problems or issues confronting educators today. Motivating students requires some understanding of student affect. Designing and operating effective classroom environments require that educators know something about the kinds of classroom environments students prefer and how they (the students) perceive the current classroom environment. Building character requires attention be paid to core values and virtues, both of which lie within the affective realm. Finally, even when focused on the cognitive domain, educators should be aware of the affective consequences of how students are taught, how they learn, and how well they learn.

In retrospect, all of these individual problems are related to a single overriding one, namely, the improvement of schooling. Ultimately, affective assessment can help to make schools more effective in accomplishing their goals and more satisfying places to live and work. Can this be accomplished? At least it is worth a serious attempt.

SUMMARY OF MAJOR POINTS

1. Affective assessment is likely to be useful in solving problems in four primary areas: motivating students, designing classroom learning environments, building students' character, and examining affective consequences of instructional activities and learning (or failing to learn).

2. Most of the explanations of poor motivation are affective in nature. Thus, being aware of students' affective characteristics or affect–tar-

get combinations may be helpful in both understanding and improving student motivation.

3. Over the past 25 years, researchers have concluded that it is the students' perceptions of their classroom learning environments, not objective descriptions of these environments that are important to understanding and improving student learning. Assessing students' perceptions, then, can enable teachers to design classroom learning environments that are more likely to facilitate high levels of student achievement.

4. In general, classroom learning environments that are characterized by cohesiveness, goal direction, organization and rule clarity, satisfaction, and a sense of belonging are most conducive to student engagement in learning and student learning per se.

5. During the 1990s there has been a renewed interest in the development of students' character (with character defined as the configuration of mental, moral, and emotional traits that make up the essence of who we are). The results of affective assessment can be used to evaluate the effectiveness of character education programs, and improve character education programs by identifying weaknesses that subsequently can be strengthened.

6. Affective consequences are an important aspect of schooling. They are what might be termed *unintended outcomes* of what happens in schools. Two unintended outcomes related to the affective domain are the enhancement of self-esteem and the effect of the latent curriculum. Affective assessment is useful in monitoring the schools' influences on these and other affective consequences.

7. To the extent that motivating students, creating effective classroom learning environments, building character, and being concerned with the affective consequences of schooling are important, perhaps essential, in school improvement, so too is affective assessment. Ultimately, affective assessment can help make schools more effective in accomplishing their goals and more satisfying places to live and work.

Appendix A

Descriptions of Various Affective Scaling Strategies

We wrote this appendix because we believe that a better understanding of affective scales is possible if you understand the procedures by which the scales are designed. In addition, the procedures outlined in this appendix should help you design your own affective scales. We begin with an overview and summary of Likert scales (see also chap. 4, this volume). Then we move to a description of Thurstone scales, Guttman scales, and Semantic Differential scales. We end with a brief discussion of Adjective Checklists as a means of collecting affective data.

LIKERT SCALES

As mentioned in chapter 4, the traditional form of the Likert scale contains a series of statements about a particular affect–target combination. Students are asked to indicate the extent of their agreement or disagreement with the position taken or point of view expressed in each statement. The traditional response categories from which students are to choose are: *Strongly Agree*, *Agree*, *Undecided* or *Not Sure*, *Disagree*, and *Strongly Disagree*. Table A.1 identifies the steps that make up the Likert strategy for scale design.

TABLE A.1

The Likert Strategy for Scale Design

Step 1	Write or select statements that are clearly either favorable or unfavorable with respect to the underlying affective characteristic.
Step 2	Have several judges react to the statements. These judges should examine each statement and classify it as positive, negative, or neutral.
Step 3	Eliminate those statements that are not unanimously classified as positive or negative (because neutral statements are not acceptable for inclusion on a Likert Scale).
Step 4	Decide on the number of alternative choices to be offered for each statement. (Note: The original Likert scale had five alternatives: SD,D, NS, A, SA.)
Step 5	Prepare the self-report instrument. Include directions. The directions should indicate that the respondents should indicate how they feel about each statement by marking SA if they strongly agree, A if they agree, NS if they are not sure, D if they disagree, and SD if they strongly disagree.
Step 6	Administer the scale to a sample of the audience for whom the instrument is intended. (Note: You should have at least 10 times as many persons as statements.)
Step 7	Compute the correlation between each statement response and the total scale score.
Step 8	Eliminate those statements whose correlation with the total scale is not statistically significant (Likert's Criterion of Internal Consistency).
Step 9	Calculate an alpha coefficient.

Step 1 states clearly one of the major identifying characteristics of a Likert scale; that is, the statements must be either favorable or unfavorable with respect to the underlying affective characteristic. In Step 2 judges are called in to examine the statements relative to their position on the underlying continuum. The judges are asked to classify each statement as being clearly favorable (positive), unfavorable (negative), or neither (neutral). To the extent possible, the judges should be members of the audience for whom the scale is intended.

Any statements not classified as positive or negative by all (or at least the vast majority) of the judges are eliminated from further consideration (Step 3). The remainder of the statements become the basis for the scale. Next, the response options are selected (Step 4). The statements plus the response options become the items. The instrument is prepared for administration and directions are written (Step 5).

Next, the instrument is administered to a sample of the audience for whom it is intended (Step 6).

The completed instruments are collected and the responses appropriately coded. The correlations between each item and the total scale score are computed (Step 7). For obvious reasons, the correlations are referred to as item-total correlations. Any item whose correlation with the total scale score is not statistically significant is eliminated (Step 8). The fact that each statement must be correlated with the total scale score is referred to as Likert's Criterion of Internal Consistency. Finally, an alpha coefficient is computed (Step 9). This provides a numerical value of the internal consistency of the entire scale.

Likert's Criterion of Internal Consistency is an interesting and important criterion for the inclusion of an item on a Likert scale. Let us consider the rationale for the criterion in some detail. As mentioned earlier in this volume, a scale is a set of related items. Likert's Criterion of Internal Consistency is an empirical procedure for examining the relatedness among items, or rather, between each item and the entire scale.

The rationale for the criterion is simple. If an item belongs on a scale, the responses to the item should be consistent with the responses to all the other items on the scale (i.e., the total scale score). The level of consistency of responses is indicated by the item-scale correlation coefficients.

As mentioned in chapter 4, the Likert strategy has been modified in many ways over the years. Most of the modifications have concerned the response options. Changes have been made in the number of response options, the strength or intensity of the response options, and the nature of the underlying scale (e.g., agree–disagree, important-not at all important, always or almost always–almost never or never; see chap. 4.)

There also have been changes in the statement format. In most cases statements on Likert scales are typically complete statements. Modifications include the use of incomplete statements. Incomplete statements require changes in the response options. The options are phrases that could complete the incomplete statement. Like traditional response options, the phrases are selected to cover the entire gamut of emotions. Consider the following two examples.

Example 1.   If I did *not* have to go to school, I would be
             a. overjoyed.
             b. glad.
             c. sad.
             d. miserable.
Example 2.   School days seem like they
             a. last forever.
             b. are long.
             c. are short.
             d. go by very quickly.

Notice that the options allow a range of responses on the part of the student similar to the range allowed by the traditional Likert-type options. Also notice that the options can be made very specific to the particular situation represented by each incomplete sentence.

It is a small step from the incomplete statement modification to the next one. In the preceding examples, the alternatives are arranged from negative to positive (or vice versa) on some underlying affective continuum. The most positive alternative is clearly at the positive pole, whereas the most negative is clearly at the negative pole. If the two middle alternatives are eliminated, you have what is called the forced-choice format. This format tends to be popular if you wish to categorize people into one of two extreme groups. As discussed in chapter 2, for example, the affective characteristic locus of control is usually discussed in terms of two classifications of people: those with an internal locus of control and those with an external locus of control. Because this characteristic is conceptualized in this manner, the forced-choice modification of the Likert technique seems appropriate. The following two examples illustrate this modification.

Example 3.   If I did well on a test it was because
            a. the test was easy.
            b. I studied hard.
Example 4.   If my teacher taught something to my class and most of
            the students didn't learn it, it was probably because:
            a. the teacher didn't do a good job of teaching
            b. the students lacked the ability to learn it.

In both examples the second response is the internal response and the first response is the external response.

Modifications of Likert scales are prevalent. When they are encountered, it is important they are recognized as modifications and not a completely different scaling technique. Such a recognition makes greater understanding of the scale, and the reasoning behind it, possible.

THE THURSTONE STRATEGY

The strategy for designing scales developed by Louis Thurstone (Thurstone & Chave, 1929) is the oldest. Items on a Thurstone scale are viewed as existing along some underlying affective continuum. Equal intervals are assumed to exist on the continuum. The items are placed on the actual instrument in a random order, and the person responding to the scale is asked to read each item. If the person agrees with the item, he or she places a checkmark in front of number corresponding to the item. If the person does not agree with the item, no checkmark is placed. Each person's score is obtained by summing the scale values of all the items checked and dividing this sum by the number of checkmarks.

In practice, Thurstone scales are rarely used, perhaps because they are time consuming and require considerable effort to develop. Nonetheless, for those interested in designing a Thurstone scale, the steps to be followed are listed in Table A.2.

Step 1 characterizes the nature of the Thurstone scales. A series of statements is to be written or selected. These statements should appear to be ordered along a continuum from *least* to *most* or from *negative* to *positive*. The selected or written statements should be short and to the point, should

TABLE A.2

The Thurstone Strategy for Scale Design

Step 1	Write or select a series of statements that appear to be ordered along a continuum from least to most, or negative to positive.
Step 2	Give the statements to a group of judges. (Note: These judges should be members of the same audience from whom the scale is intended.)
Step 3	Ask judges to sort statements into 11 piles. The directions suggest that the judges ask themselves, "If a person were to agree with this statement, where on the continuum would this person fall?" (Note: Pile 1 is least positive and Pile 11 is most positive.)
Step 4	Collect and analyze data obtained from judges.
Step 5	Compute average response (e.g., median) and degree of variability (e.g., semi-inter quartile range) for each statement.
Step 6	Eliminate those statements with large variability indexes (Note: This is Thurstone's Criterion of Ambiguity).
Step 7	Select a set of the remaining statements whose medians are spaced equally along the continuum. (Note: These medians are the statements' scale values.)
Step 8	Prepare self-report instrument. Include directions. The directions should indicate that respondents should place a checkmark beside each statement with which they agree.
Step 9	Administer these statements to a sample of the audience for whom the instrument is intended. (Note: You should have at least ten times as many persons as statements.)
Step 10	Use the Criterion of Irrelevance to eliminate additional statements, if necessary. (Note: The Criterion of Irrelevance suggests that an item with a given scale value is most likely to be endorsed by respondents whose affective characteristic is located at the same position as the scale value.)

contain only one complete thought, and should be written clearly and un-ambiguously.

The purpose of Steps 2 through 6 is to gather information about the logical relations among the statements. Step 2 is concerned with the selection of individuals who will critically examine each statement and its relation to the total scale. It is important to note that these individuals are called judges rather than experts. This is an important distinction. The individuals who critically examine the set of statements should be members of the same group of people (or audience) to whom the scale is intended to be administered, rather than people brought in from outside the group in question. For example, if the scale is intended to assess the attitudes of fourth-grade students toward school, the judges should be composed of a fairly random sample of fourth-grade students. If the scale is in tended to assess the attitudes of preservice teachers toward particular child-rearing practices, then the judges should be preservice teachers.

Making this distinction between judges and experts is also important because the use of judges has caused some controversy. Many people have thought that experts have a greater insight into the task ahead. Not true. Judges, possessing the same characteristics as other member of the intended audience, are used for one very important reason. Each statement is placed along the continuum largely on the basis of its meaning to the judges. That is, whether one statement is placed higher or lower on the continuum than another is determined by the way in which the judges perceive the meaning of the statement. Thus, the statements are arranged along the continuum according to the positive or negative meaning they have relative both to the affective characteristic and to the audience for whom the scale is intended.

The activities in Step 3 have been alluded to in the discussion of the previous step. The judges are asked to sort the statements into one of a finite number of categories or piles. The original Thurstone procedure suggested using eleven piles for this task. Modifications of the procedures have used fewer piles. These modifications have been necessary because of the conceptual or developmental level of the judges. The modifications have typically resulted in an odd number of piles, because this allows for one *neutral pile*. A neutral pile can be defined as a pile that includes statements that are neither positive nor negative relative to the underlying affective characteristic as indicated by the judges.

When 11 piles are used, Pile 1 contains the least positive statements, Pile 11 contains the most positive statements, and Pile 6 contains the neutral statements. Piles 2 through 5 include decreasingly negative (but still negative) statements. Piles 7 through 10 include increasingly positive statements.

The directions to the judges are crucial. These directions suggest that the judges ask themselves the following question. "If a person were to agree with this statement, where on the continuum would this person fall?" Note that the judges are not responding to the statements in the way they feel about the statements. Rather, they are responding to the statements according to the degree of affect they believe to be present in the statements. Because this is a crucial difference but one that is difficult to grasp for certain types of audiences (especially younger children), it is clear that the Thurstone technique should be used only for audiences who can understand this difference.

After several judges (say 15 to 20) have reacted to the statements, these reactions are collected and the data are analyzed (Step 4). The analysis consists of two parts (Step 5). First, the average reaction of the judges is computed. This average reaction is typically the *median reaction*. The median locates the statement on the continuum. For example, if a majority of the judges placed a statement in the eighth pile, then the median would be somewhere around 8. Second, a measure of the variability of the judges' reactions is computed. This measure, typically the semi-interquartile range (see Glass & Stanley, 1970, pp.77–78) indicates the degree of disagreement among the judges as to the proper placement of the statement. If a statement having a median of around 8 is placed in Pile 3 by some judges, in Pile 5 by others, and Pile 11 by still others, then the disagreement among the judges is quite large. If, on the other hand, most of the judges have placed the statement in Pile 8, with a few placing it in Pile 7 and a few more placing it in Pile 9, the disagreement among the judges is quite small.

Based on the assumptions underlying the Thurstone technique, what is desired is a series of items whose median values are at equal intervals along the continuum and whose variability is quite small. Steps 6 and 7 deal specifically with this desired state. Step 6 indicates that statements with a large variability index should be eliminated. This criterion for eliminating statements is termed the Criterion of Ambiguity by Thurstone because a large disagreement among judges suggests that the statement is ambiguous in terms of its affective meaning. Once these statements are eliminated, the remaining statements are examined. As is indicated in Step 7, this examination focuses on the identification of a set of statements whose medians are spaced equally along the continuum. For example, a perfect Thurstone scale might have one statement with a median of 1.4, another with a median of 1.9, another with a median of 2.4, another with a median of 2.9, and so on.

The statement's median value becomes the scale value for the statement. The *scale value* is the number of points awarded to the student for agreeing with the statement. The more positive the statement, the higher the scale value; the less positive the statement, the lower the scale value. Thus, in general, the higher the person's total score, the more positive the affect; the lower the person's total score, the more negative the affect.

Statements selected for inclusion on the scale are now randomly arranged on a sheet of paper, and directions are written for those responding to the statements. The directions typically indicate that the respondent should place a check mark beside each statement with which he or she agrees (Step 8). Now the instrument is administered to a sample of the audience for whom the instrument is intended to be administered (Step 9). The purpose of this administration of the instrument is to examine the quality of instrument. To do this properly, a fairly large sample of respondents is recommended. Several sources recommend at least 10 times as many respondents as there are statements on the instrument.

An examination of the quality of an instrument requires several considerations. Many of these are common to all types of affective scales and are included in chapter 4. The Thurstone technique has one unique consideration that is mentioned in Step 10. Step 10 is based on what Thurstone called the Criterion of Irrelevance, which allows for a check between the logical and empirical relations among the statements. At the risk of oversimplifying, the Criterion of Irrelevance suggests that a statement with a given scale value is more likely to be endorsed (i.e., checked) by respondents whose total score is equal to that scale value.

The meaning of the Criterion of Irrelevance can be further clarified with an example. As already indicated, each statement has a scale value assigned to it. This scale value is the median pile in which the statement has been placed by the judges. As also mentioned, the number of points indicated by the scale value is awarded to students who agree with (i.e., place a check mark beside) the statement. Only one additional piece of information is needed before we can interpret the Criterion of Irrelevance. A student's total score is computed by adding up the scale values of all of the statements endorsed by the student and dividing this number the number of statements endorsed. For example, if Fred Farson agrees with statements with scale values of 5, 7, 8, and 10, Fred would have a total score of 7.5. How was this figure arrived at? First, the four scale values were added (that is, $5 + 7 + 8 + 10$) to get 30. Next, this sum was divided by 4 (that is, the total number of statements checked) to get 7.5.

Now, each statement has a scale value, and each student has a total score. For each statement, then, it is possible to graph the responses by the sample. An example of such a graph, called a *trace-line* (Fishbein & Ajzen, 1975) or an item characteristic curve (Lord, 1952) is shown in Fig. A.1. The horizontal axis refers to the scale scores of the respondents. On a Thurstone scale, scale scores can range from 1 to 11. Furthermore, because fractions are possible (as in our example of Fred Farson), the scale scores are expressed as ranges, commonly called score groups.

The vertical axis refers to the proportion of students in any score group agreeing with the statement. That is, if there were 20 students in the 4.5-to-5.4 score group and 12 students agreed with a statement, then 60% of the score group would have agreed with the statement. This number could be represented by a large dot on the graph, as has been done in Fig. A.1. Other points on the graph represent the proportions of students in other score groups who agreed with the statement. It is crucial to note that one of these figures is necessary for *each* statement.

Notice that a series of line segments can be used to connect the points. This has been done in Fig. A.2. Figure A.2 displays a "picture" of responses to a statement with a scale value of 3.8. Now let us return to the Criterion of Irrelevance. In terms of Fig. A.2, the Criterion of Irrelevance states that the graph should peak (attain its highest point) for the score group whose scale value coincides with the scale value of the item. That is, because the statement in Fig. A.2 has a scale value of 3.8, the graph should peak directly above the place on the horizontal axis that indicates the score group of 3.5 to 4.4. Although this is the case in Fig. A.2, it is not the case in Fig. A.3.

If the graph peaks at or near where it is supposed to, there is a consistency among the logical and empirical relations among the items. If the graph fails to peak at or near where it is supposed to, there is an inconsistency among the logical and empirical considerations and the statement is deemed irrelevant. All such irrelevant statements are excluded from the scale as is indicated in Step 10 of Table A.1.

In sum, then, the Thurstone technique produces a scale that consists of statements spaced rather equally along the underlying affective continuum. The spacing of the statements is done on the basis of judges' estimates of the degree of affect present in the statement. If a large amount of disagreement exists among the judges for a particular statement, then based on Thurstone's Criterion of Ambiguity, the statement is eliminated from further consideration. A preliminary version of the scale is then administered to a sample of the intended audience, who are asked to check those statements that they agree with. The correspondence between the logically derived scale values and the empirically derived scale values is examined. If a lack of correspondence is found to exist for a given statement, the statement is eliminated from further consideration on the basis of Thurstone's Criterion of Irrelevance. Only after the preliminary version of the scale has been carefully examined and appropriate modifications (if

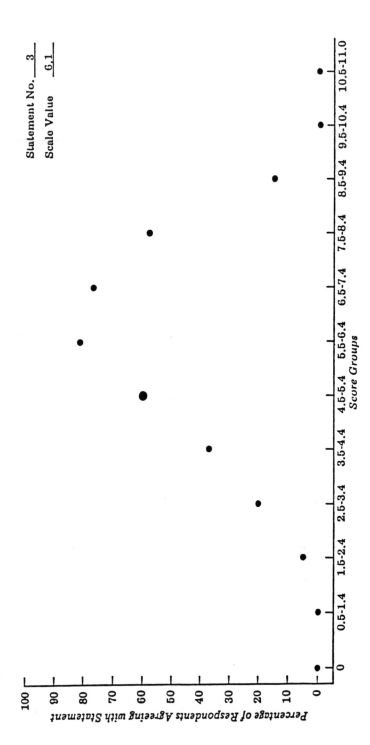

FIG. A.1 An example of the beginning of a traceline for responses to a statement on a Thurstone scale.

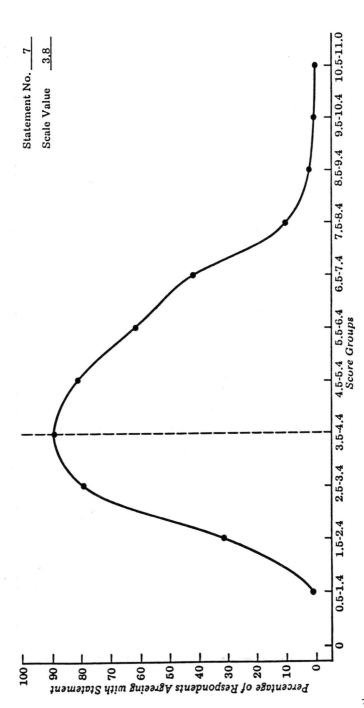

FIG. A.2 An example of a traceline for responses to a statement on a Thurstone scale (with a scale value of 3.8).

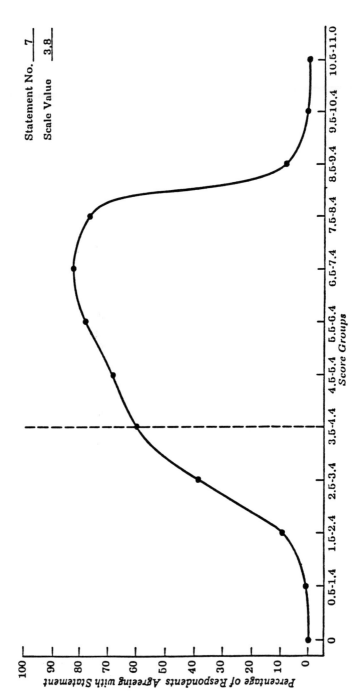

FIG. A.3   Another example of a traceline for responses to a statement on a Thurstone scale (with a scale value of 3.8).

any) have been made can the Thurstone scale be used to gather information about the affective characteristics of individuals or groups.

THE GUTTMAN STRATEGY

A scale quite similar to the Thurstone scale was developed by Louis Guttman (1944). There are two major differences between Guttman scales and Thurstone scales. First, for the Guttman scale, distances between consecutive items on the underlying continuum are not necessarily the same. Second, the items on the Guttman scale form a cumulative hierarchy. That is, for example, if a person agrees to the third item on the continuum, he or she would have to agree to the first two items. Directions and scoring procedures are both simple. Students are asked to place a checkmark by the items with which they agree; the total score is normally the number of checkmarks. Guttman scales are very difficult to develop, requiring many drafts.

The steps that comprise the Guttman technique are listed in Table A.3. The Guttman technique begins by writing or selecting statements that possess two characteristics. First, the statements must appear to be ordered along the underlying continuum from *least positive* to *most positive*. Second, if a person agrees with a statement that is located at a point somewhere along the continuum, he or she is likely to agree with all other less positive statements (Step 1). This first step clearly differentiates the Guttman technique from the Thurstone and Likert techniques. The statements are then readied for administration and directions are written (Step 2). Next, the instrument is administered to a sample of the audience for whom it is intended (Step 3). The responses are submitted to what is called a Guttman scale analysis, which generally requires a computer program. The Guttman scale analysis computes several indexes or coefficients. These coefficients are used to indicate to what extent the statements conform to the properties of a Guttman scale. In order to illustrate these properties and the utility of the coefficients, let us consider the following example.

Suppose five statements were administered to a sample of respondents. Furthermore, suppose the statements were believed to be ordered along the underlying continuum as follows: Statement 1 was the least positive; Statement 5 was the most positive, and the remaining statements were somewhere in between (in numerical order). Now if the assumptions underlying a Guttman scale are met, several potential response patterns are acceptable. The acceptable response patterns are shown in Table A.4. The As in the figure indicate agreement, the Ds indicate disagreement.

TABLE A.3

The Guttman Strategy for Scale Design

Step 1   Write or select statements that appear to have two characteristics:
a. They appear to be ordered along a continuum from least positive to most positive.
b. Agreement with a given statement implies agreement with every less positive statement.

Step 2   Prepare the instrument for administration. Prepare directions that indicate that the respondent should check each statement with which he or she agrees.

Step 3   Administer these statements to a sample of the audience for whom the instrument is intended. (Note: You should have at least ten times as many persons as statements.)

Step 4   Submit the data to the Guttman scale analysis.

Step 5   Examine the Coefficient of Reproducibility (CR) (Note: CR should be greater than 90.)

Step 6   Examine the Coefficient of Scalability (CS) (Note: CS should be greater than 60.)

Step 7   If CR is greater than 90 and CS is greater than 60, the statements comprise a Guttman scale.

Step 8   If CR is not greater than 90 or if CS is not greater than 60, then revision of the series of statements is necessary.

As can be seen in Table A.4, a person who agrees with Statement 4 must agree with Statements 1 through 3. Of course, that person may or may not agree with Statement 5. If the person does not agree with Statement 5, the result is Response Pattern V. If he or she does agree with Statement 5, the result is Response Pattern VI. In either case the cumulative nature of the Guttman scale has been supported.

Clearly there are many inappropriate response patterns. Several of these are illustrated in Table A.5. In Response Pattern VII it is theoretically impossible for a person who disagrees with Statement 2 to agree with Statement 3. Likewise, in Response Pattern VIII, it is theoretically impossible for a person who agrees with Statement 5 to disagree with Statement 3 or 4, let alone both Statements 3 *and* 4.

It is possible to calculate the number of errors in a particular response pattern. In Table A.5 response Patterns VII, VIII, and IX have one error (indicated by an asterisk). Response Pattern X, on the other hand, has two errors (also indicated by an asterisk).

The Guttman scale analysis begins with an examination of the number of inappropriate response patterns and the number of errors. Suppose that

TABLE A.4

Acceptable Response Patterns for a Five-Item Guttman Scale

Response Patterns	Statement Number (Along the Continuum)				
	1	2	3	4	5
I	D	D	D	D	D
II	A	D	D	D	D
III	A	A	D	D	D
IV	A	A	A	D	D
V	A	A	A	A	D
VI	A	A	A	A	A

TABLE A.5

Unacceptable Response Patterns for a Five-Item Guttman Scale

Response Pattern	Statement Number (Along the Continuum)				
	1	2	3	4	5
VII	A	D	A*	D	D
VIII	A	A	D	D	A*
IX	A	A	A	D	A*
X	A	D	A*	D	A*

Note. An asterisk (*) indicates responses that are in "error."

20 people responded to the five-statement Guttman scale used in the preceding illustrations. Further suppose that the only unacceptable response patterns that were identified were those listed in Table A.5 and that only one person was associated with each of the four unacceptable response patterns. First, the total number of errors is computed. In this situation this number would be five. Next the total number of responses is found by multiplying the number of statements by the number of respondents. The total number of responses would be 100 (or 20 people x 5 responses). Now the percentage of errors is computed by dividing the total number of errors (e.g., 5) by the total number of responses (e.g., 100). In the present illustration there would be a 5% error rate. This error rate is subtracted from 100% (to yield in this case 95), and this number is referred to as the Coefficient of Reproducibility (CR; Step 5 of Table A.4). Guttman (1944) suggested that the Coefficient of Reproducibility should be greater than 90; that is, the er-

ror rate should be no larger than 10% before the set of statements is considered to be a Guttman scale.

Even if the Coefficient of Reproducibility is greater than 90, however, a Guttman scale is not ensured. Rather, a second criterion is specified by the Coefficient of Scalability (Step 6). In order to explain the Coefficient of Scalability, let us continue our earlier discussion.

Guttman (1944) believed that it was impossible to interpret the magnitude of the Coefficient of Reproducibility without some knowledge of the minimum value that this coefficient can assume. He also was aware that the minimum value of the Coefficient of Reproducibility varied according to responses that the respondents made to the entire set of statements. It was suggested, therefore, that a minimum Coefficient of Reproducibility (which he called the Minimum Marginal Reproducibility, or MMR) would be computed for the scale. This value represented the smallest Coefficient of Reproducibility that was possible given the proportion of respondents agreeing and disagreeing with each statement.

Once the minimum value for the coefficient was determined, a proper interpretation of the actual value of the coefficient was possible. This interpretation was made by subtracting the minimum value from the actual value. Guttman referred to this difference simply as the Percent Improvement (PI). Guttman next computed the Possible Percent Improvement (PPI) by subtracting the minimum value from 100%.

The Coefficient of Scalability is simply the number obtained by dividing the PI by the PPI; that is, $CS = PI / PPI$. As can be seen in Step 6 of Table A.3, the Coefficient of Scalability should be greater than 60. That is to say, the actual improvement should be 60% of the possible improvement.

The set of statements can be said to be a Guttman scale, then, only if two criteria are met. The Coefficient of Reproducibility must be greater than 90, and the Coefficient of Scalability must be greater than 60 (Step 7). If either of these two criteria is not met, then the set of statements does not form a Guttman scale and appropriate revisions must be made.

Typically, two types of revisions are made. First, statements that are associated with a large number of errors are eliminated. (In Fig. A.5, Statement 5 is a good example of such a statement because three of the four response patterns contain errors at that point on the continuum.) Second, statements that are believed to represent points on the continuum different from those already represented are added to the set. In either case, the scale is administered to another sample, and the Guttman scale analysis is performed again.

In sum, then, the Guttman scale is a difficult scale to construct. The difficulty, in large part, stems from the inability of scale developers to conceptualize a cumulative set of statements. Early attempts usually prove frustrating (as the authors know from past experience). Statements may appear to be cumulative in nature, when written, but the results of the Guttman scale analysis often fail to support this initial supposition. If either the Coefficient of Reproducibility (i.e., the percentage of error-free responses) or the Coefficient of Scalability (i.e., the extent to which the improvement in the Coefficient of Reproducibility is substantial) is too low, the assumptions underlying the Guttman scale are not supported. The one advantage of the Guttman scale, however, is that modifications in statements can be made over and over again until the empirical criteria have been met.

THE SEMANTIC DIFFERENTIAL STRATEGY

The semantic differential strategy was developed by Charles Osgood (1952). The format of the items is highly visual, illustrating the underlying continuum. Above and in the center of the continuum is the target (e.g., mathematics, my classmates). Pairs of adjectives, sometimes called anchors, are placed at the two ends of the continuum. Examples of appropriate adjective pairs are *valuable–worthless*, and *boring–interesting*. Those responding a semantic differential instrument are asked to indicate their feelings towards the concept by placing an *X* somewhere along the continuum between each pair of adjectives.

Each space between the adjectives is preassigned a numerical value and each response is assigned the value corresponding with the space. The scale score is computed by summing all of the numerical values of the spaces in which an *X* was placed. Although the instructions for respondents are somewhat complicated, these scales are relatively easy to design and administer. However, a lack of context for the adjectives used to anchor each scale means that respondents may attach very different meanings to the same adjective pairs. Respondents can also become bored easily with this type of scale, thus falling into a response set if the scale is too lengthy.

The steps pertaining to the development of a semantic differential scale are displayed in Table A.6. The first step is the selection of so-called *bipolar adjectives* (Step 1). Bipolar adjectives are of pairs of adjectives whose meanings are opposites and as such would be representative of opposite poles of the underlying affective continuum. Because affective assessment represents the emotional or feeling component of life, Osgood, Suci, and Tannenbaum (1957) conducted several studies to attempt to determine those adjectives that reflected such emotional responses or reactions. They found a large set of adjectives that elicited similar responses from different samples of respondents. What these adjectives seemed to have in common was that they were emotion-laden, or what Osgood (1952) called evaluative in nature. Examples of such evaluative adjective pairs are

TABLE A.6

The Semantic Differential Strategy for Scale Design

Step 1: Choose appropriate pairs of bipolar adjectives. The pairs you choose should contain adjectives that are clearly evaluative in nature with respect to the concept (target) under consideration. (Examples of such adjectives would include good–bad, tasty–distasteful, kind–cruel, brave–cowardly, clear–hazy, honest–dishonest, beautiful–ugly, calm–agitated, valuable–worthless, pleasant–unpleasant, happy–sad, relaxed–tense, nice–awful, fair–unfair, and healthy–sick.)

Step 2: Construct a response sheet. For example:
                              My Teacher
        Fair _____ · _____ · _____ · _____ · _____ · _____ : ____ Unfair

Step 3: Administer the scale to sample of the audience for whom the instrument is intended. (Note: You should have at least 10 times as many persons as items—that is, bipolar adjective pairs.)

Step 4: Compute the correlation between each pair of bipolar adjectives and the total scale score.

Step 5: Eliminate those adjective pairs that do not correlate significantly with the total scale score.

---

good–bad; valuable–worthless; and healthy–sick. Additional examples are presented in Table A.6 (see Step 1).

Once 5 to 10 adjective pairs are selected, a response sheet is constructed. The adjectives in each pair are placed at different ends of a continuum. The continuum is then broken down into seven segments. The final response sheet consists of the 5 to 10 adjective pairs placed at the ends of the continuum with the name of the target of the affective characteristic placed at the top (Step 2). Table A.7 represents an example of a semantic differential response sheet. As can be seen, the target of the affect is classmates. Six bipolar adjective pairs constitute the body of the response sheet good–bad, cruel–kind, honest–dishonest, valuable–worthless, tense–relaxed, and nice–awful.

Now the semantic differential instrument is administered to a sample of the audience for whom the scale is intended. Respondents are instructed to place a check mark somewhere along the continuum at a place that indicates how they feel about the object at the top of the sheet (Step 3 of Table A.6). A check mark near either end of the continuum indicates strong posi-

TABLE A.7

Example of a Semantic Differential Response Sheet

My Classmates

Good	____:____:____:____:____:____:____	Bad
Cruel	____:____:____:____:____:____:____	Kind
Honest	____:____:____:____:____:____:____	Dishonest
Valuable	____:____:____:____:____:____:____	Worthless
Tense	____:____:____:____:____:____:____	Relaxed
Nice	____:____:____:____:____:____:____	Awful

tive or negative feelings, whereas a checkmark near the center of the continuum indicates neutral or ambivalent feelings.

The next two steps of the semantic differential technique (Steps 4 and 5 on Table A.6) are identical to Steps 7 and 8 of the Likert procedure. First, the correlations between each adjective pair and the total scale score are computed. Second, adjective pairs that do not correlate significantly with the total scale score are eliminated.

PROCEDURE FOR DESIGNING ADJECTIVE CHECKLISTS

The differences between a scale and bunch-of-statements (or, in this case, a bunch-of-adjectives) is most clearly seen in the comparison of semantic differential instruments with adjective checklists. Semantic differential scales are based on the selection of adjectives that are evaluative in nature and bipolar. Thus some degree of logical relation exists among the adjective pairs included. In addition, this apparent logical relation is examined using the empirical results; that is, the correlations between the responses to the adjectives and the scale score. Adjective checklists, however, may omit either or both of these considerations. When either consideration is omitted, the result is a bunch of adjectives (not a scale) that are arranged on a piece of paper and administered to a group of people.

The procedure for the development of adjective checklists is simple and straightforward. Table A.8 presents the steps involved. First, an appropriate number of adjectives is selected (Step 1). A good source of possible adjectives is Allport and Odbert's (1936) list of 17,953 trait words. The adjectives should be selected so as to relate to some single affective characteristic and some defined object toward which the affect is directed. This is not necessary. Next, the adjectives are placed on a sheet of paper (Step 2). Directions for responding to the adjectives are prepared (Step 3). Finally,

TABLE A.8

Procedure for Preparing Adjective Checklists

Step 1	Select an appropriate number of adjectives. A good source of possible adjectives is Allport and Odbert's (1936) list of 17,953 trait words.
Step 2	Place adjectives on a sheet of paper.
Step 3	Write or select directions for responding to the adjectives. (Usually directions ask the respondent to place a check mark in front of the adjectives.)
Step 4	Administer the checklist to a sample of the audience for whom the instrument is intended.

the checklist is administered to a sample of the audience for whom it is intended (Step 4).

Although adjective checklists are usually not scales and are typically used to gather a large amount of information about several things in a relatively short period of time, modifications can be made to scale adjective checklists. One such modification is that used by Bills (1975). Bills's Index of Adjustment and Values (IAV) looks like an adjective checklist. Three alterations were made to convert the instrument to an affective scale.

First, in constructing the adult form of the IAV, Bills (1975) selected a sample of adjectives that "occur frequently in client centered interviews and which seem to present clear examples of self-concept definitions" (p.61). Thus, logical relationships among the adjectives were considered.

Second, Bills (1975) embedded the adjectives within a Likert-type format (although the response sheet still maintains the appearance of an adjective checklist). The incomplete-sentence Likert format was used, with response options *seldom, occasionally, about half of the time, a good deal of the time,* and *most of the time.* This modification placed the adjectives within a frame of reference.

Finally, Bills (1975) used two empirical criteria to eliminate adjectives from the final form of the scale: stability and internal consistency. With respect to stability, the instrument was administered to a sample of college students on two occasions, three weeks apart. The consistency of responses on the two occasions was examined. Any adjectives to which responses varied more than the average student's responses to the average adjective were eliminated.

In sum, then, adjective checklists typically are not scales. They are useful in that they permit the gathering of a great deal of discrete information in a short period of time. However, because they are not scales, it is impossible to combine the information in any meaningful way (other than to simply count the number of checkmarks). However, It is possible to modify adjective checklists so that they possess the characteristics of a scale.

Appendix B
The Quality of School Life (QSL) Instrument

We would like to know how you feel about your life in primary school. **This is not a test**, and there are no right or wrong answers. What we want is your opinion, so try to answer what you think about your school life. Your answers will not be seen by anyone else.

First of all, would you please answer these questions:
Name of Your School?_____
Your Class?_____Boy or Girl?_____

Each statement on the next two pages starts with MY SCHOOL IS A PLACE WHERE ... some particular thing happens to you or you feel a particular way. You should give your opinion by ticking one of the boxes in each line to show that you **Agree, Mostly Agree, Mostly Disagree** or **Disagree** with the statement.
Try to give an answer to every statement but, if you really cannot decide, leave that one out.

Don't forget that you have to think of **My School is a Place Where** ... before each item for it to make sense, for example, **My School is a Place Where ... I feel important**.

MY SCHOOL IS A PLACE WHERE ...	Agree	Mostly Agree	Mostly Disagree	Disagree
		(Tick one box in each line)		
1. I really like to go each day.	☐	☐	☐	☐
2. My teacher is fair to me.	☐	☐	☐	☐
3. I learn to get along with other people.	☐	☐	☐	☐
4. I am a success as a student.	☐	☐	☐	☐
5. I feel unhappy.	☐	☐	☐	☐
6. Other students accept me as I am.	☐	☐	☐	☐
7. I know how to cope with the work.	☐	☐	☐	☐
8. I like to be.	☐	☐	☐	☐
9. The work is a good preparation for my future.	☐	☐	☐	☐
10. I like to do extra work.	☐	☐	☐	☐
11. I feel happy.	☐	☐	☐	☐
12. The things I learn are important to me.	☐	☐	☐	☐
13. Learning is fun.	☐	☐	☐	☐
14. I feel lonely.	☐	☐	☐	☐
15. Things I learn will help me in secondary school.	☐	☐	☐	☐
16. I am good at school work.	☐	☐	☐	☐
17. I feel proud to be a student.	☐	☐	☐	☐
18. I feel worried.	☐	☐	☐	☐
19. My teacher takes an interest in helping me with my work.	☐	☐	☐	☐
20. People trust me.	☐	☐	☐	☐
21. I have a lot of fun.	☐	☐	☐	☐
22. My teacher listens to what I say.	☐	☐	☐	☐
23. I enjoy what I do in class.	☐	☐	☐	☐
24. I am popular with other students.	☐	☐	☐	☐
25. I can learn what I need to know.	☐	☐	☐	☐
	Agree	Mostly Agree	Mostly Disagree	Disagre
26. I know I can keep up with the work.	☐	☐	☐	☐
27. I get excited about the work we do.	☐	☐	☐	☐
28. I get upset.	☐	☐	☐	☐
29. I know people think a lot of me.	☐	☐	☐	☐

(Tick one box in each line)

MY SCHOOL IS A PLACE WHERE …	Agree	Mostly Agree	Mostly Disagree	Disagree
	□	□	□	□
30. I get on well with the other students in my class.				
31. What I learn will be useful.	□	□	□	□
32. The work we do is interesting.	□	□	□	□
33. I get enjoyment from being there.	□	□	□	□
34. My teacher helps me to do my best.	□	□	□	□
35. People can depend on me.	□	□	□	□
36. Other students are very friendly.	□	□	□	□
37. I feel restless.	□	□	□	□
38. My teacher treats me fairly in class.	□	□	□	□
39. What I learn will be useful to me when I leave school.	□	□	□	□

If you want to tell us anything else about your life at school, please write it here.

Descriptions of the Seven QSL Scales

Scale Name	Brief Description and Sample Item	Question Numbers
General Satisfaction	General feelings of well being at school "I feel happy."	Q1, 8, 11, 17, 21, 33
Negative Affect	General negative feelings about school "I get upset."	Q5, 14, 18, 28, 37
Teachers	A feeling about the adequacy of their interaction with the teacher "My teacher helps me do my best."	Q2, 19, 22, 34, 38
Social Integration	A sense of belonging; a feeling of self worth and the ability to get along with others "I get on well with the other students in my class."	Q3, 6, 20, 24, 29, 30, 35, 36
Opportunity	A future-oriented scale about a belief in the relevance of schooling "The work is a good preparation for my future."	Q9, 12, 15, 25, 31, 39

| Achievement | A sense of confidence in one's ability to be successful in school work "I am a success as a student." | Q4, 7, 16, 26 |
| Adventure | A sense of self-motivation in learning and the belief that learning is enjoyable for its own sake "I enjoy what I do in class." | Q10, 13, 23, 27, 32 |

Note. Keep in mind that each of the statements in quotes is preceded by the phrase, "My school is a place where.... "

References

Ainley, J., & Bourke, S. F. (1992). Student views of primary schooling. *Research Papers in Education, 7*(2), 107–128.

Allport, G., & Odbert, H. (1936). Trait names: A psycho-lexical study. *Psychological Monographs, 1* (entire).

Anderson, L. W. (1992). In my opinion … measuring children's traits and abilities. *Children's Health Concerns, 21*(3), 136–139.

Anderson, L. W. (1981). *Assessing affective characteristics in the schools.* Boston: Allyn and Bacon.

Anderson, L. W., Ryan, D. W., & Shapiro, B. J. (1989). *The IEA classroom environment study.* Oxford: Pergamon.

Anderson, T. W., & Finn, J. D. (1996). *The new statistical analysis of data.* New York: Springer-Verlag.

Andrich, D., & Masters, G. N. (1988). Rating scale analysis. In J. P. Keeves (Ed.), *Educational research, methodology and measurement: An international handbook* (pp. 297–302). Oxford: Pergamon Press.

Australian Association for Research in Education (AARE).(1995). *Code of ethics for research in education.* Coldstream, Victoria, Australia: Author.

Bateson, D. J. (1990). Science achievement in semester and all-year courses. *Journal of Research in Science Teaching, 27,* 233–240.

Berlack, H. (1992). The need for a new science of assessment. In H. Berlack (Ed.), *Toward a new science of educational testing and assessment.* Albany, NY: SUNY Press.

Berndt, T. J., & Miller, K. E. (1990). Expectancies, values, and achievement in junior high school. *Journal of Educational Psychology, 82,* 319–326.

Bills, R. E. (1975). *A system for assessing affectivity.* Tuscaloosa, AL: University of Alabama Press.

Binet, A., & Simon, T. (1916). *The development of intelligence in children.* (E. S. Kite, Trans.). Baltimore: Williams and Wilkins.

Bloom, B. S. (1981). *All our children learning.* New York: McGraw-Hill.

Bloom, B. S. (1976). *Human characteristics and school learning.* New York: McGraw-Hill.

Bloom, B. S., Hastings, J. T., & Madaus, G. F. (1971). *Handbook of formative and summative evaluation of student learning.* New York: McGraw-Hill.

Bolte, C. (1994). Conception and application of a learning climate questionnaire based on motivational interest concepts from chemistry instruction at German schools. In D. L. Fisher (Ed.)., *The study of learning environments, (Vol. 8*; pp. 182–192). Oxford: Pergamon Press.

Bourke, S. F. (1984). *The teaching and learning of mathematics.* Melbourne, Australia: Australian Council for Educational Research.

Bourke, S., & Frampton, J. (1992). *Assessing the quality of school life: Some technical considerations.* Joint AARE and NZARE Conference Papers, ISSN 1324–9339. Published on the Internet by the Australian Association for Research in Education (AARE) at http://www.swin.edu.au/aare/conf92/bours92.183.

Brophy, J. (1987). Synthesis of research on strategies for motivating students to learn. *Educational Leadership, 45*(2), 40–48.

Cohen, J. (1977). *Statistical power analysis for the behavioral sciences, 2nd edition.* Hillsdale, NJ: Lawrence Erlbaum Associates.

Crandall, V. C., Crandall, V. J., & Katkovsky, W. (1965). A children's social desirability questionnaire. *Journal of Consulting Psychology, 29*, 27–36.

Cronbach, L. J. (1951). Coefficient alpha and the internal structure of tests. *Psychometrika, 16*, 297–334.

Cronbach, L. J. (1970). *Essentials of psychological testing. (3rd ed.).* New York: Harper and Row.

Crowne, D. P., & Marlowe, D. (1960). A new scale of social desirability independent of psychopathology. *Journal of Consulting Psychology, 24*, 349–354.

Davis, G. (1981). *Educational psychology.* Reading, MA: Addison-Wesley.

de Charms, R. (1976). *Enhancing motivation: Change in the classroom.* New York: Irvington Publishers.

Dreeben, R. (1968). *On what is learned in school.* Reading, MA: Addison-Wesley.

Durkheim, E. (1925). *Moral education: A study in the theory and application of the sociology of education.* New York: The Free Press.

Eccles, J. P., Adler, T., & Meece, J. L. (1984). Sex differences in achievement: A test of alternative theories. *Journal of Personality and Social Psychology, 46*, 25–43.

Elam, S. M., Rose, L. C., & Gallup, A. M. (1994). The 26th Phi Delta Kappan/Gallup Poll of the public's attitudes toward public schools. *Phi Delta Kappan, 76*(1), 41–56.

Edwards, A. L. (1962). The social desirability hypothesis: Theoretical implications for personality measurement. In S. Messick & J. Ross (Eds.), *Measurement in personality and cognition.* (pp. 57–83). New York: John Wiley & Sons.

Fanelli, G. C. (1977). Locus of control. In S. Ball (Ed.), *Motivation in education.* (pp.). New York: Academic Press.

Feather, N. (Ed.). (1982). *Expectations and actions.* Hillsdale, NJ: Lawrence Erlbaum Associates.

Finn, J. (1989). Withdrawing from school. *Review of Educational Research, 59*, 117–142.

Fishbein, M., & Ajzen, I. (1975). *Belief, attitude, intention, and behavior: An introduction to theory and research.* Reading, MA: Addison-Wesley.

Fiske, D. W. (1971). *Measuring the concepts of personality.* Chicago: Aldine Press.

Francis, L. J., & Greer, J. E. (1992). Measuring Christian moral values among Catholic and Protestant adolescents in Northern Ireland. *Journal of Moral Education, 21*, 59–65.

Fraser, B. J. (1998). Classroom environment instruments: Development, validity, and applications. *Learning Environments Research, 1*, 7–33.

Fraser, B. J., Anderson, G. J., & Walberg, H. J. (1982). *Assessment of learning environments: Manual for Learning Environment Inventory (LEI) and My Class Inventory (MCI).* Perth, Australia: Western Australian Institute of Technology.

Fraser, B. J., Giddings, G. J., & McRobbie, C. J. (1993). Assessing the climate of science laboratory classes. In B. J. Fraser (Ed.), *Research implications for science and mathematics teachers, (Vol. l; pp. 41–50).* Perth, Western Australia: Curtin University of Technology.

Fraser, B. J., Giddings, G. J., & McRobbie, C. J. (1995). Evolution and validation of a personal form of an instrument for assessing science laboratory classroom environments. *Journal of Research in Science Teaching, 32*, 399–422.

Gardner, R. C., & MacIntyre, P. D. (1993). On the measurement of affective variables in second language learning. *Language Learning, 43*, 157–194.

Gehman, W. S. (1957). A study of the ability to fake scores on the Strong Vocational Interest Blank for Men. *Educational and Psychological Measurement, 17*, 65–70.

Germann, P. J. (1988). Development of the attitude toward science in school assessment and its use to investigate the relationship between science achievement and attitude toward science in school. *Journal of Research in Science Teaching, 25*, 689–703.

Getzels, J. W. (1966). The problem of interests: A reconsideration. *Supplementary Education Monographs, 66*, 97–106.

Gibbs, L. & Earley, E. (1994). Using children's literature to develop core values. *Phi Delta Kappa Fastback* (Whole No. 361).

Glaser, R. (1963). Instructional technology and the measurement of learning outcomes. *American Psychologist, 18*, 519–521.

Glass, G. V. (1976). Primary, secondary, and meta-analysis. *Educational Researcher, 5*, 3–8.

Glass, G. V., & Stanley, J. C. (1970). *Statistical methods and psychology.* Englewood Cliffs, NJ: Prentice-Hall.

Goodenow, C., & Grady, K. (1993). The relationship of school belonging and friends' values to academic motivation among urban adolescent students. *Journal of Experimental Education, 62*, 60–71.

Gordon, L. V. (1960). *Survey of interpersonal values.* Chicago: Science Research Associates.

Greenberg, B. C., Abdula, A. L., Simmons, W. L., & Horvitz, D. G. (1969). The unrelated question in a randomized response model, theoretical framework. *Journal of the American Statistical Association, 64*, 520–539.

Guttman, L. (1944). A basis for scaling qualitative data. *American Sociological Review, 9*, 139–150.

Hadfield, O. D., Martin, J. V., & Wooden, S. (1992). Mathematics anxiety and learning style of the Navajo middle school student. *School Science and Mathematics, 92*, 171–176.

Halderson, C., Kelley, E. A., Keefe, J. W., & Berge, P. S. (1989). *Comprehensive Assessment of School Environments: Technical manual*. Reston, VA: NASSP.

Hall, C. S., & Lindzey, G. (1970). *Theories of personality, (2nd ed.)*. New York: John Wiley & Sons.

Hesburgh, T. M. (1979). *The Hesburgh papers: Higher values in higher education*. Mission, Kansas: Andrews and McMeel.

Higgins, A. (1991). The Just Community approach to moral education: Evolution of the idea and recent findings. In W. Kurtines & J. Gewirtz (Eds.), *Handbook of moral behavior and development, Vol. 3, Application*. Hillsdale, NJ: Lawrence Erlbaum Associates.

Higgins-D'Alessandro, A., & Sadh, D. (1998). The dimensions and measurement of school culture: Understanding school culture as the basis for school reform. *International Journal of Educational Research, 27*, 553–569.

Hively, W. (1974). Introduction to domain-referenced testing. *Educational Technology, 74*(1), 5–10.

Holmes-Smith, P., & Rowe, K. J. (1994, January). *The development and use of congeneric measurement models in school effectiveness research*. Paper presented at the International Congress for School Effectiveness and Improvement, World Congress Centre, Melbourne, Australia.

Huebner, E., & Dew, T. (1987). Preliminary validation of the positive and negative affect schedule with adolescents, *Journal of Psychoeducational Assessment, 3*, 15–22.

Jöreskog, K. G., & Aish, A. M. (1993). *Structural equation modeling with ordinal variables*. Chicago: Scientific Software, Inc.

Jöreskog, K. G., & Sörbom, D. (1993a). *LISREL 8: Structural equation modeling with the SIMPLIS command language*. Hillsdale, NJ: Lawrence Erlbaum Associates.

Jöreskog, K. G., & Sörbom, D. (1993b). LISREL 8: User's reference guide. Chicago: Scientific Software, Inc.

Jöreskog, K. G., & Sörbom, D. (1993c). *PRELIS 2: User's reference guide*. Chicago: Scientific Software, Inc.

Keith, P. B., Wetherbee, M. J., & Kindzia, D. L. (1995). *Identifying unmotivated students: Planning school-wide interventions*. Paper presented at the Annual Meeting of the National Association of School Psychologists, Chicago.

Keller, J. M. (1994). Motivation in instructional design. In T. Husen & T. N. Postlethwaite (Eds.), *The international encyclopedia of education, (2nd ed.*; pp. 3943–3947) Oxford, England: Pergamon Press.

Kifer, E. (1977). An approach to the construction of affective evaluation instruments. *Journal of Youth and Adolescence, 6*, 205–214.

Klausmeier, H. J. & Goodwin, W. (1971). *Learning and human abilities: Educational Psychology, (4th ed.).* New York: Harper & Row.

Kloosterman, P. & Stage, F. K. (1992). Measuring beliefs about mathematical problem solving. *School Science and Mathematics, 92,* 109–115.

Kounin, J. S. (1970). *Discipline and group management in classrooms.* New York: Holt, Rinehart, and Winston.

Kramer, J. J., & Conoley, J. C. (Eds.). (1992). *The eleventh mental measurement yearbook.* Lincoln: University of Nebraska Press.

LaPiere, R. T. (1934). Attitudes vs. actions. *Social Forces, 13,* 230–237.

Lefcourt, H. (1976). *Locus of control: Current trends in theory and research.* New York: Halstead Press.

Lickona, T. (1997). Educating for character: A comprehensive approach. In A. Molnar (Ed.), *The construction of children's character* (pp. 45–62). Chicago: University of Chicago Press.

Likert, R. (1932). A technique for the measurement of attitudes. *Archives of Psychology,* No. 140.

Lind, G., & Wakenhut, R. (1985). Testing for moral judgment competence. In G. Lind, H. A. Hartmann, & R. Wakenhut (Eds.), *Moral development and the social environment* (pp. 79–105). Chicago: Precedent Publishing.

Lord, F. M. (1952). A theory of test scores. *Psychometrika Monographs, 7* (entire).

Ma, H. K. (1989). Moral orientation and moral judgment in adolescents in Hong Kong, Mainland China and England. *Journal of Cross-Cultural Psychology, 20,* 152–177.

Macpherson, R. J. S. (Ed.). (1995). Accountability research in education: Current developments. *International Journal of Educational Research, 23,* 475–567.

Marsh, H. W. (1994). Student evaluation of teaching. In T. Husen & T. N. Postlethwaite (Eds.), *International encyclopedia of education (2nd ed.;* pp. 6627–6635). Oxford, England: Pergamon Press.

Masters, J. R. (1974). The relationship between the number of response categories and reliability of Likert-type questionnaires. *Journal of Educational Measurement, 11* (l), 49–53.

Maxwell, T. W. (1996). Accountability: The case of accreditation in British Columbia's public schools. *Canadian Journal of Education, 21,* 18–34.

McKenna, M. C., & Kear, D. J. (1990). Measuring attitude toward reading: A new tool for teachers. *Reading Teacher, 43,* 626–639.

Messick, S. J. (1979). Potential uses of non-cognitive measurement in education. *Journal of Educational Psychology, 71,* 281–292.

Moos, R. H. (1979). *Evaluating educational environments: Procedures, measures, findings, and policy implications.* San Francisco: Jossey-Bass.

Moos, R. H., & Trickett, E. J. (1987). *Classroom Environment Scale manual (2nd ed.).* Palo Alto, CA: Consulting Psychologists Press.

Morrison, H., Gardner, J., Reilly, C., & McNally, H. (1993). The impact of portable computers on pupils' attitudes toward study. *Journal of Computer Assisted Learning, 9,* 130–141.

Noddings, N. (1997). Character education and community. In A. Molnar (Ed.), *The construction of children's character* (pp. 1–16). Chicago: University of Chicago Press.

Oppenheim, A. N. (1992). *Questionnaire design, interviewing and attitude measurement.* London: Pinter.

Overly, N. V. (Ed.). (1970). *The unstudied curriculum.* Washington, DC: Association for Supervision and Curriculum Development.

Osgood, C. E. (1952). The nature and measurement of meaning. *Psychological Bulletin, 49,* 197–237.

Osgood, C. E., Suci, G., & Tannenbaum, P. (1957). *The measurement of meaning.* Urbana, IL: University of Illinois Press.

Paulhus, D. L. (1984). Two-component models of socially desirable responding. *Journal of Personality and Social Psychology, 46,* 598–609.

Paulhus, D. L. (1988). *Assessing self-deception and impression management in self-reports: The balanced inventory of desirable responding.* Unpublished manual, University of British Columbia, Vancouver, Canada.

Pellicer, L. O., & Anderson, L. W. (1994). *Handbook for teacher leaders.* Thousand Oaks, CA: Corwin.

Popham, W. J. (1994). Educational assessment's lurking lacuna: The measurement of affect. *Education and Urban Society, 26,* 404–416.

Power, F. C., & Higgins, A. (1992). The just community approach to classroom participation. In A. Garrod (Ed.), *Learning for a lifetime: Moral education in theory and practice.* (pp. 101–122). Westport, CT: Praeger.

Power, F. C., & Khmelkov, V. T. (1998). Character development and self-esteem: Psychological foundations and educational implications. *International Journal of Educational Research, 27,* 583–642.

Prawat, R. S., & Anderson, A. L. H. (1994). The affective experience of children during mathematics. *Journal of Mathematical Behavior, 13,* 201–222.

Public Agenda Foundation. (1996). Public broadly embraces the need for higher standards, rigorously enforced. *American Education, 20*(1), 16–17.

Purkey, W. W., Cage, B., & Graves, M. (1973). The Florida Key: A scale to infer learner self-concept. *Educational and Psychological Measurement, 33,* 979–984.

Purpel, D. E. (1997). The politics of character education. In A. Molnar (Ed.), *The construction of children's character.* (pp. 140–153). Chicago: University of Chicago Press.

Raven, J. (1992). A model of competence, motivation, and behaviors, and a paradigm for assessment. In H. Berlack (Ed.), *Toward a new science of educational testing and assessment.* (pp. 81–97). Albany, NY: SUNY Press.

Rest, J. R. (1979). *Development in judging moral issues.* Minneapolis: University of Minnesota Press.

Robinson, J. P., Shaver, P. R., & Wrightsman, L. S. (1991). *Measures of personality and social psychological attitudes (Vol. 1).* San Diego, CA: Academic Press.

Rokeach, M. (1973). *The nature of human values.* New York: Free Press.

Sarason, I. G. (1986). Test anxiety, worry, and cognitive interference. In R. Schwarzer (Ed.), *Self-related cognitions in anxiety and motivation* (pp. 19–34). Hillsdale, NJ: Lawrence Erlbaum Associates.

Schiefele, U., & Csikszentmihalyi, M. (1995). Motivation and ability as factors in mathematics experience and achievement. *Journal for Research in Mathematics Education, 26,* 163–181.

Schubert, W. H. (1997). Character education from four perspectives on curriculum. In A. Molnar (Ed.), *The construction of children's character* (pp. 17–30). Chicago: University of Chicago Press.

Schwarzer, R. (Ed.). (1986). *Self-related cognitions in anxiety and motivation*. Hillsdale, NJ: Lawrence Erlbaum Associates.

Seligman, M. E. P. (1975). *Helplessness: On depression, development, and death*. San Francisco: Freeman.

Selznick, P. (1992). *The moral commonwealth*. Berkeley, CA: University of California Press.

Shavelson, R. J., Hubner, J. J., & Stanton, G. C. (1976). Self-concept: Validation of construct interpretations. *Review of Educational Research, 46*, 407–441.

Simpson, R. D., & Troost, K. M. (1982). Influences on commitment to and learning of science among adolescent students. *Science Education, 66*, 763–781.

Smith, R. E. (1989). Effects of coping skills training on generalized self-efficacy and locus of control. *Journal of Personality and Social Psychology, 56*, 238–233.

Spielberger, C. D. (1972). Conceptual and methodological issues in ancient research. In C. D. Spielberger (Ed.), *Anxiety: Current trends in theory and research* (pp. 1–18). New York: Academic Press.

Stanley, J., & Hopkins, K. (1972). *Educational and psychological measurement and evaluation (4th ed.)*. Englewood Cliffs, NJ: Prentice-Hall.

Steller, A. W. & Lambert, W. K. (1996). Teach the children well. *The Executive Educator, 18*, 25–28.

Taylor, P. C., Fraser, B. J., & Fisher, D. L. (1997). Monitoring constructivist classroom learning environments. *International Journal of Educational Research, 27*, 293–302.

Thorndike, R. L. (1982). *Applied psychometrics*. Boston: Houghton-Mifflin.

Thorndike, R. L., & Hagen, E. P. (1977). *Measurement and evaluation in psychology and education*. New York: Wiley.

Thorndike, R. L., & Thorndike, R. M. (1994). Reliability in educational and psychological measurement. In T. Husen & T. N. Postlethwaite (Eds.), *The International Encyclopedia of Educational Research (2nd ed.; pp. 4981–4995)*. Oxford, Pergamon Press.

Thurstone, L. L., & Chave, E. J. (1929). *The measurement of attitude*. Chicago: University of Chicago Press.

Townsend, T. (1996). School effectiveness and improvement initiatives and the restructuring of education in Australia. *School Effectiveness and School Improvement, 7*, 114–132.

Tyler, R. W. (1973). Assessing educational achievement in the affective domain. *Measurement in Education, 4*(3), 108.

Walberg, H. J. (1968). Structural and affective aspects of classroom climate. *Psychology in the Schools, 5*, 247–253.

Walberg, H. J., & Anderson, G. J. (1968). Classroom climate and individual learning. *Journal of Educational Psychology, 59*, 414–419.

Watson, M., Battistich, V., & Solomon, D. (1998). Enhancing students' social and ethical development in schools: An intervention program and its effects. *International Journal of Educational Research, 27*, 571–586.

Wehlage, G. (1989). Dropping out: Can schools be expected to prevent it? In L. Weis, E. Farrar, & H. Petrie (Eds.), *Dropouts from school* (pp. 1–19). Albany, NY: SUNY Press.

Weiner, B. (1992). Motivation. In M. Alkin (Ed.), *Encyclopedia of educational research (4th ed.;* pp. 860–865). New York: Macmillan.

Wicker, A. W. (1969). Attitudes vs. actions: The relationship between verbal and overt behavioral responses to attitude objects. *Journal of Social Issues, 25,* 41–78.

Zeller, R. A. (1994). Validity. In T. Husen & T. N. Postlethwaite (Eds.), *The international encyclopedia of educational research (2nd ed.;* pp. 6569–6576). Oxford, Pergamon Press.

Index